Berlitz

African
PHRASE BOOK

12 key languages spoken across Africa

Algeria, Angola, Botswana, Cameroon, Congo, Egypt, Gambia, Ivory Coast, Kenya, Madagascar, Morocco, Mozambique, Niger, Nigeria, Senegal, South Africa, Tanzania, Zaïre, Zimbabwe

How best to use this phrase book

This phrase book is designed to provide you with the essential key phrases you'll need for travelling in and across Africa.

● **Colour margins** will help you locate quickly the language that you require.

● Each language is divided into essential **topic sections**. The following content table will help you find your way around:

Basic expressions	Shops, stores & services incl. bank, post office, telephone
Hotel-Accommodation	Time, Date and Numbers
Eating out	Emergency
Travelling around	Guide to pronunciation
Sightseeing	

● Each expression appears with a transliteration next to it. Simply read this imitated pronunciation as if it were English, stressing the syllables printed in bold type. For further help, consult the **Guide to pronunciation** at the back of each language section.

● In the **Eating out** section, a selection of popular traditional dishes are listed alphabetically, followed by brief explanations, to help you decipher dishes appearing on a menu.

● Throughout the book, this symbol ☞ suggests phrases your listener can use to answer you, simply by pointing to the appropriate answer.

Note: Where languages vary slightly according to gender, parentheses ( ) indicate the version to be spoken *by* a female speaker; brackets [ ] indicate the form to be spoken *to* a female listener.

Acknowledgements: We would like to thank Saidi el-Gheithy (*Centre for African Language Learning*) and Dr Benjamin Akíntúndé Oyètadé (*Lecturer in Yoruba, SOAS, University of London*).

First edition 1997 Printed in Spain

Arabic

Basic expressions

Yes/No.	نعم / لا.	naAHm/laa
Please.	من فضلك / فضلك.	min faDlak (faDlik)
Thank you.	شكرا.	shukraan
I beg your pardon.	آسف/آسفة.	'aasif/'aasifa

Introductions

Good morning.	صباح الخير.	sabaaH al-khayr
Good afternoon.	مساء الخير.	masaa al-khayr
Good-bye.	إلى اللقاء.	'ilaa-liqaa
My name is …	اسمي...	'ismee
Pleased to meet you.	تشرّفنا.	tasharrafnaa
What's your name?	ما اسمك؟	maa 'ismak ('ismik)
How are you?	كيف حالك؟	keef Haalak (Haalik)
Fine thanks. And you?	بخير الحمد لله، وأنت؟	bi-khayr al-Hamdu li-llaah. wa'antaa ('anti)
Where do you come from?	أنت مَن أين؟	'anta ('anti) min 'ayna
I'm from …	أنا من...	'anaa min
Australia	استراليا	'ustraalia
Britain	بريطانيا العظمى	breeTaaniya l-AHuZmaa
Canada	كندا	kanadaa
South Africa	جنوب افريقيا	janoob 'ifReeqiyaa
United States	الولايات المتحدة	'al-wilaayaat al-muttaHida
I'm with my…	أنا مع...	'anaa maAHa
wife	زوجتي	zaojatee
husband	زوجي	zaojee
family	أسرتي	'usRatee
boyfriend/girlfriend	صديقي / صديقتي	sadeeqee/sadeeqatee

GUIDE TO PRONUNCIATION, see page 17/EMERGENCIES, see page 16

Questions

When?/How?	متى؟ / كيف؟	mataa/keef
What?/Why?	ما؟ / لماذا؟	maa/limaadhaa
Who?/Which?	من؟ / أي؟	man/ayy
Where is/are…?	أين الـ...؟	ayna l…
Where can I find …?	أين أجد...؟	ayna ajid
How much is it?	بكم هذا؟	bikam haadhaa
Can you help me?	ممكن تساعدني؟ / تساعديني؟	mumkin tusaaAHidnee (tusaaAHideenee)
What does this mean?	ما معنى هذا؟	maa maAHnaa haadhaa
I understand.	أنا أفهم.	ana 'afham
I don't understand.	أنا لا أفهم.	'ana laa 'afham
Please repeat that.	ممكن تكرر / تكرري هذا.	mumkin tukarrir (tukarriree) haadhaa
Can you translate this for me?	ممكن تترجم لي/ تترجمي لي.	mumkin tutarjim lee (tutarjimee lee)
Can I have …?	أريد ... من فضلك / فضلك.	'ureed … min faDlak (faDlik)
Do you speak English?	هل تتكلم انجليزي؟	hal tatakallam ingileezee
I don't speak Arabic.	أنا لا أتكلم العربية جيدا.	'anaa laa 'atakallam al-AHarabiya jayyidan

It's …

It's …	إنه...	'innahu
better/worse	أحسن / أسوأ	'aHsan/'aswa'
big/small	كبير / صغير	kabeer/Sagheer
cheap/expensive	رخيص / غال	rakhees/ghaali
good/bad	كويس / سيء	kwayyis/sayyi'
hot/cold	ساخن / بارد	saakhin/baarid
near/far	قريب / بعيد	qareeb/baAHeed
vacant/occupied	خال / مشغول	khaali/mashghool

Hotel–Accommodation

I've a reservation.	عندي حجز.	AHandee Hajz
Here's the confirmation.	هذا تأكيد الحجز.	haadhaa ta'keed al-Hajz
Do you have any vacancies?	هل عندك غرفة خالية؟	hal AHindak ghurfa khaaliya
I'd like a … room …	أريد غرفة...	'ureed ghurfa …
single/double	لشخص / لشخصين	lishakhs/lishakhsayn
with twin beds	بسريرين	bisareerayn
with a double bed	بسرير كبير	bisareer kabeer
with a bath/shower	بحمام / بدش	biHammaam/bidush
We'll be staying …	سنبقى	sanabqaa
overnight only	الليلة فقط	al-leela faqaT
a few days	بعض الأيام	baAHD l-'ayyam
a week	أسبوع	'usbooAH

Decision

May I see the room?	ممكن أرى الغرفة؟	mumkin 'araa l-ghurfa
That's fine. I'll take it.	حسنا، سآخذها.	Hasanan sa'akhudhhaa
No. I don't like it.	لا. لا تعجبني.	laa. laa tuAHjibnee
It's too…	هي... كثيرا	hiya … katheeran
dark/small	مظلمة / صغيرة	muzlima/sagheera
noisy	يوجد ضوضاء	yoojad Dawdaa'
Do you have anything …?	هل عندك شيء...؟	hal AHindak shay'
bigger	أكبر	'akbar
cheaper	أرخص	'arkhas
quieter	أهدأ	'ahda'
May I please have my bill?	أريد حسابي من فضلك.	'ureed Hisaabee min faDlak
It's been a very enjoyable stay.	كانت إقامة ممتعة جدا.	kaanat 'iqaama mumtiAHa jiddan

DAYS OF THE WEEK, see page 15

Eating out

I'd like to reserve a table for 4.	أريد أن أحجز طاولة (ترابيزة) لأربعة أشخاص.	'ureed 'an 'aHjiz Taawila (tarabayza) li-'arbaAHa 'ashkhaas
We'll come at 8.	سنأتي الساعة ثمانية.	sana'tee s-saaAHa thmaaniya
I'd like breakfast/ lunch/dinner.	أريد الفطار / الغداء / العشاء من فضلك.	'ureed al-fiTaar/al-ghadaa'/al-AHashaa' min faDlak
What do you recommend?	بماذا تنصحني؟	bimaadhaa tansaHnee
Do you have vegetarian dishes?	هل عندك وجبات نباتية؟	hal AHindak wajbaat nabaatiyya

Breakfast

May I have some …?	أريد...	'ureed
bread/butter	خبز / زبدة	khubz/zubda
cheese	جبنة	jibna
eggs	بيض	bayD
jam	مربى	murabba
rolls	خبز صغير	khubz Sagheer

Starters

بطارخ	baTaarikh	red fish roe
زيتون	zaytoon	olives
جمبري (قريدس)	gambaree ('araydis)	prawns/shrimps
ورق عنب محشي	waRaq AHinab maHshee	stuffed vine leaves

Meat

I'd like some …	أريد	'ureed
beef	بقري	baqaree
chicken	فراخ	firaakh
lamb	ضاني	Daanee
veal	بتلو	betello

NUMBERS, see page 16

ريش	riyaash	spicy grilled chops
كباب	kabaab	chunks of grilled meat
كفتة	kufta	grilled meatballs
مقلوبة	maqlooba	meat and aubergine (eggplant) with rice

شاورمة (shaawirma) roasted meat cut from spit, served on a bun or with rice

فتة (fatta) boiled mutton and rice mixed with bread crumbs and broth

barbecued	مشوي على الفحم	mashwee ahalaa l-fahm
fried	مقلي	muqlee
grilled	مشوي	mashwee
roasted	روستو	roostoo
underdone (rare)	قليل السوا جدا	qaleel as-sawa jiddan
medium	نصف سوا	nisf sawa
well-done	مستوي	mustawee

Fish and seafood

كابوريا	kaabooriyyaa	crab
سمك موسى	samak moosa	sole
كفتة سمك	kuftit samak	deep-fried balls of fish, rice and parsley
سلطة تونة	salaTit toona	tuna salad

كباب سمك (kabaab samak) charcoal-grilled chunks of fish with pieces of tomato and sweet peppers

Vegetables

aubergine/eggplant	باذنجان	baadhinjaan
green beans	فاصوليا	faasoolyaa
courgette/zucchini	كوسة	koosa
lentils	عدس	AHads
potatoes	بطاطس	baTaaTis
rice	رز	ruzz

شوربة عدس	shurbit AHads — lentil soup
محشي (mahshee)	vegetables stuffed with mixture of minced meat, rice, onion and herbs
ملوخية (mulookhiyya)	spicy soup of greens flavoured with garlic; usually served with rice and meat from the stock
سلطة زبادي (salata zabaadee)	diced cucumber with dressing of yoghurt, olive oil, garlic and mint

Fruit & dessert

apple	تفاح	tuffaaH
dates	بلح	balaH
figs	تين	teen
grapes	عنب	AHinab
orange	برتقال	burtuqaal
ice-cream	جيلاتي (آيس كريم)	jeelaatee (ays krim)

بقلاوة (baqlaawa)	"baklava": thin layers of pastry, filled with nuts, almonds and pistachios, steeped in syrup

Drinks

(hot) chocolate	شوكولاتة (ساخنة)	shookoolaata (saakhina)
coffee	قهوة	qahwa
black	بدون لبن	bidoon laban
with milk	باللبن	bil-laban
fruit juice	عصير فواكه	AHaseer fawaakih
mineral water	مياه معدنية	miyaah maAHdaniyya
tea	شاي	shaay
herbal tea	شاي عشبي	shaay AHushbee

Paying

I'd like to pay.	أريد أن أدفع	'ureed 'an 'adfaAH
I think you made a mistake in the bill.	أظن أنه يوجد خطأ في الفاتورة (الحساب).	'azunn 'annahu yoojad khaTa' fee l'faatoora (l-Hisaab)
We enjoyed it, thank you.	تمتعنا بالأكل كثيرا، شكرا.	tamattaHnaa bil-'akl katheeran, shookran

NUMBERS, see page 16

Travelling around

Plane

Is there a flight to Amman?	هل توجد رحلة إلى عمان؟	hal toojad rihla 'ilaa AHamman
What time do I check in?	متى أتسجل؟	mataa 'atasajil
I'd like to … my reservation.	أريد أن... حجزي.	'ureed 'an … Hajzee
cancel/change/ confirm	ألغ / أغير / أؤكد	'ulghee/'ughayyir/ 'u'akkid

Train

I want a ticket to Cairo.	أريد تذكرة إلى القاهرة.	'ureed tadhkira 'ilaa l-qaahira
single (one-way)	ذهاب	dhahaab
return (roundtrip)	ذهاب وإياب	dhahaab wa 'iyaab
first/second class	درجة أولى / ثانية	darja oola/thaaniya
When is the … train to Aswan?	متى يقوم القطار إلى أسوان؟	mataa yaqoom al-qiTaar 'ilaa 'aswaan
first	الأول	al-'awwal
next	القادم	al-qaadim
last	الأخير	al-'akheer
Is this the right train to Port-Said?	هل هذا هو القطار لبور سعيد؟	hal haadhaa huwa al-qiTaar li-boor saAHeed

Bus–Coach

What bus do I take to the centre?	أي اوتوبيس يذهب إلى وسط البلد؟	'ayy 'utoobees yadhhab 'ilaa wasT al-balad
How much is the fare to …?	كم ثمن التذكرة إلى...	kam thaman at-tadh kira 'ilaa
Will you tell me when to get off?	ممكن تقول لي متى أنزل من فضلك؟	mumkin taqool lee mataa 'anzil min faDlak
How long is the journey	كم من الوقت تأخذ الرحلة؟	kam min l-waqt ta'khudh ar-riHla

TELLING THE TIME, see page 15

Taxi

Where can I find a taxi?	أين أجد تاكسي؟	'ayna 'ajid taaksi
How much is it to...?	كم أدفع إلى...	kam 'adfaAH 'ilaa
Take me to this address.	وصلني إلى هذا العنوان.	wassalnee 'ilaa haadhaa l-AHunwaan
Please stop here.	قف هنا من فضلك.	qif hunaa min faDlak

Car hire (rental)

I'd like to hire (rent) a car.	أريد تأجير سيارة.	'ureed ta'jeer sayyara
I'd like it for a day/ week.	أريدها ليوم / لأسبوع.	'ureeduhaa liyaom/ li'usbooAH
Where's the nearest filling station?	أين أقرب محطة بنزين؟	'ayna 'aqrab maHaTTat binzeen
Full tank, please.	املأ لي من فضلك.	'imlaa' lee min faDlak
Give me ... litres of petrol (gasoline).	أعطني... لتر بنزين من فضلك.	'aAHTeenee ... litr binzeen min faDlak
How do I get to ...?	ممكن تصف لي الطريق إلى...	mumkin tasif lee at-tareeq 'ilaa
I've had a breakdown at...	أنا عندي عطل في...	'ana 'AHindee AHaTal fee
Can you send a break-down truck?	ممكن إرسال سيارة نجدة؟	mumkin 'irsaal sayyaarat najda
How long will it take?	كم من الوقت يأخذ هذا الشغل؟	kam min al-waqt ya'khudh haadhaa sh-shughl

☞ You're on the wrong road.	أنت في الطريق الخطأ. ☜
Go straight ahead.	اتجه إلى الأمام
It's down there on the ...	إنه هناك على...
left/right	الشمال / اليمين.
opposite/behind ...	أمام / خلف
next to/after ...	بجانب/بعد
north/south/east/west	شمال / جنوب / شرق / غرب

NUMBERS, see page 16

Sightseeing

Where's the tourist office?	أين مكتب السياحة؟	'ayna maktab as-siyaaHa
Is there an English-speaking guide?	هل يوجد مرشد سياحي يتكلم اللغة الانجليزية؟	hal yoojad murshid siyaaHee yatakallam al-loogha al-ingileezee
Where is/are the ...?	أين...؟	'ayna
beach	الشاطئ	l-shaaTi'
city centre/downtown	وسط البلد	waST al-balad
market/bazaar	السوق	l-sooq
mosque	المسجد	l-masjid
museum	المتحف	l-matHaf
old town	المدينة القديمة	l-madeena al-qadeema
pyramids	الأهرام	l-'ahraam
ruins	الأطلال	l-'aTlaal
tomb	القبر	l-qabr
When does it open/close?	متى يفتح ؟ / يقفل؟	mataa yaftaH/yuqfil
How much is the entrance fee?	كم سعر الدخول؟	kam siAHr ad-dukhool

Entertainment

What's playing at the theatre?	ماذا يوجد في المسرح؟	maadhaa yoojad fee l-masraH
How much are the seats?	بكم التذاكر؟	bikam at-tadhaakir
Would you like to go out with me tonight?	هل تحب (تحبين) الخروج معي الليلة؟	hal tuHibb (tuHibbeen) al-khurooj maAHee al-layla
Is there a discoteque in town?	هل يوجد مرقص (ديسكو) في البلد؟	hal yoojad marqas (deeskoo) fee l-balad
Would you like to dance?	هل تحب أن ترقص؟ (تحبين أن ترقصي؟)	hal tuHibb 'an tarqus (tuHibbina 'an tarqusee)
Thank you. It's been a wonderful evening.	شكرا. كانت سهرة ممتازة.	shukran kanat sahra mumtaaza

TELLING THE TIME, see page 16/DATE, see page 15

Shops, stores and services

Where's the nearest …?	أين أقرب...؟	'ayna 'aqrab …
baker's	مخبز	makhbaz
bank	بنك	bank
bookshop/bookstore	مكتبة	maktaba
chemist's/drugstore	صيدلية (أجزخانة)	Saydaliyya ('ajzikhaana)
department store	محل تجاري	maHall tijaaree
grocery	محل بقالة	maHall baqqaala
market	سوق	sooq
newsagent	محل بيع الجرائد	maHal bayAH al-jaraa'id
post office	مكتب البريد (البوستة)	maktab al-bareed (al-boosta)
supermarket	سوبرماركت	soobar maarkit
toilets	تواليت	tooaaleet

General expressions

Where's the main shopping area?	أين الحي التجاري الرئيسي؟	'ayna l-Hayy at-tijaaree ar-ra'eesee
Do you have any …?	هل تبيع...؟	hal tabeeAH …
Do you have anything …?	هل عندك شئ...؟	hal AHindak shay' …
cheaper/better	أرخص / أحسن	'arkhas/'aHsan
larger/smaller	أكبر / أصغر	'akbar/'asghar
Can I try it on?	ممكن أقيس هذا؟	mumkin 'aqees haadhaa
How much is this?	بكم هذا؟	bikam haadhaa
Please write it down.	من فضلك اكتبها	min faDlak 'iktibhaa
I don't want to spend more than …	لا أريد أن أصرف أكثر من...	laa 'ureed 'an 'aSrif 'akthar min …
No, I don't like it.	لا، لا تعجبني.	laa, laa tuAHjibnee
I'll take it.	سآخذها.	sa'a akhudh-haa
Do you accept credit cards?	هل تقبل كروت مصرفية؟	hal taqbal kuroot maSrafiyya

NUMBERS, see page 16

black	أسود	'aswad
blue	أزرق	'azraq
brown	بني	boonnee
green	أخضر	'akhdar
orange	برتقالي	burtuqaalee
red	أحمر	'ahmar
yellow	أصفر	'asfar
white	أبيض	'abyad

I want to buy...	أريد	'ureed
aspirin	أسبرين	'asbireen
insect cream	طارد للحشرات	Taarid lil-Hasharaat
newspaper	جريدة	jareeda
English/American	انجليزية / أمريكية	ingiliziya/amrikiya
sun-tan cream	كريم للشمس	kreem lish-shams
soap	صابون	saaboon
a half-kilo of apples	نصف كيلو تفاح	nisf kiloo tuffaaH
a litre of milk	لتر لبن	litr laban
I'd like ... film for this camera.	أريد... فيلم لهذه الكاميرا.	'ureed feelam lihaadhihi l-kaameeraa

Souvenirs

carpets	سجاجيد	sajaajeed
handkerchief	منديل	mandeel
oriental lamp	مصباح شرقي	misbaaH sharqee
robe (full length)	جلابية	gallabiyya
water pipe	شيشة (نرجيلة)	sheesha (narjeela)

At the bank

Where's the nearest exchange office?	أين أقرب مكتب صرافة؟	'ayna 'aqrab maktab Sarraafa
I want to change some dollars/pounds.	أريد تحويل...	'ureed taHweel ...
What's the exchange rate?	ما سعر التحويل؟	maa siAHr at-taHweel

At the post office

I want a…-piastre stamp.	طابع ب... قرش من فضلك.	TaabiAH bi… qirsh min faDlak
What's the postage for a postcard to...?	بكم الطابع لكارت بوستال إلى...؟	bikam aT-TaabiAH li-kart boostaal 'ilaa
Is there any mail for me? My name is…	هل توجد خطابات لي؟ اسمي...	hal toojad khiTaabaat li. 'ismee

Telephoning

Where's the nearest public phone.	أين أقرب كابينة تليفون؟	'ayna 'aqrab kaabinat talifoon
Hello. This is… speaking.	آلو. أنا...	haaloo. 'ana …
I want to speak to…	أريد أن أتكلم مع...	'ureed 'an 'atakallam maAHa …
Please speak louder/ more slowly.	تكلم بصوت عال / ببطء من فضلك	takallam bisaot AHaali/ bibuT' min faDlak
When will he/she be back?	متى سيرجع؟ / سترجع؟	mataa sayarjaAH/ satarjaAH
Will you tell him/her that I called?	ممكن تخبره / تخبريها بأني اتصلت؟	mumkin tukhbiru/ tukhbirhaa bi-'annanee t-taSalt
My name is …	اسمي...	'ismee

Time

It's ...	إنها...	'innahaa
five past one	الواحدة وخمس دقائق	al-waaHida wa khams daqaa'iq
quarter after three	الثالثة والربع	athaalitha wa r-rubAH
twenty after four	الرابعة وعشرين دقيقة	ar-raabiAH wa AHishreen daqeeqa
half-past six	السادسة والنصف	as-saadisa wa n-nisf
ten to ten	العاشرة إلا عشر دقائق	al-AHaashira 'illa AHashr daqaa'iq
noon/midnight	الثانية عشر ظهرا / منتصف الليل	ath-thaaniya AHashar zuhran/moontaSaf l-layl

NUMBERS, see page 16

in the morning	في الصباح	fee S-sabaaH
during the day	بعد الظهر	baaHd aZ-Zuhr
at night	في المساء	fee l-masaa

Sunday	الأحد	al-'ahad
Monday	الأثنين	al-'ithnayn
Tuesday	الثلاثاء	ath-thulathaa'
Wednesday	الأربعاء	al-'irbiahaa'
Thursday	الخميس	al-khamees
Friday	الجمعة	al-jumaha
Saturday	السبت	as-sabt
January	يناير	yanaayir
February	فبراير	fabraayir
March	مارس	maaris
April	أبريل	'abreel
May	مايو	maayoo
June	يونيو	yooniyoo
July	يوليو	yooliyoo
August	أغسطس	'aghustus
September	سبتمبر	sibtambar
October	اكتوبر	'uktoobar
November	نوفمبر	noofambar
December	ديسمبر	dissambar

yesterday	أمس	'ams
today	اليوم	al'yaom
tomorrow	غدا	ghadan

Numbers

0	صفر	sifr
1	واحد	waaHid
2	اثنين	'ithnayn
3	ثلاثة	thalaatha
4	أربعة	'arbaAHa
5	خمسة	khamsa
6	ستة	sitta
7	سبعة	sabAHa
8	ثمانية	thamaaniya
9	تسعة	tisAHa
10	عشرة	AHashra

11	احدى عشر	'iHdaa AHashar
12	اثنا عشر	ithnaa AHashar
13	ثلاثة عشر	thalaathata AHashar
14	أربعة عشر	arbaAHata AHashar
15	خمسة عشر	khamsata AHashar
16	ستة عشر	sittata AHashar
17	سبعة عشر	sabAHata AHashar
18	ثمانية عشر	thamaaniyata AHashar
19	تسعة عشر	tisAHata AHashar
20	عشرين	AHishreen
21	واحد وعشرين	waaHid wa AHishreen
30	ثلاثين	thalaatheen
40	اربعين	'arbaAHeen
50	خمسين	khamseen
60	ستين	sitteen
70	سبعين	sabAHeen
80	ثمانين	thamaaneen
90	تسعين	tisaAHeen
100	مية	mi'a
1000	ألف	'alf
first	أول	'awwal
second	ثاني	thaanee

Emergency

Call the police	اطلب البوليس	'uTlub al-boolees
Get a doctor	اطلب الدكتور	'uTlub ad-duktoor
Go away	امشي	'imshee
HELP	النجدة	an-najda
I'm lost	ضليت الطريق	Dalleet aT-Tareeq
STOP THIEF	امسك حرامي	'imsik Haraamee
My … have been stolen.	سرقت...	suriqat …
I've lost my …	فقدت...	faqadt …
briefcase	محفظتي	miHfazatee
handbag	حقيبة يدي	Haqeebat yadee
passport	جواز سفري	jawaaz safaree

TELEPHONING, see page 14

Guide to Arabic pronunciation

Consonants

Letter	Approximate pronunciation	Symbol	Example
أ	glottal stop	’	ra’aa
ب	like **b** in **b**oy	b	baab
ت	like **t** in **t**en	t	taaj
ث	like **th** in **th**in	th	thoom
ج	like **j** in **j**am	j	jaar
ح	like **h** in **h**oot; with emphasis	H	Hadeed
خ	like **ch** in Scottish lo**ch**	kh	khubz
د	like **d** in **d**ad	d	darja
ذ	like **th** in **th**at	dh	dhakee
ر	like rolled Scottish **r**	r	raajul
ز	like **z** in **z**ebra	z	zayt
س	like **s** in **s**it	s	sabab
ش	like **sh** in shine	sh	shaykh
ص	like **s** in **s**un, with emphasis	S	Sabr
ض	like **d** in **d**uck, with emphasis	D	Dayf
ط	like **t** in **t**ough, with emphasis	T	Tayyaara
ظ	like **z** in **z**oo, with emphasis	Z	Zareef
ع	like **ah** blocked in the throat	AH	rafeeAH
غ	a soft **r**, like gargling	gh	ghalee
ف	like **f** in **f**eed	f	fa’r
ق	a **k** from deep in the throat	q	qalb
ك	like **k** in **k**ilo	k	kitaab
ل	like **l** in **l**et	l	lateef
م	like **m** in **m**eet	m	min
ن	like **n** in **n**eat	n	naar
ه	like **h** in **h**ear	h	haram
و	like **w** in **w**ell	w	ward
ي	like **y** in **y**ell	y	yaktub

Vowels

ـَ	like **a** in h**a**t, but short	a	sabr
ـُ	like **u** in b**u**t	u	yaktub
ـِ	like **i** in b**i**ll	i	mit
ـَا	like **a** in c**a**r (long)	aa	naar
ـِي	like **ee** in m**ee**t (long)	ee	reef
ـُو	like **oo** in m**oo**n (long)	oo	noor
ـَوْ	like **aow** in mi**aow**	ao	yaom
ـَيْ	like **ay** in d**ay**	ay	bayt

French

Basic expressions *Expressions courantes*

Yes/No.	**Oui/Non.**	wee/nawng
Please.	**S'il vous plaît.**	seel voo pleh
Thank you.	**Merci.**	mehrsee
I beg your pardon?	**Pardon?**	pahrdawng

Introductions *Présentations*

Good morning/ Good afternoon.	**Bonjour.**	bawngzhoor
Good night.	**Bonne nuit.**	bon nwee
Good-bye.	**Au revoir.**	oa rervwahr
My name is …	**Je m'appelle …**	zher mahpehl
Pleased to meet you.	**Enchanté(e).**	ahngshahngtay
What's your name?	**Comment vous appelez-vous?**	kommahng voo zahperlay voo
How are you?	**Comment allez-vous?**	kommahng tahlay voo
Fine thanks. And you?	**Très bien, merci. Et vous?**	treh byang mehrsee. ay voo
Where do you come from?	**D'où êtes-vous?**	doo eht voo
I'm from …	**Je viens de …**	zher vyang der
Australia	**l'Australie**	loastrahlee
Britain	**la Grande-Bretagne**	lah grahngd brertañ
Canada	**le Canada**	ler kahnahdah
USA	**les États-Unis**	lay zaytah zewnee
I'm with my …	**Je suis avec …**	zher swee ahvehk
wife	**ma femme**	mah fahm
husband	**mon mari**	mawng mahree
family	**ma famille**	mah fahmeey
boy/girlfriend	**mon ami(e)**	mawng nahmee
I'm on my own.	**Je suis seul(e).**	zher swee surl
I'm on business/holiday (vacation).	**Je suis en voyage d'affaires/ en vacances.**	zher swee zahng vwahyahzh dahfehr/ zahng vahkahngss

GUIDE TO PRONUNCIATION/EMERGENCIES, see page 31

Questions *Questions*

Where is/are …?	**Où est/sont …?**	oo eh/sawng
How?	**Comment?**	kommahng
Why?	**Pourquoi?**	poorkwah
When?	**Quand?**	kahng
What is this/that?	**C'est quoi ça?**	seh kwarh sah
Who is this/that?	**C'est qui ça?**	seh kee sah
Which?	**Lequel (Laquelle)?**	lerkehl (lahkehl)
Where can I get/find …?	**Où puis-je trouver …?**	oo pweezh troovay
How far?	**À quelle distance?**	ah kehl deestahngss
How long?	**Combien de temps?**	kawngbyang der tahng
How much?	**Combien?**	kawngbyang
Can you help me?	**Pouvez-vous m'aider?**	poovay voo mehday
What does this mean?	**Que veut dire ceci?**	ker vur deer serssee
I understand.	**Je comprends.**	zher kawngprahng
I don't understand.	**Je ne comprends pas.**	zher ne kawngprahng pah
Please speak slowly.	**Parlez lentement, s'il vous plaît.**	pahrlay lahngtaymahng seel voo pleh
Can you translate this for me?	**Pouvez-vous me traduire ceci?**	poovay voo mer trahdweer serssee
Can I have …?	**Puis-je avoir …?**	pweezh ahvwahr
Do you speak English?	**Parlez-vous anglais?**	pahrlay voo ahnggleh
I don't speak French.	**Je ne parle pas français.**	zher ner pahrl pah frawngssay

A few useful words *Quelques mots usuels*

It's …	**C'est …**	seh
better/worse	**meilleur/pire**	mehyurr/peer
big/small	**grand/petit**	grahng/pertee
cheap/expensive	**bon marché/cher**	bawng mahrshay/shehr
good/bad	**bon/mauvais**	bawng/moaveh
hot/cold	**chaud/froid**	shoa/frwah
near/far	**près/loin**	preh/lwang
right/wrong	**juste/faux**	zhewst/foa
vacant/occupied	**libre/occupé**	leebr/okkewpay

Hotel–Accommodation *Hôtel*

We've a reservation.	**Nous avons réservé.**	noo zahvawng rayzehrvay
Do you have any vacancies?	**Avez-vous des chambres disponibles?**	ahvay voo day shahngbr deesponeebl
I'd like a … room.	**Je voudrais une chambre …**	zher voodreh ewn shahngbr
single	**pour une personne**	poor ewn pehrson
double	**pour deux personnes**	poor dur pehrson
with twin beds	**avec des lits jumeaux**	ahvehk day lee zhewmoa
with a double bed	**avec un grand lit**	ahvehk ang grahng lee
with a bath	**avec salle de bains**	ahvehk sahl der bang
with a shower	**avec douche**	ahvehk doosh
We'll be staying …	**Nous resterons …**	noo rehsterrawng
overnight only	**juste cette nuit**	zhewst seht nwee
a few days	**quelques jours**	kehlker zhoor
a week	**une semaine**	ewn sermehn

Decision *Décision*

May I see the room?	**Puis-je voir la chambre?**	pweezh vwahr lah shahngbr
That's fine. I'll take it.	**D'accord. Je la prends.**	dahkor. zher lah prahng
No. I don't like it.	**Non, elle ne me plaît pas.**	nawng ehl ner mer pleh pah
It's too …	**Elle est trop …**	ehl eh troa
dark/small	**sombre/petite**	sawngbr/perteet
noisy	**bruyante**	brweeyahngt
Do you have anything …?	**Avez-vous quelque chose de …?**	ahvay voo kehlker shoaz der
better/bigger	**mieux/plus grand**	myur/plew grahng
cheaper	**meilleur marché**	mehyurr mahrshay
quieter	**plus tranquille**	plew trahngkeel
May I have my bill, please?	**Puis-je avoir ma note, s'il vous plaît?**	pweezh ahvwahr mah not seel voo pleh
It's been a very enjoyable stay.	**Le séjour a été très agréable.**	ler sayzhoor ah aytay treh zahgrayahbl

DAYS OF THE WEEK, see page 30

Eating out *Restaurant*

I'd like to reserve a table for 4.	**Je voudrais réserver une table pour 4 personnes.**	zher voodreh rayzehrvay ewn tahbl poor kahtr pehrson
We'll come at 8.	**Nous viendrons à 8 heures.**	noo vyangdrawng ah weet urr
I'm hungry/thirsty.	**J'ai faim/soif.**	zhay fang/swahrf
I'd like …	**Je voudrais …**	zher voodreh
breakfast/lunch/ dinner	**le petit déjeuner/ le déjeuner/le dîner**	ler pertee dayzhurnay/ler dayzhurnay/ler deenay
Do you have a set menu/local dishes?	**Avez-vous un menu/ des plats locaux?**	ahvayvoo ang mehnew/ deh plah loakoa
What do you recommend?	**Que me recommandez-vous?**	ker mer rerkommahngday voo
Do you have vegetarian dishes?	**Avez-vous des plats végétariens?**	ahvay voo day plah vayzhaytahryang

Breakfast *Petit déjeuner*

May I have some …?	**Puis-je avoir …?**	pweezh ahvahr
bread/butter	**du pain/du beurre**	dew pang/dew burr
cheese	**du fromage**	dew fromahzh
ham and eggs	**des œufs au jambon**	day zur oa zhahngbawng
jam	**de la confiture**	der lah kawngfeetewr
rolls	**des petits pains**	day pertee pang

Starters *Hors-d'œuvre*

aloco	ahloakoa	sliced, deep-fried plantain (*Ivory Coast*)
avocat-vinaigrette	ahvoakah veenehgreht	avocado salad
brochettes	broasheht	meat snack (*Niger, Mali, Senegal, Ivory Coast*)
foura	foorrah	small balls of fermented millet
loobia	loobyah	hot red sauce (*Algeria*)
merguez	mehrgehz	spicy sausage (*Algeria, Morocco*)
nempti	nehmptee	thin millet pancake (*Mali*)

NUMBERS, see page 30

Meat *Viande*

I'd like some …	**Je voudrais …**	zher voodreh
beef	**du bœuf**	dew burf
chicken	**du poulet**	dew pooleh
goat	**de la chèvre**	der lah shehvr
lamb	**de l'agneau**	der lahñoa
pork	**du porc**	dew por
veal	**du veau**	dew voa
bouillon	booyawng	mutton or beef stew
djekoume	jaykoomay	chili chicken (*Togo*)
kedjenou	kayjaynoo	steamed chicken (*Ivory Coast*)
mechoui	mayshooee	whole roast mutton, filled with couscous
mermez	mehrmehz	stewed mutton (*Algeria*)
viande de brousse	vyahng der brooss	any bush meat dish
yassa	yahssah	chicken dish (*Senegal*)

baked/boiled	**au four/bouilli**	oa foor/booyee
fried/grilled	**frit/grillé**	free/greeyay
roast/stewed	**rôti/à l'étouffée**	roatee/ah laytoofay
underdone (rare)	**saignant**	sehñahng
medium	**à point**	ah pwang
well-done	**bien cuit**	byang kwee

Fish and seafood *Poissons et fruits de mer*

acheke-poisson	ahchaykay-pwarhssawng	cassava with deep-fried fish (*Ivory Coast*)
adokouin	ahdoakooeeng	shellfish with a prawn sauce (*Togo*)
chep-bu-djen	chehboojehn	rice with fish
gboma	boamah	spinach and seafood dish (*Togo*)
merou	mayrroo	grouper (large sea fish)
moutsella	mootsaylah	spicy fish and vegetables (*Algeria, Morocco*)

Vegetables *Légumes*

beans	**haricots verts**	ahreekoa vehr
cabbage	**choux**	shoo
potatoes	**pommes (de terre)**	pom (der tehr)
rice/spinach	**riz/épinards**	ree/aypeenahr
banane-arachide grillée	bahnan ahrahsheed greeyay	braised plantain with grilled peanuts
foutou/foufou	footoo/foofoo	pounded yam or plantain

Fruit and dessert *Fruits et desserts*

apple/banana	**pomme/banane**	pom/bahnahn
lemon/orange	**citron/orange**	seetrawng/orahngzh
ice-cream	**creme-glacée**	crehm glahsay
halva	hahlvah	sweet sesame seed cake
makrouf	mahkroof	wheat biscuit (*Algeria*)
thiacry	teeahcree	couscous, sour milk and sugar (*Senegal*)

Drinks *Boissons*

beer	**une bière**	ewn byehr
(hot) chocolate	**un chocolat (chaud)**	ang shokolah (shoa)
coffee	**un café**	ang kahfay
black/with milk	**noir/crème**	nwahr/krehm
fruit juice	**un jus de fruits**	ang zhew der frwee
millet beer	**chapalo**	chahpahloa
mineral water	**de l'eau minérale**	der loa meenayrahl
tea	**un thé**	ang tay
wine	**du vin**	dew vang
red/white	**rouge/blanc**	roozh/blahng

Paying *L'addition*

I'd like to pay.	**L'addition, s'il vous plaît.**	ahdeessyawng seel voo pleh
I think there's a mistake in the bill.	**Je crois qu'il y a une erreur dans l'addition.**	zher krwah keel ee ah ewn ehrurr dahng lahdeessyawng
Our compliments to the cook/our host.	**Nos compliments au chef/à notre hôte.**	noa kawngpleemahng oa shehf/ah nohtr oht

NUMBERS, see page 30

Travelling around *Excursions*

Plane *Avion*

Is there a flight to Bamako?	**Y a-t-il un vol pour Bamako?**	ee ahteel ang vol poor bahmahko
What time do I check in?	**À quelle heure est l'enregistrement?**	ah kehl urr eh lahngrerzheestrermahng
I'd like to … my reservation.	**Je voudrais … ma réservation.**	zher voodreh … mah rayzehrvahssyawng
cancel/change	**annuler/changer**	ahnnewlay/shahnzhay
confirm	**confirmer**	kawngfeermay

Train *Train*

I want a ticket to N'djamena.	**Je voudrais un billet pour N'djamena.**	zher voodreh ang beeyeh poor njahmehnah
single (one-way)	**aller**	ahlay
return (roundtrip)	**aller-retour**	ahlay rertoor
first/second class	**première/deuxième classe**	prermyehr/durzyehm klahss
How long does the journey (trip) take?	**Combien de temps dure le trajet?**	kawnbyang der tahng dewr ler trahzheh
When is the … train to Lome?	**Quand part le … train pour Lome?**	kahng pahr ler … trang poor lomeh
first/next	**premier/prochain**	prermyay/proshang
last	**dernier**	dehrnyay
Is this the right train for Dakar?	**C'est bien le train pour Dakar?**	seh byang ler trang poor dakahr

Bus–Coach *Bus–Autocar*

Is there a bus today?	**Y a-t-il un bus aujourd'hui?**	ee ahteel ang bewss oazhurdwee
What bus do I take to the town centre?	**Quel bus va au centre-ville?**	ehl boos vah oh sahngtr veel
How much is the fare to …?	**Quel est le prix du trajet jusqu'à …?**	kehl eh ler pree dew trahzheh zhewskah
Will you tell me when to get off?	**Pourriez-vous me dire quand je dois descendre?**	pooryay voo mer deer kahng zher dwah dehssahngdr

TELLING THE TIME, see page 29

Taxi *Taxi*

How much is it to …?	**Quel est le tarif pour …?**	kehl eh ler tahreef poor
Take me to this address.	**Conduisez-moi à cette adresse.**	kawngdweezay mwah ah seht ahdrehss
Please stop here.	**Arrêtez-vous ici, s'il vous plaît.**	ahrehtay voo eessee seel voo pleh
Please wait for me. I'll be 10 minutes.	**Attendez-moi, s'il vous plait. J'en ai pour dix minutes.**	atahngday mwarh seel voo pleh. zhahng ay poor dee meenewt

Car hire (rental) *Location de voitures*

I'd like to hire (rent) a car.	**Je voudrais louer une voiture.**	her voodreh looay ewn vwahtewr
I'd like it for a day/week	**Je l'utiliserai un jour/une semaine.**	zher lewteeleezerray ang zhoor/ewn sermehn
Where's the nearest filling station?	**Où est la station-service la plus proche?**	oo eh lah stahssyawng sehrveess lah plew prosh
Give me … litres of petrol (gasoline).	**Donnez-moi … litres d'essence.**	donnay mwah … leetr dehssahngss
How do I get to …?	**Comment-puis-je aller à …?**	kommahng pweezh ahlay ah
I've had a breakdown at …	**Je suis tombé(e) en panne à …**	her swee tawngbay ahng pahn ah
Can you send a break-down truck?	**Pourrait-on avoir une remorque?**	pooreh tawng avwarhr ewn raymohrk
Can you mend it?	**Pouvez-vous réparer la voiture?**	poovayvoo raypahray lah vwahtewr

☞ You're on the wrong road.	**Vous êtes sur la mauvaise route.** ☜
Go straight ahead.	**Allez tout droit.**
It's down there on the left/right.	**C'est là-bas à gauche/droite.**
next to/after …	**à côté de/au-delà de …**
north/south/east/west	**nord/sud/est/ouest**

NUMBERS, see page 30/EMERGENCIES, see page 31

Sightseeing *Visites touristiques*

Where's the tourist office?	**Où se trouve l'office du tourisme?**	oo ser troov loffeess dew tooreezm
Is there an English-speaking guide?	**Y a-t-il un guide qui parle anglais?**	ee ahteel ang geed kee pahrl ahngglеh
Where is the …?	**Où se trouve …**	oo ser troov
church/mosque	**l'église/la mosquée**	laygleez/la moskay
city centre	**le centre (de la ville)**	ler sahngtr (der lah veel)
harbour	**le port**	ler por
market	**le marché**	ler mahrshay
museum	**le musée**	ler mewzay
When does it open/close?	**Quelle est l'heure d'ouverture/de fermeture?**	kehl eh lur doovehrtewr/ der fehrmertewr
How much is the entrance fee?	**Combien coûte l'entrée?**	kawngbyang koot lahngtray

Entertainment *Divertissements*

What's playing at the theatre?	**Que joue-t-on au théâtre?**	ker zhootawng oa tayahtr
How much are the seats?	**Combien coûtent les places?**	kawngbyang koot lay plahss
Would you like to go out with me tonight?	**Voulez-vous sortir avec moi ce soir?**	voolay voo sorteer ahvehk mwah ser swahr
Would you like to dance?	**Voulez-vous danser?**	voolay voo dahngssay

Shops, stores and services *Boutiques, magasins et services*

Where's the nearest…?	**Ou se trouve … le/la plus proche?**	oo ser troov … ler/lah plew prohsh
baker's	**la boulanger**	ler boolahnzhay
butcher's	**le boucher**	ler booshay
chemist's/pharmacy	**la pharmacie**	lah fahrmahssee
department store	**le rayon**	ler rehyawng
grocery	**l'épicerie** *(f)*	laypeesserree
post office	**le bureau de poste**	ler bewroa der pohst
supermarket	**le supermarché**	ler sewpehrmahrshay
toilets	**les toilettes**	lay twarhleht

General expressions *Expressions courantes*

Where's the main shopping area?	**Où se trouve le Commerce?**	oo ser troov ler kohmmehrss
Do you have anything …?	**Avez-vous quelque chose …?**	ahvayvoo kehlker shoaz
cheaper/better	**moins cher/mieux**	moawng shehr/myur
larger/smaller	**plus grand/plus petit**	plew grahng/plew pertee
Can I try it on?	**Puis-je essayer?**	pwee zhayssayyer
How much is this?	**C'est combien ?**	seh kombyang
Please write it down.	**Écrivez-le, s'il vous plaît.**	aykreevay ler seel voo pleh
That's too much.	**C'est trop.**	seh troa.
How about … francs?	**Que diriez-vous de … francs?**	ker deereeayvoo der … frawng
No, I don't like it.	**Non, ça ne me plaît pas.**	nawng sah ner mer pleh pah
I'll take it.	**Je le prends.**	zher ler prahng
Do you accept credit cards?	**Acceptez-vous les cartes de credit?**	ahksehptay voo leh kahrt der kraydee

black	**noir**	nwarhr	orange	**orange**	oarahngzh
blue	**bleu**	blur	red	**rouge**	roozh
brown	**brun**	brang	yellow	**jaune**	zhoan
green	**vert**	vehr	white	**blanc**	blahng

I want to buy…	**Je veux acheter…**	zher vur ahshaytay
anti-malaria tablets	**des comprimés anti-paludique**	deh kompreemay ahngtee pahlewdeek
aspirin	**de l'aspirine**	der lahsspeereen
batteries	**des piles**	deh peel
newspaper	**un journal**	ang zhoornahl
English	**anglais**	ahnggleh
American	**américain**	ahmehrreekang
shampoo	**du shampooing**	dew shahmpooawng
sun-tan cream	**de la crème solaire**	der lah krehm soalehrr
soap	**du savon**	dew sahvawng
toothpaste	**de la pâte dentifrice**	der lah paht dahngteefreess

NUMBERS, see page 30

a half-kilo of apples	**un demi-kilo de pommes**	ang daymee keeloa der pohm
a litre of milk	**un litre de lait**	ang leettr der leh
I'd like … film for this camera.	**Je voudrais une pellicule … pour mon appareil-photo.**	zher voodreh ewn payleekewl … poor mawng ahpahreh-foatoa
black and white	**blanc et noir**	blahng eh nwarhr
colour	**couleur**	koolur

Souvenirs *Souvenirs*

batik art	**art batik**	ahr bahteek
desert cross pendant	**la Croix d'Agadez**	lah krwah dahgahdehz
leather goods	**objets en cuir**	ohbzheh ahng kweer
miniature statues	**statuettes**	stahteweht
pottery	**poterie**	poatayree
traditional clothing	**vêtements traditionels**	vehtaymahng trahdeessyawngnehl
traditional jewellery	**bijoux traditionels**	beezhoo trahdeessyawngnehl
traditional masks	**masques traditionels**	mahssk trahdeessyawngnehl

At the bank À la bank

Where's the nearest bank/currency exchange office?	**Où se trouve le bureau de change le plus proche?**	oo ser troov ler bewroa der shahngzh ler plew prohsh
What's the exchange rate?	**Quel est le taux de change?**	keh leh ler toa der shahngzh
I want to change some dollars/pounds into francs.	**Je veux convertir quelques dollars/ livres en francs.**	zher vur kawngvehrteer kehlker doalahr/leevr ahng frawng

At the post office *Au bureau de poste*

I want to send this by …	**Je veux expédier ceci par …**	zher vur ehxpaydeeay serssee pahr
airmail	**avion**	ahveeawng
express	**exprès**	ehkspreh
I want … -franc stamps.	**Je veux des timbres de … francs.**	zher vur deh tangbr der … frawng

NUMBERS, see page 30

What's the postage for a letter/postcard to America?	**Quel est le tarif postal pour une lettre/carte postale pour l'Amérique?**	kehl ay leh tahreef pohstahl poor ewn lehtr/kahrt pohstahl poor lahmayreek
Is there any mail for me? My name is …	**Y a-t-il du courrier pour moi? Mon nom c'est …**	yahteel dew kooreeay poor mwarh. mawng nawng seh

Telephoning *Téléphoner*

Where's the nearest public phone?	**Où se trouve le téléphone publique le plus proche?**	oo ser troov ler taylayfon pewbleek ler plew prohsh
May I use your phone?	**Est-ce que je peux appeler?**	ehss ker zher pur ahpehlay
I want to make an international call to …	**Je veux faire un appel international en/au …**	zher vur fehr ang ahpehl angtehrnahsseeaw-ngnahl ahng/oa
Hello. This is … speaking.	**Allô. C'est … à l'appareil.**	ahloa. seh … ah lahpahrehy
I want to speak to …	**Je veux parler à …**	zher vur pahrlay ah
When will he/she be back?	**Quand est-ce qu'il/elle revient?**	kahng tehss keel/kehl rayvyang
Will you tell him/her that I called?	**Dites-lui que j'ai appelé(e).**	deet lwee ker zhay ahpaylay

Time and date *Heure et date*

It's …	**Il est …**	eeleh
five past one	**une heure cinq**	ewn urr sangk
quarter past three	**trois heures et quart**	trwarh zurr eh kahr
twenty past five	**cinq heures vingt**	sang kurr vang
half-past seven	**sept heures et demi**	seht urr eh daymee
twenty-five to nine	**neuf heures moins vingt-cinq**	nurv urr moawng vang sangk
ten to ten	**dix heures moins dix**	deez urr mwang deess
noon/midnight	**midi/minuit**	meedee/meenwee
in the morning	**le matin**	ler mahtang
during the day	**pendant la journée**	pahngdahng lah joornay
in the evening	**le soir**	ler swarh
at night	**la nuit**	lah nwee

Sunday	**dimanche**	deemahngsh
Monday	**lundi**	langdee
Tuesday	**mardi**	mahrdee
Wednesday	**mercredi**	mehrkraydee
Thursday	**jeudi**	zhurdee
Friday	**vendredi**	vahngdraydee
Saturday	**samedi**	sahmaydee
January	**janvier**	zhahngveeay
February	**fevrier**	fayvreeay
March	**mars**	mahrss
April	**avril**	ahvreel
May	**mai**	may
June	**juin**	zhwang
July	**juillet**	zhweeyeh
August	**aout**	oot
September	**septembre**	sehptahngbr
October	**octobre**	ohktohbr
November	**novembre**	noavahngbr
December	**decembre**	dayssahngbr

yesterday	**hier**	yehr
today	**aujourd'hui**	oazhoadwee
tomorrow	**demain**	dermang
spring/summer	**printemps/été**	prangtanhg/aytay
autumn (fall)/winter	**automne/hiver**	oatohn/eevehr

Numbers *Les nombres*

0	**zero**	zayroa	11	**onze**	awngz
1	**un**	ang	12	**douze**	dooz
2	**deux**	dur	13	**treize**	trehz
3	**trois**	trwarh	14	**quartorze**	kahrtohrz
4	**quatre**	kahtr	15	**quinze**	kangz
5	**cinq**	sangk	16	**seize**	sehz
6	**six**	seess	17	**dix-sept**	deeseht
7	**sept**	seht	18	**dix-huit**	deezweet
8	**huit**	weet	19	**dix-neuf**	deeznurf
9	**neuf**	nurf	20	**vingt**	vang
10	**dix**	deess	21	**vingt et un**	vang tehang

30	**trente**	trahngt
40	**quarante**	kahrahngt
50	**cinquante**	sangkahngt
60	**soixante**	swahssahngt
70	**soixante dix**	swahssahngt deess
80	**quatre-vingts**	kahtr vang
90	**quatre-vingt-dix**	kahtr vang deess
100	**cent**	sahng
1,000	**mille**	meel
first	**premier**	permeeay
second	**deuxième**	durzyehm
once	**une fois**	ewn fwarh
twice	**deux fois**	dur fwarh
a half	**un demi**	ang daymee

Emergency *Urgences*

Call the police	**Appelez la police**	ahpehlay lah poaleess
Get a doctor	**Appelez un médecin**	ahpehlay ang mehdsang
Go away	**Allez vous en**	ahlay voo zahng
HELP	**AU SECOURS**	oa saykoor
I'm ill	**Je suis malade**	zher swee mahlahd
I'm lost	**Je me suis perdu(e)**	zher mer swee pehrdew
STOP THIEF	**AU VOLEUR**	oa voalur
My … has been stolen.	**… a été volé.**	… ah aytay voalay
I've lost my…	**J'ai perdu …**	zhay pehrdew
handbag	**mon sac à main**	mawng sahkamang
passport	**mon passeport**	mawng pahsspohr
luggage	**mes baggages**	may bahggahzh
wallet	**mon portefeuille**	mawng pohrterfur

Guide to French pronunciation

Consonants

Letter	Approximate pronunciation	Symbol	Example	
b, c, d, f, k, l, m, n, p, s, t, v, x, z		as in English		
ch	like **sh** in **sh**ut	sh	**cherche**	shersh
ç	like **s** in **s**it	s	**ça**	sah

TELEPHONING, see page 29

g	1) like **s** in pleasure	zh	**manger**	mahngzhay
	2) like **g** in go	g	**garçon**	gahrsawng
gn	like **ni** in onion	ñ	**ligne**	leeñ
h	always silent		**homme**	om
j	like **s** in pleasure	zh	**jamais**	zhahmeh
qu	like **k** in **k**ill	k	**qui**	kee
r	rolled in the back of the mouth	r	**rouge**	roozh
w	usually like **v** in voice	v	**wagon**	vahgawng

Vowels

a, à or **â**	between **a** in hat and father	ah	**mari**	mahree
é or **ez**	like **a** in late	ay	**été**	aytay
è, ê, e	like **e** in get	eh	**même**	mehm
e	sometimes like **er** in other	er	**je**	zher
i	like **ee** in meet	ee	**il**	eel
o	generally like **o** in hot	o	**donner**	donner
	but sometimes as in wr**o**te	oa	**rose**	roaz
ô	like **o** in wrote	oa	**Rhône**	roan
u	round your lips and say **ee**	ew	**cru**	krew

Sounds spelt with two or more letters

ai, ay, ey	like **a** in late	ay	**j'ai**	zhay
aient, ais ait, aï, ei	like **e** in get	eh	**chaîne**	shehn
eu, eû, œu	like **ur** in **fur**, but with lips rounded, not spread	ur	**peu**	pur
oi, oy	like **w** followed by the **a** in **hat**	wah	**moi**	mwah
ou, oû	like **oo** in **look**	oo	**nouveau**	noovoa
ui	like **wee** in between	wee	**traduire**	trahdweer

Nasal sounds

am, an, em, en	something like **arn** in **tarn**ish	ahng	**tante**	tahngt
ien	sounds like **yan** in **yank**	yang	**bien**	byang
im, in, aim, ain, eim, ein, um, un	like **ang** in **rang**	ang	**instant**	angstahng
om, on	like **ong** in **song**	awng	**maison**	mayzawng

Hausa

Basic expressions *Kalamomi na yau da gobe*

Yes./No.	**I./A'a.**	ee/ah-a
Please.	**Don Allah.**	dohn allah
Thank you.	**Na gode.**	nah gawday
I beg your pardon?	**Don Allah, me ka ce?**	dohn allah mee ka chay

Introductions *Gaishe-gaishe*

Good morning.	**Barka da kwana.**	barkah da quahna
Good afternoon.	**Barka da yamma.**	barkah da yamma
Good night.	**A kwana lafiya.**	a quahna lahpiyah
Good-bye.	**Sai watarana.**	sigh watarahnah
May I introduce …?	**Ko zan gabatar da…?**	kaw zahn gabahtar da
My name is …	**Sunana …**	soonahnah
Pleased to meet you.	**Sannunka.**	sannunka
What's your name?	**Me ne ne sunanka?**	may nay nay sunanka
How are you?	**Kana lafiya?**	kanah lahpiyah
Fine thanks. And you?	**Lafiya k'alau. Kai fa?**	lahpiyah Kala^{oo}. kigh fa
Where do you come from?	**Daga ina ka fito?**	daga eenah ka pitaw
I'm from …	**Na fito daga …**	nah pitaw daga
Australia	**Ostareliya**	ohstrayliya
Britain	**Birtaniya**	burtahniya
Canada	**Kyanada**	kairnadah
South Africa	**Afirka ta Kudu**	afeerka ta kudu
USA	**Amirka/Amerika**	ameerka/amayrika
I'm with my …	**Ina tare da …**	eenah tahreh da
wife/husband	**matata/mijina**	mahtahtah/mijeenah
children	**yayana**	air-air-nah
parents	**iyayena**	iyahyeenah
boyfriend	**saurayina**	sowrayeenah
girlfriend	**budurwata**	budurwahtah
I'm on my own.	**Ni kad'ai na ke.**	nee kaDigh na kay
I'm on holiday/on business.	**Na zo hutu/aiki.**	nah zaw hootoo/ighkee

GUIDE TO PRONUNCIATION/EMERGENCIES, see page 47

Questions *Tambayoeyee*

Where is/are …?	**Ina …?**	eenah
How?/When?	**Yaya?/Yaushe?**	yahyah/ya^{oo}sheh
Why?	**Don me?**	dohn may
Which?	**Wane?/Wace?/ Wad'anne?**	wohneh/wohcheh/ wohᴅanneh
Where can I find …?	**Ina zan sami …?**	eenah zan sahmi
How far?/Is it far?	**Da nisa?**	da neesah
How long?	**Kwana nawa?**	quahnah nohwa
How much?	**Nawa?**	nohwa
Can I have …?	**A ba ni …?**	a bah ni
Can you help me?	**Don Allah, ko za ka taimake ni?**	dohn allah kaw zah ka timakayneh
What does this mean?	**Me ne ne ma'anar wannan?**	mee nay nay ma-anar wohnan
I understand.	**Na gane.**	nah gahnay
I don't understand.	**Ban gane ba.**	ban gahnay ba
Please speak slowly.	**Don Allah ka yi magana sannu-sannu.**	dohn allah ki maganah sannu-sannu
Can you translate this for me?	**Ko za ka iya fassara mini wannan?**	kaw zah ka iya passarah mini wohnan
Do you speak English?	**Kana jin turanci?**	kanah jin tooranchee
I don't speak Hausa.	**Ba na jin Hausa.**	bah nah jin ha^{oo}sa

It's … *Ta fi …*

It's …	**Ta fi …**	tah pi
better/worse	**kyau/muni**	kya^{oo}/moonee
big/small	**girma/k'aranci**	girmah/ᴋarenchee
cheap/expensive	**arha/tsada**	arhah/tsahdah
It's …	**Akwai …**	akoy
good/bad	**kyau/ba kyau**	kya^{oo}/bah kya^{oo}
hot/cold	**zafi/sanyi**	zahpee/sanyee
vacant/occupied	**daki/ba kowa**	dahkee/bah kawwah
It's early/late.	**An yi sauri/latti.**	an yi sa^{oo}ry/lattee
It's far/near.	**Da nisa./Ba nisa.**	da neesah/bah neesah

Hotel–Accommodation *Kama 'Dakin Otel*

We've reserved two rooms.	**Mun kama daki biyu.**	moon kahma dahkeẹ biyoo
Here's the confirmation.	**Ga rasit din kama daki.**	gah rasit din kahma dahkee
Do you have any vacancies?	**Akwai d'aki?**	akoy Dahkee
I'd like a … room.	**Ina son d'aki …**	eenah sohn Dahkee
single/double	**k'arami/babba**	Karamee/babbah
with twin beds	**mai gado biyu**	migh gadaw biyu
with a double bed	**mai babban gado**	migh babban gadaw
with a bath	**mai bahon wanka**	migh bah-hohn wohnkah
with a shower	**mai shawa**	migh shahwah
We'll be staying …	**Za mu yi …**	zah mu yee
overnight only	**kwan d'aya kawai**	quan Dayair kawigh
a few days	**yan kwanaki**	airn quanakee
a week (at least)	**(a k'alla) mako guda**	(a Kalla) mahkaw gudah
Is there a campsite near here?	**Akwai fagen fakewa nan kusa?**	akoy pagen pakaywah nain kusa

Decision *Yanke shawara*

I'd like to see the room.	**Ina son in ga d'akin.**	eenah sohhn en ga Dahkin
That's fine. I'll take it.	**Ya yi. Zan d'auka.**	yah yee. zen Daookah
No. I don't like it.	**A'a. Ba na sonsa.**	ah-a. bah nah sohnsa
It's too …	**Ya cika …**	yah chika
cold/hot	**zafi/sanyi**	zahpee/sanyee
dark/small	**duhu/k'arami**	duhoo/Karamee
Do you have anything …?	**Akwai wanda ya fi …?**	akoy wanda ya pi
better/bigger	**kyau/girma**	kyow/girmah
cheaper/quieter	**arha/kammala**	arhah/kammalah
May I please have my bill?	**A kawo bil?**	a kahwaw bil
It's been a very enjoyable stay.	**Na ji dad'in zamana sosai.**	nah ji dahDin zamahnah sawsigh

NUMBERS, see page 46/DAYS OF THE WEEK, see page 45

Eating out *Cin Abinci Waje*

I'd like to reserve a table for 4.	**Ina son in kama tebur na mutum hudu.**	eenah sohn in kahma taybur na mutum hudu
We'll come at 8.	**Za mu zo da k'arfe takwas.**	zah mu zoor da Karfay taquas
I'd like breakfast/ lunch/dinner.	**Ina son karin kumallo/abincin rana/abincin dare.**	eenah sohn karin kumallaw/abinchin rahna/abinchin daree
Do you have a set menu/local dishes?	**Kuna da shiryayyen abinci/na Hausawa?**	kunah da shiryayyen abinchi/na ha^{oo}sahwah
Do you have vegetarian dishes?	**Kuna abincin da ba nama?**	kunah abinchin da bah nahmah

Breakfast *Karin kumallo*

May I have some …?	**Ina son …?**	eenah sohn
bread/butter	**biredi/buluban**	braydee/blooban
cereal	**kwampilas (Nasco®)**	quampilas (nascaw)
ham and eggs	**doya da kwai**	dawyah da quay
jam/rolls	**jam/d'an biredi**	jam/Dan braydee

Starters *K'walama kafin cin abinci*

dak'uwa	daKuwah	snack made from tigernuts or groundnuts
fankaso	pankahsoh	flour cake
fyarfesu	pyarpaysoo	pepper soup
nakiya	nahkiyah	cake made from flour, honey and peppers
suya	sooyah	kebab meat coated in groundnut flour
waina	wighna	fried rice cake

Meat *Nama*

I'd like some …	**Ina son naman…**	eenah sohn nahman
beef	**shanu**	sharnoo
chicken	**kaza**	kahzah
goat	**akuya**	aqueer
lamb	**rago/tunkiya**	rahgoh/tinkiyah
veal	**maraka**	marakaha

miyar nama	miyar nahmah	meat stew
dunk'ulen nama	dunkulen nahmah	meat balls
soyen nama	sohyen nahmah	peppered fried meat

baked/boiled	**gasasshe/dafaffe**	gasasshay/dapappay
fried/grilled	**soyayye/gasasshe**	sohayyay/gasasshay
roast/stewed	**gasasshe/romo**	gasashshay/rawmaw
underdone (rare)	**d'ima**	Dimah
medium	**dafu ba sosai ba**	dapu bah sawsay ba
well-done	**dafu sosai**	dapu sawsay

Fish and seafood *Kifi da naman ruwa*

fyarfesun kifi	pyarpaysoon keepee	fish pepper soup
gasasshen kifi	gasasshen keepee	grilled fish
miyar kifi	miyar keepee	fish stew
soyen kifi	sawyen keepee	fried fish

Vegetables *Kayan Lambu*

beans	**wake**	wahkay
cabbage	**kabeji**	kahbayjee
carrots	**karaz**	karaz
lentils	**yan wake**	airn wahkay
onion	**albasa**	albasah
peas	**d'anyen wake**	Danyen wahkay
potatoes	**dankali**	dankalee
rice	**shinkafa**	sheenkahpah
spinach	**alayyaho**	allayahoh
miyan agushi	miyenn agushee	stew of melon seeds and spinach
miyan taushe	miyenn ta^{oo}shay	stew of spinach, pumpkin and sorrel

Fruit and dessert *Yayan itachei da kayan zak'i*

apple	**tuffa**	tuppah
banana	**ayeba**	ayeba
lemon	**lemon tsami**	laymohn tsahmee
orange	**lemon zak'i**	laymohn zahKee
plum	**d'inya/tsada**	Dinyah/tsahder
cake/ice-cream	**fanke/ayis-kirim**	pankay/ahyis kireem

alkaki	alkahkee	sweet wheaten dessert
fura da nono	purah da nawnaw	cooked millet balls
salak d'in yayan itace	salak Din air-air-an itahchay	fruit salad

Drinks *Abin Sha*

beer	**giya**	giyah
(hot) chocolate	**shayin cakuleti**	shahyin chahkulaytee
coffee	**kofi**	kawpee
black	**(baki) ba madara**	(bakee) bah madarah
with milk	**da madara**	da madarah
fruit juice	**ruwan**	ruwan
apple	**tuffa**	tuppah
orange	**lemon zaki**	laymohurn zahkee
mineral water	**ruwan kwalba (soda)**	ruwan qualba (sohda)
tea	**ti**	tee
wine	**giya**	giyah
red/white	**ja/fara**	jah/parah
vodka	**giyar vodka**	giyar vohdka

Complaints and Paying *Koke-koke da Biya*

This is too …	**Wannan ya cika …**	wohnan yah chika
bitter/sweet	**d'aci/zaki**	Dahchee/zahkee
That's not what I ordered.	**Ba shi na yi oda ba.**	bah shee na yi awdah ba
I'd like to pay.	**Ina son in biya.**	eenah sohn en biyah
I think you made a mistake in the bill.	**Ina jin ka yi kuskure a lissafi.**	eenah jee kah yi kuskuray a lissahpee
Can I pay with this credit card?	**Ko zan iya biya da kati?**	kaw zan eyah biyah da kahtee
We only accept cash.	**Muna karb'ar kud'i kawai.**	munah karBar kuDee kawigh
Is service included?	**Da kudin sabis a ciki?**	da kudin sahbis a chikee
We enjoyed it, thank you.	**Tubarkalla, mun gode.**	tubarkallah mun gawday
Our compliments to the cook/our host.	**A gaida mana kuuku/ mai d'aukar bak'uncinmu.**	a gaydah mana kookoo/migh Da^{oo}kar bahKunchinmu

Travelling around *Zagaya Gari*

Plane *Jirgin Sama*

Is there a flight to Kano?	**Akwai jirgi zuwa Kano?**	akoy jirdee zuwa kanaw
What time do I check in?	**Yaushe ne lokacin cakin?**	yoosheh nay lawkachin checking
I'd like to … my reservation on flight no. …	**Ina son in … kujerata a jirgi mai lamba …**	eenah sohn in … kujeerahtah a jirgee migh lambah
change	**canza**	chainza
confirm	**tabbatar da**	tabbatar da

Train *Jirgin k'asa*

I want a ticket to Kano.	**Ina son tikiti zuwa Kano.**	eenah sohn tikitee zuwah kanaw
single (one-way)	**zuwa kawai**	zawwah kawigh
return (roundtrip)	**zuwa da dawowa**	zawwah da dahwawwah
first/second class	**fes/sakan kilas**	pes/sekohn klass
How long does the journey (trip) take?	**Me ne ne tsawon lokacin tafiyar?**	may nay nay tsawohn lohkerchin tapiyah
When is the… train to Zaria?	**Yaushe ne jirgin … zuwa Zaria?**	yawshay nay jirgin … zuwa zahiyah
first/next	**farko/na gaba**	parkaw/na gaba
last	**na k'arshe**	na Karshay
Is this the right train to Jos?	**Wannan shi ne jirgin zuwa Jos?**	wohnan shee nay jirgeen zuwa jaws
There's no train today.	**Babu jirgi yau.**	bahbu jirgee yaw

Bus–Coach *Bas*

Is there a bus today?	**Akwai bas yau?**	akoy bus yaw
What bus do I take to the centre?	**Wace bas zan dauka zuwa tsakar gari?**	wohchay bus zan da^oo^kah zuwa tsakar garee
How much is the fare to…?	**Nawa ne zuwa …?**	nohah nay zuwa

TELLING THE TIME, see page 45

Will you tell me when to get off?	**Don Allah ko za ka gaya mini lokacin da zan sauka?**	dohn allah kaw zah ka gayah mini lohkerchin da zen sawka

Taxi *Tasi*

How much is it to …?	**Nawa ne zuwa …?**	nohwa nay zuwa
Take me to this address.	**Kai ni adireshin nan.**	kigh ni adiraysheen nain
Please stop here.	**Don Allah tsaya nan.**	dohn allah tsayah nain
Please wait for me. I'll be 10 minutes.	**Don Allah jira ni. Ba zan wuce minti goma ba.**	dohn allah jirah ni. ba zen wucheh mintee gawma ba

Car hire (rental) *Hayar Mota*

I'd like to hire (rent) a car.	**Ina son in dauki hayar mota.**	eenah sohn en da^{oo}ki hayar mohrtar
I'd like it for a day/ week.	**Zan dauka kwana/ mako guda.**	zen da^{oo}kah quahnah/ mahkaw gudah
Where's the nearest filling station?	**Ina ne gidan mai mafi kusa?**	eenah nay giden migh mapee kuser
Full tank, please.	**A cika tanki.**	a cheeka tankee
Give me … litres of (gasoline).	**Ba ni lita … na fetur.**	bah ni litreh … na petrol paytur
How do I get to …?	**Yaya zan kai …?**	yahyah zen kigh
I've had a breakdown at …	**Mota ta lalace a …**	mohrtar tah lahlahchay a
Can you send a mechanic/break-down truck?	**Ko za ka turo makanike/motar ja?**	kaw zah ka tooraw mekaniky/mohrtar jah

☞ You're on the wrong road.	**Kana kan hanyar da ba ita ba.** ☜
Go straight ahead.	**Bi hanyar nan sak.**
It's down there on the left/right.	**Tana can haka a dama/hagu.**
next to/after …	**kusa da/gaban**
north/south/east/west	**Arewa/Kudu/Gabas/Yamma**

NUMBERS, see page 46

Sightseeing *Ganin Gari*

Where's the tourist office?	**Ina ne ofishin kula da bak'i?**	eenah nay awpisheen kuler da bahKee
Is there an English-speaking guide?	**Ko akwai d'an rakiya mai jin Turanci?**	kaw aquigh Dan rakiyah migh jin toorenchee
Where is/are the…?	**Ina …?**	eenah
botanical gardens	**gadenaa tsire-tsire take**	gahdenar tsiray-tsiray takay
castle	**gidan Sarauta**	gidan sara^{oo}tah
Emir's palace	**fadar sarki**	pahdar sarkee
church	**coci**	chawchee
city centre	**kanwuri**	kanwuree
harbour	**tashar jirgin ruwa**	tashayr jirgin ruwah
market	**kasuwa**	kahsuwah
museum	**gidan tarihi**	gidan taheehee
president's palace	**fadar shugaban k'asa**	pahdar shoogaban Kasah
shops	**shaguna suke**	shahgunah sookay
zoo	**gidan dabbobi**	giden dabbawbee
When does it open/close?	**Yaushe ake budewa/rufewa?**	ya^{oo}shay akay boodaywah/rufaywah
How much is the entrance fee?	**Nawa ne kudin shiga?**	nohwa nay kudin shigah

Entertainment *Shak'atawa*

Which film is showing at the cinema?	**Wane fim ake nunawa a silima?**	wanay peem akay noonahwah a silimah
How much are the seats?	**Nawa ne kudin kujera?**	nohwa nay kudin kujayrah
Would you like to go out with me tonight?	**Kana/Kina son fita tare da ni yau da dare?**	kanah/keenah sohn pitah tahreh da nee yaw da daray
Is there a discotheque in town?	**Ko akwai gidan Disko a gari?**	koh akoy gidan diskaw a garee
Would you like to dance?	**Ko za ki so mu yi rawa?**	kaw zah ki saw mu yi rawah
Thank you. It's been a wonderful evening.	**Na gode. Na ji dad'in wannan dare.**	nah gawday. nah ji daDin wohnan daray

Shops, stores and services *Shaguna, Kantuna, da Ire-irensu*

Where's the nearest …?	**Ina ne … mafi kusa?**	eenah nay… mapee kusa
baker's	**gidan biredi**	giden braydee
bookshop	**kantin litattafai**	kanteen leetattapigh
butcher's	**wajen fawa**	wohjen pahwa
chemist's	**kemis**	kemis
dentist	**likitan hak'ori**	likitan haᴋawree
department store	**babban kanti**	babban kantee
grocery	**waje yan tumatur**	wohjen airn tumahtur
hairdresser/barber	**makitsiya/ma'aski**	makitsiyah/ma-askee
newsagent	**bendo**	bendaw
post office	**gidan waya (fas ofis)**	giden wayah (pohs ohpis)
supermarket	**kasuwa**	kahsuwah
toilets	**makewayi**	makaywayee

General expressions *Matambayi ba ya B'ata*

Where's the main shopping area?	**Ina ne babbar kasuwa?**	eenah nay babbar kahsuwah
Do you have any …?	**Ko kana da …?**	kaw kanah da
Do you have anything…?	**Ko kana da wani da ya fi…?**	kaw kanah da wohni da ya pi
cheaper/better	**arha/kyau**	arhah/kya^{oo}
larger/smaller	**girma/k'ank'anta**	girmah/ᴋanᴋanta
Can I try it on?	**In gwada?**	en guadah
How much is this?	**Nawa ne wannan?**	nohwa nay wohnan
Please write it down.	**Don Allah rubuta shi.**	dohn allah rubootah shi
That's too much.	**Yana da tsada.**	yenah da tsahdah.
How about … Naira?	**Ka bari Naira …?**	kah baree nighrah
No, I don't like it.	**A'a, ba na sonsa.**	ah-a bah nah sohnsa
I'll take it.	**Na saya.**	nah sayah
Do you accept credit cards?	**Ana biya da Kati?**	anah beeya da kahtee
Can you order it for me?	**Ko za ka yi mini odarsa?**	kaw zah ka yee mini ohrdersa

NUMBERS, see page 46

black	**bak'i**	baKee
blue	**shud'i**	shoodee
brown	**k'asa-k'asa**	Kasa-Kasa
green	**kore**	kooray
orange	**ruwan goro**	ruwan gawraw
red	**ja**	jah
yellow	**rawaya**	rahwayah
white	**fari**	paree

I want to buy …	**Ina son in sayi …**	eenah sohn en sayee
anti-malaria tablets	**maganin zazzabi**	mahganin zazzabee
aspirin	**aspirin**	aspirin
batteries	**batur**	bahtur
bottle opener	**ofana**	awpanah
newspaper	**jaridar**	jareedar
English/American	**Turanci/Amirka**	toorenchee/ameerka
shampoo	**shamfu**	shampoo
sun-tan cream	**man kariyar rana na shafawa**	mahn kahiyar rahnah na shahpahwah
soap	**sabulu**	sahbuloo
toothpaste	**makilin®**	mahkleen
a half-kilo of apples	**kabin-kilon tuffa**	rebin kilawn tuppah
a litre of milk	**litar madara**	leetar madarah
I'd like … film for this camera.	**Ina son fim mai … na wannan kyamara.**	ennar sohn peem migh … na wohnan kyamarah
black and white	**baki da fari**	bakee da paree
colour	**kala**	kalah
I'd like a hair-cut.	**Ina son ciko.**	eenah sohn cheekaw

Souvenirs *Tsaraba*

akwama	aquahmah	leather handbag
alabai	alabigh	leather wallet
kaftani da wando	kaptahnee da wandaw	kaftan and trouser set
malfa	malpah	straw-hat
riga da yar ciki	reegah da air-ar chikee	gown and shirt set
takalmin yara	tahkelmeen yahah	children's open leather shoes
zanna	zannah	embroidered cap

At the bank *A Banki*

Where's the nearest bank/currency exchange office?	**Don Allah, ina ne banki/ofishin canja kudi?**	dohn allah eenah nay bankee/ohrepishin chanja kudee
I want to change some dollars/pounds into Naira.	**Ina son in canja dala/ fam zuwa Naira.**	eenah sohn en chahnja dohlar/pam zuwah nighra
What's the exchange rate?	**Nawa ake canjawa?**	nohwa akay chanjahwah

At the post office *A Gidan Waya [Fas Ofis]*

I want to send this by …	**Ina son in aika wannan ta …**	eenah sohn en ighka wohnan ta
airmail	**iyamel**	"airmail"
express	**esfiress**	"express"
registered mail	**rajistattar wasika**	rejistettar waseekah
I want…-Naira stamps.	**Ina son kan sarki [sitam] na Naira …**	eenah sohn kahn sarkee [stam] na nighra
What's the postage for a letter/postcard to America?	**Nawa ne kudin aika takarda/kati zuwa Amurka?**	nohwa nay kudin ighka takardah/kartee zuwa amurka
Is there any mail for me? My name is …	**Ina da wasika? Sunana …**	eenah da waseekah. soonahnah
Can I send a telegram/fax?	**Ina iya aika da talgiram/faks?**	eenah iya ighkah da talgram/pax

Telephoning *Buga Waya*

Where's the nearest public phone?	**Ina ne ofishin buga waya mafi kusa?**	eenah nay ohrepishin buga wayah mapee kusa
I want to make an international call to…	**Ina son in buga waya zuwa …**	eenah sohn en buga wayah zuwa
Hello. This is … speaking.	**Halo … Ne ke magana.**	helloh … nay kay maganah
I want to speak to…	**Ina son in yi magana da …**	eenah sohn en yi maganah da
Will you tell him/her that I called?	**Ko za ka/ki gaya masa/mata cewa na bugo?**	kaw zah ka/ki gayah masa/mata chaywah nah bugaw

NUMBERS, see page 46

Time and date *Lokaci*

What's the time/hour?	**K'arfe nawa?**	Karpay nohwa
It's ...	**Yanzu ...**	yenzoo
five past one	**d'aya da minti biya**	daya da mintee biyar
quarter past three	**d'aya da kwata**	daya da quatah
twenty past five	**biyar da minti ashirin**	biyar da mintee ashireen
half-past seven	**bakwai da rabi**	bakoy da rabee
twenty-five to nine	**tara saura ashirin da biyar**	tarah sawrah ashireen da biyar
ten to ten	**goma saura goma**	gooma sawrah gohma
noon/midnight	**sha biyun rana/dare**	shah biyoon rahna/daray
in the morning	**da safe**	da saapay
during the day	**yau**	yo^{oo}
in the evening	**da maraice**	da marighchay
at night	**da dare**	da daray
yesterday	**jiya**	jiya
today	**yau**	ya^{oo}
tomorrow	**gobe**	gawbeh

Sunday	**Lahadi**	la-hadee
Monday	**Litinin**	leetineen
Tuesday	**Talata**	talahtah
Wednesday	**Laraba**	lahrabah
Thursday	**Alhamis**	alhamees
Friday	**Jumma'a**	jumma-ah
Saturday	**Asabar**	assabar
January	**Janairu**	janighru
February	**Fibrairu**	pibrighru
March	**Maris**	mahris
April	**Afrilu**	apreelu
May	**Mayu**	mahyu
June	**Yuni**	yoonee
July	**Yuli**	yoolee
August	**Agusta**	agusta
September	**Satumba**	satumbah
October	**Oktoba**	ohktohber
November	**Nuwamba**	nuwambah
December	**Disamba**	desember

Numbers *Lambobi*

0	**sifili**	sipilee
1	**d'aya**	Daya
2	**biyu**	biyu
3	**uku**	uku
4	**hud'u**	huDu
5	**biyar**	biyar
6	**shida**	shida
7	**bakwai**	bakoy
8	**takwas**	taquas
9	**tara**	tara
10	**goma**	gawma
11	**sha d'aya**	shah Daya
12	**sha biyu**	shah biyu
13	**sha uku**	shah uku
14	**sha hud'u**	shah huDu
15	**sha biyar**	shah biyar
16	**sha shida**	shah shida
17	**sha bakwai**	shah bakoy
18	**sha takwas**	shah taquas
19	**sha tara**	shah tara
20	**ashirin**	ashireen
21	**ashirin da d'aya**	ashireen da Daya
30	**talatin**	talahteen
40	**arba'in**	arba-een
50	**hamsin**	hamseen
60	**sittin**	sitteen
70	**saba'in**	saba-een
80	**tamanin**	tamahneen
90	**casa'in**	chasa-een
100	**d'ari**	Daree
101	**d'ari da d'aya**	Daree da Daya
200	**d'ari biyu**	Daree biyu
500	**d'ari biyar**	Daree biyar
1,000	**dubu**	duboo
100,000	**dubu dari**	duboo daree
1,000,000	**miliya d'aya**	milliohn Daya
first	**na d'aya**	na Daya
second	**na biyu**	na biyu
once	**sau d'aya**	sa^{oo} Daya
twice	**biyu**	biyu

a half	**rabi**	rabee
a quarter	**kwata**	quartah
one third	**sulusi**	sulusee

Emergency *Hadari*

Call the police	**Kira yan sanda**	kirah airn sandah
Get a doctor	**Kira likita**	kirah likita
Go away	**Tafi**	tapi
HELP	**TAIMAKO**	tighmakaw
I'm ill	**Ban da lafiya**	ban da lahpiyah
I'm lost	**Na b'ata**	nah Batah
Leave me alone	**Rabu da nii**	rabu da nee
STOP THIEF	**HA B'ARAWO**	hah Barahwaw
My … have been stolen.	**An sace mini …**	an sahchay mini
I've lost my …	**Na b'atad da …**	nah Batad da
handbag	**handibagena**	handibageenah
passport	**fasfo d'eenaa**	paspaw Deenah
luggage	**kayana**	kahyahnah
wallet	**alabaina**	alabaynah
Where can I find a doctor who speaks English?	**Ina zan sami likitan dake jin Turanci?**	eenah zohn sahmi likitan dakay jin toorenchee

Guide to Hausa pronunciation

Consonants

Letter	Approximate pronunciation	Symbol	Example	
b, d, g, h, j, k. l, m, n, r, s, t, w, y, z	as in English			
c	like **ch** in **ch**urch	ch	**ce**	chay
f	like **p** in **p**ower	p	**fari**	paree

TELEPHONING, see page 44

Special consonants

b'	similar to **b** but more forceful	B	**b'ata**	Batah
d'	similar to **d** in **d**og, but more forceful	D	**d'aya**	Daya
k'	similar to **k** in **k**ite, but more forceful	K	**k'alau**	Kala^{oo}
kw	like **qu** in **qu**ick	qu	**kwan**	quan
ts	similar to **s** but more forceful; like **ts** in **tsetse**	ts	**tsada**	tsahdah

Vowels

a	usually:			
	1) like **a** in **a**t	a	**ban**	ban
	2) like **a** in c**a**r	ah	**kwana**	quahna
	3) like **ai** in p**ai**n	ai	**nan**	nain
	4) like **o** in t**o**ne	oh	**wane**	wohneh
e	1) like **e** in b**e**d	e/eh	**fagen**	pagen
			wace	wohcheh
	2) like **a** in g**a**me	ay	**gode**	gawday
i	1) like **i** in s**i**t	i	**rasit**	rasit
	2) like **ee** in sh**ee**n	ee	**ina**	eenah
o	1) like **o** in t**o**ne	oh	**don**	dohn
	2) like **aw** in s**aw**	aw	**fito**	pitaw
u	1) like **u** in p**u**t	u	**guda**	gudah
	2) like **oo** in m**oo**d	oo	**turanci**	toorenchee

Diphthongs

ai	like **igh** in s**igh**	igh	**mai**	migh
au	like **ou** in **ou**t	a^{oo}	**kyau**	kyaoo
ya	aspirated and with some force, as in **air**	air	**yayana**	airairnah

Malagasy

Basic expressions *Fiteny andavanandro*

Yes.	**Eny./En, En.**	**ayn**'/ay^{n} ay^{n}
No.	**Tsia./An, An.**	ts'/a^{n} a^{n}
Please.	**Azafady.**	**azafad**'
Thank you.	**Misaotra tompoko.**	**m**'sa^{oo}tr' toompk'
I beg your pardon?	**Ahoana tsara hoe./ Azafady.**	a-oana **tsara** o/ azafad'

Introductions *Fifankalalana*

Good morning/ Good afternoon.	**Manao ahoana tompoko.**	ma-na-**oana** **toompk**'
Good night.	**Tafandria mandry tompoko.**	ta-fan**dree** ma^{n}dr' **toomp**'k
Good-bye.	**Veloma tompoko.**	vay**looma** **toompk**'
My name is …	**… no anarako.**	**noo** anara-k'
Pleased to meet you.	**Faly mahafantatra anao.**	fal' **mafantatr**' **ana**^{oo}
What's your name?	**Iza no anaranao?**	ee-za noo anara**na**^{oo}
How are you?	**Manao ahoana ianao?**	ma-na-**oan** **ee-na**^{oo}
Where do you come from?	**Avy aiza ianao**	av' ayz' **ee-na**^{oo}
I'm from …	**Avy any …**	**a**vee-**a**nee
Australia	**Australie**	**o**stra-lee
Britain	**Angletera**	an-glay**tay**ra
Canada	**Kanada**	ka-na**da**
USA	**Etazonia**	ay-ta**zoo**nee
I'm with my …	**Miaraka amin'ny … aho.**	**miara**-km-nee … a'
wife/husband	**vadiko**	**va**dee-k'
children	**zanako**	**za**na-k'
parents	**ray amandreniko**	re man**dray**nee-k'
boyfriend/girlfriend	**namako**	**na**-ma-k'
I'm on vacation.	**Maka rivotra aho.**	**ma**ka-**ree**vootr'a
I'm on business.	**Miasa aho.**	mia-**sa**^{oo}

GUIDE TO PRONUNCIATION, see page 63/EMERGENCIES, see page 62

Questions *Fanontaniana*

How?	**Ahoana no …?**	a^{oo}na **noo**
When?	**Rahoviana?**	**roa**veen'
Why?	**Nahoana?**	na-oan'
Which?	**Iza?**	**eez**
What is this/that?	**Inona ity/ito?**	een'**eetee/eetoo**
Who is this/that?	**Iza io/iny**	eez**eeo**/eez**ee**nee
Where is/are …?	**Aiza ny/Aiza i' …?**	ayz nee/ay**zee**
Where can I get/find …?	**Aiza no mety ahazoko/ahitako …?**	ayz noo may-tee **azo**-koo/a-**eetak**'
How long …?	**Afirihana no …?**	**afreen**'
How much …?	**Ohatrinona …?**	o-**treen**'
Can I have …?	**Mba omeo kely … aho azafady?**	mba o-may-oo kay-lee … **a' azafad**'
Can you help me?	**Azafady mba atorohy ahy kely ity?**	aza**fa**dee mba a-too-roo-ee a' kay**leetee**
What does this mean?	**Inona no dikan'ity?**	ee-noo-na noo dee-kan'eetee
I understand.	**Azoko.**	a-zoo-koo
I don't understand.	**Tsy azoko.**	tsee a-zoo-k'
Please speak slowly.	**Mitenena miadana azafady.**	mee-tay**nay**na mee-da-na **azafad**'
Can you translate this for me?	**Adikao kely amiko ity azafady?**	a-dee**ka^{oo}** kay-lee ameek'-**eetee azafad**'
Do you speak English?	**Miteny anglisy ve ianao?**	mee**tay**nee-an-glee-s' vay **ee**-na^{oo}
I don't speak Malagasy.	**Tsy miteny malagasy aho.**	tsee mee-tay-n' malaga-see a^{oo}

A few useful words *Fomba fiteny sasantsany*

big/small	**lehibe/kely**	lay**bay/kay**lee
cheap/expensive	**mora/lafo**	**moora/laf**'
early/late	**aloha loatra/tara**	**aloo'** loatr'/**tar**'
good/bad	**tsara/ratsy**	**tsar**'/**rats**'
hot/cold	**mafana/mangatsiaka**	**ma**fa-na/man-ga-**tseek**'
near/far	**akaiky/lavitra**	a-ka-ee-k'/la-vee-tr'
next/last	**aorian'ny/farany**	a^{oo}reen'/**fara**-nee
right/wrong	**marina/diso**	**ma**ree-n'/**dee**soo

Hotel–Accommodation *Hotely*

We've reserved two rooms.	**Namandrika efitra roa izahay.**	na-man-dree-**kay**-fee-tr' **roo** zay
Do you have any vacancies?	**Misy efitra tsy misy olona ve ato aminareo?**	mee-see ay-fee-tra tsee mee-s'ol'-na vay atoo amee-na-ray-oo
I'd like a … room.	**Mila efitra … aho.**	mee-la ay-fee-tra … a^{oo}
single	**tokana**	**to**-ka-na
double	**ho an'olona roa**	oo an'ol'na roo
with twin beds	**misy fandriana anankiroa**	mee's fan-dree-na-a-nan-kee-roa
with a double bed	**misy fandriana lehibe ho an'olon-droa**	mee-s' fan**dree**na lay-bay oo-an'olon'droa
with a bath	**misy efitra fandroana**	mee-see ay-fee-tra fan**dro**ana
with a shower	**misy douche**	mee-see doo-see
We'll be staying overnight only.	**Indray alina ihany izahay no hipetraka.**	ee^{n}dray a-lee-na ee-anee zay noo ee-pay-tra-ka
We'll be staying a few days.	**Hipetraka andro vitsivitsy izahay.**	ee-pe-tra-k'an-dro vee-tsee-vee-ts'eezay

Decision *Fanapahankevitra*

May I see the room? vay	**Mba azonay jerena ve ny efitrano, azafady?**	mba azo**nay** jay**ray**na ny ay-fee**tra**no azafa**dee**
That's fine. I'll take it.	**Mety tsara fa ho raisiko.**	me-t' tsa-ra fa o **ray**-s'-koo
No. I don't like it.	**An, an, tsy tiako ilay izy.**	an an tsee **tee**-koo lay eez'
It's too …	**… loatra.**	loa-tr'
cold/hot	**Mangatsiaka/Mafana**	man-gat**see**-ka/**ma**fa-na
dark/small	**Maizina/Kely**	**may**zeena/kay-lee
Do you have anything …?	**Soa dia misy … kokoa?**	soa-dee-mee-s' … koo-**koa**
better/bigger	**tsaratsara/lehibebe**	tsa-ra**tsara**/lay**bay**bay
cheaper	**moramora**	moo-ra-moo-ra
May I please have my bill?	**Azafady kely hoe ny noty?**	azafad' kay-lee o nee **no**-tee

NUMBERS, see page 62

Eating out *Misakafo any ivelany*

I'd like to reserve a table for 4.	**Mba hamandrika latabatra ho an'olona efatra azafady.**	mba a-**man**-dree-ka lata**b**atr-o an'**ol'**-a **ay**-fa-tra azafadee
We'll come at 8.	**Tonga eo izahay amin'ny valo.**	toong'ay-oo 'zay a**meen'**n' valoo
I'd like breakfast/ lunch/dinner.	**Mila sakafo maraina/ antoandro/hariva.**	mee-la sa-**ka**foo ma-**ray**^{n}a/a-toa-dr'/a-ree-va

The staple food is rice (*vary*), eaten for breakfast (*vary sosoa*), for lunch (*vary maina*) and dinner (*vary amin'anana*). It is always eaten with an accompaniment of *loaka* – fish or meat mixed with vegetables.

Do you have a set menu?	**Misy menu mano-kana ve?**	mee-s'may-noo ma**noo**ka-na vay
Do you have local dishes?	**Misy sakafo avy eto antoerana?**	mee-s' sa-**ka**-f' avee-aytoo a^{n}-**to**-ra-n'
What do you recommend?	**Inona no tsara ho haninay?**	ee-n'a noo tsa-ra a-n'-nay
Do you have vegetarian dishes?	**Misy sakafo tsy misy hena ve?**	mees' sa-**kaf'** tsee mee-see **ay**na vay

Breakfast *Sakafo maraina*

May I have some …?	**Mba itondray kely … aho azafady?**	mba ee-too^{n}**dray**kay-lee … a^{oo} azafadee
bread/butter	**mofo/dobera**	moo-f'/d**bay**ra
jam	**konfitiora**	ko^{n}-fee-tee-r'
rolls	**petypain**	pe-tee-pay^{n}

Snacks *Hanin-Kotrana*

katsaka (**ka**tsa-ka)	loose grains of maize cooked in milk and sugar
koba (koo-ba)	mixture of ground peanuts and sugar, covered in rice flour paste and wrapped in banana leaves
menakely (may-na**kayl'**)	small doughnut made from fried rice flour and dip
mofo sakay (moo-f' sa-kay)	small cake made with finely shredded greens and hot Malagasy pepper

NUMBERS, see page 62

Meat *Hena*

I'd like some …	**Omeo kely … aho azafady.**	o-may-oo kayl' … **a^{oo}** azafad'
beef/chicken	**hen'omby/akoho**	ayno^{m}-b'/**akoo**
goat/lamb	**hen'osy/hen'ondry**	ayn'oos'/en'o^{n}-dr'
pork	**henakisoa**	ay-na kee**soo**
veal	**henan-jana-komby**	ayna-**dza**-na-ko^{m}-b'

hena ritina (ayna **ree**tee-na) — meat, generally beef and pork, boiled until the water has completely dried out

romazava (roo-mazava) — beef cooked with vegetables, garlic and tomatoes

varanga (va**ran**-ga) — sirloin steamed and shredded, then dried and fried; usually reserved for special occasions

baked	**natono**	na**too**n'
boiled	**nampangotrahana**	na^{m}-pa^{n}-goa-tra-ha-na
fried	**nendasina**	nay^{n}-da-seen'
grilled	**natono**	na-toon'
roast	**hena voatsatsika**	ay-na voa-tsa-tseek'
stewed	**alain-dro**	a-lay^{n}-dr'
underdone (rare)	**mantamanta**	**ma^{n}**ta-**ma^{n}**ta
medium	**antonintoniny**	a^{n}-too-ee^{n}-**too**nee-nee
well-done	**masaka tsara**	**ma**sa-ka tsa-r'

Fish and seafood *Trondro sy hazandrano*

drakaka (**dra**ka-ka) — medium-sized, purple crab from the south west

patsa (**pa**ts') — tiny red or white shrimps, dried and cooked, mixed with meat or served on their own

vango (va^{n}-goo) — fish from the south west; bony but delicious

Vegetables *legioma*

beans	**tsaramaso**	**tsa**ra-ma-soo
cabbage	**laisoa**	lay**soa**
carrots	**karaoty**	kara**^{oo}t'**

lentils	**ndengo**	**nday**^{n}goo
onion	**tongolo**	too^{n}**gool'**
peas	**pity poa**	peet'**poa**
potatoes	**ovy**	**oo**vee
rice	**vary**	**var'**
spinach (greens)	**anana**	**ana**-n'

lasary (lasaree)	mixed salad of shredded onions, tomatoes and *dania*, seasoned with salt and pepper
lasary karaoty (lasar kara^{oo}**t'**)	salad of carrots, french beans and cabbage

Fruit & dessert *Voankazo*

apple	**paoma**	pa^{oo}ma
banana	**akondro**	a-**koo**^{n}droo
lemon	**voasarimakirana**	voa**sar'**ma-**keer**a-na
orange	**voasary**	**voa**saree
plum	**paiso rakena**	pay-soo ra**kay**na
strawberries	**fraizy**	fray-**zee**
cake	**mofomamy**	moo**foo**mamee
flan	**fla**	fla
honey cake	**jalebo**	dzalayboo
ice-cream	**glasy**	**gla**see

Drinks *Zava-pisotro*

beer	**labiera**	la-**bee-ay**ra
(hot) chocolate	**kakao**	kaka^{oo}
coffee	**kafe**	ka**fay**
with(out) milk	**(tsy) misy ronono**	(ts') mees' roo**noo**noo
fruit juice	**ranomboankazo**	ran'boa**kaz'**
apple	**ranopaoma**	ran'**pa**^{oo}ma
orange	**ranomboasary**	ran'boa**sar'**
mineral water	**ranovisy**	ra-noo**vee**see
tea	**dite**	**deetay**
wine	**divay**	**deevay**
red/white	**mena/fotsy**	**may**na/foo-ts'
vodka	**vodka**	vo-dee-ka
water	**rano**	**ran**oo

betsabetsa	bay-tsa**bay**tsa	alcoholic banana drink
ranovola	ran'**voo**la	rice water
toaka gasy	toa-ka gas'	Malagasy rum

Complaints and paying *Fitarainana sy fandoavambola*

This is too … bitter/sweet	**… loatra ity. Mamy/Mangidy**	loat'rtee ma'/ma^{n}**geedee**
That's not what I ordered.	**Tsy ity mihitsy no nangatahako.**	ts' eetee **meen**tsee noo na^{n}gata-akoo
I'd like to pay.	**Azafady mba omeo amin'izay ny faktiora.**	azafad' mba o-**may-oo** ameen'eezay nee fak**teer'**
I think you made a mistake in the bill.	**Misy diso ny fitambarany.**	mees' deeso nee feeta^{m}baranee
Can I pay with this credit card?	**Azo aloa amin'ity karta de kredi ity ve?**	azoo aloa ameen'**eetee** karta day kraydee**tee** vay
We only accept cash.	**Tsy mandray afa tsy lelavola izahay.**	tsee ma^{n}**dray** afa tsee lay-lavol'zay
Is service included?	**Efa voakaoty ato ve ny servisy.**	ayfa voa**ka^{oo}**tee a**too** vay nee serveesee
We enjoyed it, thank you.	**Tena afa-po izahay fa misaotra indrindra.**	tayna afa-poo zay fa meesa^{oo}tra '**dreen**dra
Our compliments to the cook/our host.	**Misoatra ny mpahandro/ny tompontrano.**	**mee**soa-tran' mpa-handroo/nee toom-poon-tranoo

Travelling around *Mitety tany*

Plane *Fiaramanidina*

Is there a flight to Toamasina?	**Misy vol mankany Toamasina ve?**	mees' vool' ma^{n}kan' toamaseena vay
What time do I check in?	**Amin'ny firy no tsy maintsy tonga eny amin'ny aeroport?**	ameen'nee **feeree** noo **tsee may^{n}**tsee too^{n}gay-nee ameen'aeroporo
I'd like to … my reservation on flight no. …	**Saika mba … toerana amin'ny vol …**	sayka mba … to-**rana** ameeny vol
cancel	**tsy andeha indray**	tsee an**day-a** 'dray
change	**hanova**	a**noo**va
confirm	**hanamafy**	anama**fee**

NUMBERS/TELLING THE TIME, see page 61

Train *Masinina*

I want a ticket to Antsirabe.	**Mba omeo kely billet ho any Antsirabe aho azafady.**	mba o-**may-oo** kayl' bee-ay oo anee-antsee-rabay a^{oo} azafad'
single (one-way)	**mandroso ihany**	ma^{n}-**droo**soo ee-anee
return (roundtrip)	**mandroso sy miverina**	ma^{n}-**droo**soo see mee-**vay**-reena
first class	**premiera**	pray-mee-**ay**-r'
economy	**ekonomi**	ay-koa-**noa**-mee
How long does the journey (trip) take?	**Adiny firy vao tonga any?**	adeenee feeree va^{oo} $too^{n}g$'anee
When is the… train to Toamasina?	**Amin'ny firy ny masinina… mankany Toamasina no mandeha?**	ameen'**fee**ree nee maseena … ma^{n}kanee toamaseena noo manday
first	**voalohany**	voa-**loo**-anee
next	**manaraka**	man**a**raka
last	**farany**	faranee
Is this the right train to Andasibe?	**Ity ve no masina mankany Andasibe?**	'tee vay noo mas**ee**na ma^{n}kanee **'^{n}da**seebay
There's no train today.	**Tsy misy masinina androany.**	tsee meesee **maseen'**a^{n}droo-**anee**

Bus–Coach *Bus–Taxibe*

Is there a … today?	**Misy … ve anio?**	mees' … vay **ani^{oo}**
What bus do I take to the centre?	**Inona ny aotobisy mankany antanana.**	eenoo**na** nee $a^{oo}$to**bee**see ma^{n}kanee a^{n}**tanana**
How much is the fare to …?	**Ohatrinona ny mankany …?**	o-tree**na** nee ma^{n}kan'
Will you tell me when to get off?	**Lazao kely aiza aho notokony hiala azafady.**	**$laza^{oo}$** kayl' **ayza** a^{oo} **noa-toa**-koa-nee ee-la **azafa**dee

Taxi *Taxi*

How much is it to …?	**Ohatrinona ny mankany …?**	o-tree**na** nee ma^{n}**kan**'
Take me to …	**Any an …**	anee a^{n}

NUMBERS, see page 62

Please stop here.	**Eo aho ajanona azafady.**	ay-oo a^{oo} **adza**noona aza**fa**dee
Please wait for me.	**Andraso kely aho azafady.**	a^{n}draso **kay**-lee a^{oo} aza**fa**dee
I'll be 10 minutes.	**Folo minitra na fahefak'adiny ihany.**	fool'mee**nee**tra na fayfa**k'a**deenee ee-nee

Car hire–Automobile rental *Manofa aotomobilina*

I'd like to hire (rent) a car.	**Te hanofa aotomobilina aho azafady.**	tay anoofa a^{oo}to**mo**bee-ee'a^{oo} aza**fa**dee
I'd like it for a day/week.	**Indray andro ihany/ mandritra ny herinandro.**	'dray androo ee-anee/ma^{n}**dree**tree nee ayreena^{n}droo
Where's the nearest filling station?	**Aiza ny lasantsy akaiky indrindra eto?**	ayza nee la**sa**^{n}tsee akayk'ee^{n}dree^{n}dr'aytoo
Full tank, please.	**Fenoy azafady.**	fay**noo-ee** aza**fa**dee
Give me … litres of petrol (gasoline).	**Omeo kely tsotra … litatra, azafady.**	'may-oo kaylee tsoo**tra** … lee**tatr**'a^{oo} aza**fa**dee
How do I get to…?	**Ahoana no ahatongavako any…?**	a^{oo}-ana noo atoo^{n}ga**va**koo anee
I've had a breakdown at …	**Simba ao … ny fiara.**	**see**^{m}ba a^{oo} … nee **fee**-ra
Can you send a mechanic?	**Azonao andefasana mekanisien?**	azoona^{oo} a^{n}day**fa**sana mayka**nee**see-ayn
Can you mend it?	**Azonao amboarina ve?**	azoona^{oo} a^{m}boa**ree**na vay

☞ You're on the wrong road.	**Diso lalana ianao.** ☜
Go straight ahead.	**Mandehana mahitsy foana.**
It's down there on the left/right.	**Ao ambany ankavian-dalana ao/ankavanana.**
next to/after …	**eo akaikin'ny …/ ao aorinan'ny**
north/south	**avaratra/atsimo**
east/west	**atsinanana/andrefana**

EMERGENCIES, see page 62

Sightseeing *Mitsangatsangana*

Where's the tourist office?	**Aiza ny birao'ny fisahantany?**	ayza nee **bra^{oo}**-nee feesa**ha**^{n}tanee
Is there an English-speaking guide?	**Misy gida mahay miteny anglisy ve?**	mees' **gee**da ma-hay mee**tay**nee anglees' vay
Where is/are the …?	**Aiza ny …?**	ay**za** nee
botanical gardens	**zaridaina**	zaree**dayn**'
castle	**rova**	roov'
church	**fiangonana**	fee^{n}**go**na-na
city centre	**ampovoantanàna**	a^{m}poovoata**na**na
harbour	**seranana**	say**ra**nana
market	**tsena**	**tsay**na
museum	**muze**	**moo**zay
president's palace	**ambohitsirohitra**	a^{m}bootsee**o**-eetra
shops	**mpivarotra**	mpee**va**rootr'
town council	**lapan'ny tanàna**	lapan'ta**na**na
When does it open/close?	**Amin'ny firy no mivoha/mihidy?**	ameen'**fee**ree no mee**voo/mee**dee
How much is the entrance fee?	**Ohatrinona ny fidirana?**	oatree**na** nee fee**dee**rana

Entertainment *Fialamboly*

What's playing at the theatre?	**Inona no fampisehoana ao?**	eena nee fa^{m}peeseùn' a^{oo}
How much are the seats?	**Ohatrinona ny fidirana?**	o-tree**na** nee feedee**ra**na
Would you like to go out with me tonight?	**Afaka miara mivoaka amiko ve ianao rahariva?**	afaka miara mee**voa**ka ameekoo vay **ee**-na^{oo} rareeva
Is there a discotheque in town?	**Misy boaty ve any an-tanana any?**	mees' **boa**tee vay anee an-ta**na**na anee
Thank you. It's been a wonderful evening.	**Misaotra fa tena nahafinaritra be.**	meesa^{oo}tra fa tayna nafee**na**reetr'

fanorona (fa**noor**') traditional Malagasy game for two players; similar to draughts

hira gasy (eeragas') open-air, opera-like performance with dances, songs and lyrics

DAYS OF THE WEEK, see page 61/NUMBERS, see page 62

Shops, stores and services *Mpivarotra, tsenakely, stasio*

Where's the nearest…?	**Aiza ny … akaiky indrindra eto?**	**ay**za nee … akaykee**dree^{n}**dr'ayto
baker's	**mpanaomofo**	**mpana^{oo}moof**'
butcher's	**mpivarokena**	mpee**va**rookayn'
chemist's	**mpivaropanafody**	mpee**va**roo^{m}pana**food**'
grocery	**tsenakely**	tsayna**kayl**'
newsagent	**mpivarotra gazety**	mpee**va**rootr **gazayt**'
post office	**paositra**	**pa^{oo}**seetr'
supermarket	**supermarse**	soopayr**mar**say
toilets	**kabine**	kabeenay

General expressions *Fiteny andavanandro*

Where's the main shopping area?	**Aiza ny tsena be?**	**ay**z nee**tsayn**'
Do you have any…?	**Misy … ve ato aminareo?**	**mees**' … vay atoo ameen**a**ray-oo
Do you have anything …?	**Mba misy … kokoa noho ity ve?**	mba **mees**' … koo**koa** noo **eetee** vay
better/cheaper	**tsaratsara/moramora**	tsara**tsa**ra/moo**ra**moora
larger/smaller	**lebebe/kelikely**	lay**bay**bay/kaylee**kay**lee
How much is this?	**Ohatrinona ity?**	oatree**n** **eetee**
Please write it down.	**Soraty kely azafady.**	soo-**ra**-tee **kayl** **azafad**'
No, I don't like it.	**Tsy tiako.**	tsee **teek**'
I'll take it.	**Ho entiko ity.**	oo **e^{n}**teekoo **'tee**

black/blue	**mainty/manga**	may^{n}t'/ma^{n}g'
brown	**volon-takatra**	vooloon-ta**ka**tr'
green	**maintso**	may^{n}ts'
orange	**volondaoranjy**	voo**loon**dora^{n}dz
red/yellow	**mena/mavo**	mayn'/mav'

I want to buy …	**Te hividy …**	tay eeveed'
anti-malaria tablets	**nivakina**	neeva**keen**'
aspirin	**aspirina**	aspee**reen**'
batteries	**pila**	**pee**la
newspaper	**gazety**	**gazayt**'
English/American	**anglisy/amerikana**	a^{n}glees'/amayree**kan**'
post card	**karta paositaly**	karta pa^{oo}see**ta**lee

shampoo	**savony fanasana loha**	savoon' fana**sa**na loo
sun-tan cream	**menaka fiarovana amin'ny hainandro**	**may**naka fee**roo**van' ameen'ay**na^{n}dr'**
soap	**savony**	savoon
toothpaste	**dantifrisy**	da^{n}tee**free**see
a half-kilo of apples	**paoma atsasakilao**	pa^{oo}ma atsakee**la^{oo}**
a litre of milk	**ronono ray litra**	roo**noo**noo ray **lee**tr'

At the bank *Any amin'ny banky*

Where's the nearest bank?	**Aiza ny banky akaiky indrindra eto?**	ayza nee bankee akaykee'dree^{n}dr'ayto
I want to change some dollars/pounds into Malagasy francs.	**Te hanakalo dollars/ sterling ho vola gasy aho.**	tay ana**ka**loo dolara/seetereeleengee oo **voola gas**' a^{oo}
What's the exchange rate?	**Ohatrinona ny dollars/sterling iray?**	o-tree**na** nee dolara/seetereeleengee

At the post office *Any amin'ny paositra*

I want to send this by …	**Tiako mba alefa … kely ity azafady.**	**tee**koo mba **a**layfa … kayl'**tee** aza**fa**dee
airmail	**alefa fiaramanidina**	alayfa fiarama**nee**deena
express	**express**	ek**spre**see
I want …-franc stamps.	**Omeo kely timbra … ariary aho azafady.**	omay-oo **kay**lee **tee^{m}**bra … aree**ree** a^{oo} aza**fa**dee
What's the postage for a letter to America?	**Ohatrinona ny mandefa taratasy any Etazonia?**	o-**tree**'na nee ma^{n}day fa tara**ta**see an'ayta**zo**nee
Is there any mail for me? My name is …	**Misy taratasy ho ahy ve ao azafady? I … no anarako.**	mees' tara**ta**see oo-a vay a^{oo} aza**fa**d'. ee … noo **ana**-ra-koo

Telephoning *Mitelefaonina*

Where's the nearest public phone?	**Aiza no misy telefaonina eto akaiky eto?**	ayza noo **mee**see **tay**layfo'na eto akaykee **ay**to
Hello. This is … speaking.	**Allo. I … ihany ity.**	**a**loa. ee … ee-anee **ee**tee
I want to speak to …	**Mba omeo kely ahy i …**	mba **o**-may-oo kayl' **a ee**

NUMBERS, see page 62

When will he/she be back?	**Rahoaviana izy no hiverina ao?**	**roa**veen' eez noo ee**vay**reena^{oo}

Time and date *Ora/lera sy fotoana*

What's the time?	**Amin'ny firy izao?**	ameen' **feer**' 'za^{oo}
It's …	**Amin'ny …**	ameen'
five past one	**iray latsaka dimy**	ray **lat**sa-ka **deem**'
quarter past three	**telo sy fahefany**	**tay**l'see **fay**fanee
twenty past five	**dimy sy fahatelony**	deem'see fa-**tay**lonee
half-past seven	**fito sy sasany**	**feet**' see **sa**sanee
twenty-five to nine	**sivi latsaka fahatelony**	seev'**lat**sa-ka **fa**tay**lo**nee
ten to ten	**folo latsaka folo**	**fool**' **lat**sa-ka fool'
twelve o'clock	**roa ambin'ny folo**	room-bee-fool'
in the morning	**ny maraina**	nee ma**rayn**'
during the day	**amin'ny antoandro**	ameen' **a**^{n}too-**andr'**
in the evening	**amin'ny hariva/ rahariva**	ameen' a**reev**'/ra-**reev**
at night	**amin'ny alina**	ameen'**a**lee-na

Sunday	**Alahady**	la**had**
Monday	**Alatsinainy**	la-tsee**nayn**'
Tuesday	**Atalata**	ta**lat'**
Wednesday	**Alarobia**	la-roo**bee**
Thursday	**Alakamisy**	la-ka**mees**'
Friday	**Azoma**	zoo-**ma**
Saturday	**Asabotsy**	sa-boo-ts'
January	**Janoary**	dza-nu**ar**'
February	**Febroary**	fe-broo-**ar'**
March	**Martsa**	**mar**ts
April	**Aprily**	a**pree**lee
May	**Mey**	may
June	**Jiona**	**dzoo**na
July	**Jolay**	dzoo**lay**
August	**Aogositra**	**o**goseetr'
September	**Septambra**	sep**tam**br'
October	**Oktobra**	ok**to**br'
November	**Novambra**	no**vam**br'
December	**Desambra**	de**sam**br'

yesterday	**omaly**	**oomal'**
today	**anio**	**ani^{oo}**
tomorrow	**rahampitso**	ra^{m}**peets'**
hot season	**ohatoana**	**oo**toana
rainy season	**fahavaratra**	**faha-vara-tr'**
cold season	**ririnina**	**ree**reen

Numbers *Isa*

0	**naotra**	na^{oo}-tr'
1	**isa/iray**	ees'/'ray
2	**roa**	roo
3	**telo**	**tayl'**
4	**efatra**	ayfa-tr'
5	**dimy**	**dee**mee
6	**enina**	**ayn**na
7	**fito**	**feet**
8	**valo**	val'
9	**sivy**	**seev'**
10	**folo**	**fool'**
11	**iraik ambin'ny folo**	**'rayka**^{m}been'**fool'**
12	**roa ambin'ny folo**	**rooma**^{m}been'**fool'**
13	**telo ambin'ny folo**	**tel'**a^{m}been'**fool'**
14	**efatra ambin'ny folo**	efa-tram a^{m}been'**fool'**
15	**dimy ambin'ny folo**	**deem**'a^{m}been'**fool'**
16	**enina ambin'ny folo**	enee-na^{m}been'**fool'**
17	**fito ambin'ny folo**	**feet'a**^{m}been'**fool'**
18	**valo ambin'ny folo**	**val'** a^{m}**been**'fool'
19	**sivy ambin'ny folo**	**see**v a^{m}been'fool'
20	**roapolo**	roa**pool'**
21	**iraika amby roapolo**	**'ray**kamb'**roa**pool'
30	**telopolo**	**tayl'pool'**
40	**efapolo**	ayfa**pool'**
50	**dimampolo**	deema^{m}**pool'**
60	**enimpolo**	enee^{m}**pool'**
70	**fitopolo**	**feetpool'**
80	**valopolo**	**valpool'**
90	**sivyfolo**	**seevfool'**
100	**zato**	**zat'**
101	**iraika amby zato**	'ray-ka^{m}bee-zat'
200	**roanjato**	roa^{n}**dzat'**
500	**dimanjato**	deema^{n}**dzat'**
1,000	**arivo**	**areev**

100,000	**iray hetsy**	**'ray** ets'
1,000,000	**iray tapitrisa**	**'ray** ta-ptrees
first	**voalohany**	**voa**-loo-anee
second	**faharoa**	**faroo**
once	**indray mandeha**	'dray **ma^{n}**-day
twice	**in-droa**	ee^{n}-droo
a half	**hatsasany/tapany**	**atsasanee/ta**pa-nee
a quarter	**fahefany**	fa-**ayfan'**
one third	**am-pahatelony**	a^{m}pa**tay**loo-nee

Emergency *Loza/fahatairana*

Call the police	**Antsoy ny polisy**	**an**tsoo-ee nee po**lees'**
Get a doctor	**Antsoy ny dokotera**	**a^{n}**-tsoo-ee nee do-koo-**tayr'**
May I use your phone?	**Afaka mampiasa ny telefaonina ve aho azafady?**	afa-ka **ma^{m}**peesa nee **tay**lay**fo**neena vay a^{oo} aza**fa**dee
Go away	**Mandeha mandeha**	ma^{n}**day ma^{n}**day
HELP	**Miantso vonjy./ Vonjeo e. Vonjeo e.**	mia^{n}-ts' **vo^{n}**dzee/ vo^{n}-dzay **ay**. vo^{n}-dzay **ay**
I'm ill	**Marary aho/Tsy tsaratsara aho**	ma**rar'** a^{oo}/tsee **tsara**-tsara a^{oo}
I'm lost	**Very aho**	**vayr'** a^{oo}
Leave me alone	**Avelao aho/'mbela ery**	**a**vay-la^{oo} a^{oo}/'mbay-**la** ay**ree**
STOP THIEF	**Mpangalatra e**	mpa^{n}-ga-la-tr'ay
My … have been stolen.	**Nisy nangalatra ny …**	**nees'** na^{n}**ga**la-tra nee
I've lost my …	**Very ny …**	**vayr'nee**
handbag	**poketrako**	po-**kay**tra-k'
passport	**pasipaoroko**	pa-see**pa^{oo}**r'koo
luggage	**ny entako**	nee e^{n}**ta**koo
wallet	**portamoneako**	por-**ta**-mo-nay-koo
Where can I find a doctor who speaks English?	**Aiza no mety ahitako dokotera miteny anglisy?**	**ayz** noo **mayt'** a-ee**ta**koo do-koo-**tay**ra mee**tayn'** an-**glees'**

TELEPHONING, see page 60

Guide to Malagasy pronunciation

The letters **c, q, u, x** and **w** do not exist in Malagasy.

Consonants

Letter	Approximate pronunciation	Symbol		Example
b, d, f, g, h, k, l, m, n, p, t, v, z	as in English			
j	like **dge** in ju**dge**	dz	**jalebo**	dzalayboo
r	strongly rolled	r	**vary**	var'
s	like **ss** in possible	s	**laisoa**	lay**soa**
y	like **ee** in **knee**; appears only at the end of words	ee	**ity**	ee**tee**

The letter **h** is often silent; where this occurs it is omitted from the phonetic transcription.

Groups of consonants

dr	like **dr** in **dr**iver	dr	**drakaka**	**dra**ka-ka
ts	soft, like **ts** in **ts**ar	ts	**tsy**	**tsee**

Certain combinations of vowels and consonants ending in **m** or **n** should be pronounced nasalized; these are indicated by a superscript character, eg. **mandry** ($ma^{n}dr'$).

Vowels

a	like **a** in f**a**ther	a	**vadiko**	**va**dee-k'
e	like **ay** in **day**	e	**veloma**	vay**looma**
i	like **ee** in **knee**	ee	**iza**	**ee**-za
o	1) like **oo** in p**oo**l	oo	**tongolo**	too^{n}**gool'**
	2) similar to **o** in b**o**ld	o	**omeo**	o-**may-oo**

Vowels (and **y**) at the end of a word are usually silent and are indicated in the phonetic transcription by an apostrophe, eg. **azafady** (aza**fad**').

Diphthongs

ao/aho	like **ow** in n**ow**	a^{oo}	**avalao**	**a**va-la^{oo}
oa	like **oa** in b**oa**st	oa	**ianoa**	ee-**noa**
ia	like **ee** in b**ee**	ee	**tiako**	**tee**k'
ai	like **ay** in m**ay**	ay	**aiza**	ayz

Portuguese

Basic expressions *Expressões correntes*

Yes/No.	**Sim/Não.**	seeng/nahng^{w}
Please.	**Por favor/Se faz favor.**	poor fer**voar**/ser fahsh fer**voar**
Thank you.	**Obrigado(-a).**	oabri**ggah**doo(-er)
I beg your pardon?	**Diga?**	**dee**gher

Introductions *Apresentações*

Good morning.	**Bom dia.**	bawng **deeer**
Good afternoon.	**Boa tarde.**	**boa**er **tahr**der
Good evening/night.	**Boa noite.**	**boa**er **noy**ter
Good-bye.	**Adeus.**	er**deh**oosh
My name is …	**Chamo-me …**	**sher**moo mer
Pleased to meet you.	**Muito prazer em conhece-lo [la].**	**moong**^{y}too prer**zehr** ayhng^{y} koonyer**sseh** loo [ler]
What's your name?	**Como se chama?**	**koa**moo ser **sher**mer
How are you?	**Como está?**	**koa**moo ish**tah**
Fine thanks. And you?	**Bem, obrigad(-a). E o Senhor [a Senhora]?**	bayhng^{y} oabri**ggah**doo (-er). ee oo sin**nyoar** [er sin**nyoar**er]
Where do you come from?	**Donde é?**	**dawng**der eh
I'm from …	**Sou …**	soa
Australia	**de Austrália**	der owsh**trah**lyer
Britain	**de Grã-Bretanha**	der grahng brer**tah**nyer
Canada	**do Canadá**	doo kerner**dah**
South Africa	**de África do Sul**	der **ah**frikker doo sool
USA	**dos Estados Unidos**	doosh ish**tah**doosh oo**nee**-doosh
I'm with my …	**Estou com …**	ish**toa** kawng
wife	**a minha mulher**	er **mee**nyer mool**yehr**
husband	**o meu marido**	oo **meh**oo mer**ree**doo
family	**familia**	fer**mee**llyer

GUIDE TO PRONUNCIATION/EMERGENCIES, see page 79

Questions *Perguntas*

When?	**Quando?**	**kwahng**doo
Why?	**Porquê?**	poor**keh**
Which?	**Qual?**	kwahl
Who's there?	**Quem e?**	kayng^{y}eh
What is this/that?	**O que e isto/aquilo?**	oo ker eh **ish**too/er**kee**loo
Where is/are …?	**Onde é/são …?**	**awng**der eh/sahng^w
Where can I get …?	**Onde posso arranjar …?**	**awng**der **po**ssoo errahng**zhahr**
How?	**Como?**	**koa**moo
How far?	**A que distância?**	er ker dish**tahng**syer
How long?	**Quanto tempo?**	**kwahng**too **tayng**poo
How much (many)?	**Quanto(s)?**	**kwahng**too(sh)
Can you help me?	**Pode ajudar-me?**	**po**dder erzhoo**dahr** mer
What does this/ that mean?	**O que quer dizer isto/aquilo?**	oo ker kehr di**zehr** **eesh**too/er**kee**loo
I understand.	**Compreendo.**	kawng**pryayng**doo
I don't understand.	**Não compreendo.**	nahng^w kawng**pryayng**doo
Please speak slowly.	**Fale devagar, por favor.**	**fah**ler derver**gahr** poor fer**vohr**
Can you translate this for me?	**Pode traduzir-me isto?**	**po**dder trerdoo**zeer** mer **eesh**too
Can I have …?	**Queria …?**	ker**ree**er
Do you speak English?	**Fala inglês?**	**fah**ler eeng**glaysh**
I don't speak Portuguese.	**Não falo português.**	nahng^w **fah**loo poortoo**gehsh**

It's … *E/Esta …*

better/worse	**melhor/pior**	mill**yor**/pee**ohr**
big/small	**grande/pequeno**	**grahng**der/per**keh**noo
cheap/expensive	**barato/caro**	ber**rah**too/**kah**roo
good/bad	**bom/mau**	bawng/mow
hot/cold	**quente/frio**	**kehng**ter/**free**oo
near/far	**perto/longe**	**pehr**too/**lawng**zher
right/wrong	**certo/errado**	**sehr**too/**irrah**doo
vacant/full	**livre/ocupado**	**lee**vrer/okkoo**pah**doo

Hotel–Accommodation *Hotel*

I've a reservation.	**Mandei reservar.**	mahngday rerzerr**vahr**
Do you have any vacancies?	**Tem quartos vagos?**	tayhng^{y} **kwahr**toosh **vah**goosh
I'd like a … room.	**Queria um quarto …**	ker**ree**er oong **kwahr**too
single	**de solteiro**	der sohl**tay**roo
double	**de casal**	der ker**zahl**
with twin beds	**com duas camas**	kawng **doo**ersh **ker**mersh
with a double bed	**de casal**	der ker**zahl**
with a bath/shower	**com banho/duche**	kawng **bah**nyoo/**doo**sher
with a balcony	**com varanda**	kawng ver**rahng**der
We'll be staying …	**Ficamo …**	fi**kkah**moosh
overnight only	**só esta noite**	saw **ehsh**ter **noy**ter
a few days	**alguns dias**	ahl**goongsh dee**ersh
a week	**uma semana**	**oo**mer ser**mah**ner

Decision *Decisão*

May I see the room?	**Posso ver o quarto?**	**po**ssoo vehr oo **kwahr**too
That's fine. I'll take it.	**Está bem. Fico com ele.**	ish**tah** bayng^{y}. **fee**koo kawng **ay**ler
No. I don't like it.	**Não, não gosto dele.**	nahng^{w} nahng^{w} **gosh**too **day**ler
It's too …	**É muito …**	eh **moong**^{y}too
cold/hot	**frio/quente**	**free**oo/**kehng**ter
dark/small	**escuro/pequeno**	ish**koo**roo/per**keh**noo
noisy	**barulhento**	berroo**lyayng**too
Do you have anything …?	**Tem algo …?**	tehng^{y} **ahl**goo
better/bigger	**melhor/maior**	mi**llyor**/mer**yor**
cheaper	**mais barato**	mighsh ber**rah**too
quieter	**mais sossegado**	mighsh soosser**gah**doo
May I please have my bill?	**Pode trazer-me a conta, por favor?**	**po**dder trer**zehr** mer er **kawng**ter poor fer**voar**
It's been a very enjoyable stay.	**Tivemos uma estadia muito agradável.**	tiv**veh**moosh **oo**mer ishter**deeer moong**^{y}too ergrer**dah**vehl

DAYS OF THE WEEK, see page 97

Eating out *Restaurant*

I'd like to reserve a table for 4.	**Queria reservar uma mesa para quatro pessoas.**	kerreeer rerzerr**vahr** oomer **meh**zer **per**rer **kwah**troo perssoaersh
We'll come at 8.	**Viremos às 8.**	vir**reh**moosh ahsh 8
I'd like …	**Queria …**	kerr**ee**er
breakfast	**tomar o pequeno almoço**	too**mahr** oo per**kay**noo ahl**moa**ssoo
lunch	**o almoçar**	oo ahlmoa**ssahr**
dinner	**o jantar**	oo zhahng**tahr**
Do you have any local dishes?	**Tem pratos tipicos?**	tehng^{y} **prah**toosh **tee**pikoosh
What do you recommend?	**O que me recomenda?**	oo ker mer rerko**mehng**der
Do you have vegetarian dishes?	**Tem pratos vegetarianos?**	tahng^{y} **prah**toosh verzherter**ryah**noosh

Breakfast *Pequeno almoço*

May I have some …?	**Pode trazer-me …?**	**po**dder trer**zehr** mer
bread	**pão**	pahng^{w}
butter	**manteiga**	mahng**tay**ger
eggs	**ovos**	**o**vvoosh
jam	**doce de fruta**	**doa**sser der **froo**ter
rolls	**papo-secos**	**pah**poo **say**koosh

Starters *Acepipe*

castanhas de caju	kersh**ter**nyersh der kah**zhoo**	cashew nuts
cocktail de camarao	kohk**tayhl** der kermer**rahng**^{w}	prawn cocktail
ovos cozido	**o**vvoosh koo**zee**doosh	boiled eggs

Soups *Sopas*

caldo verde	**kahl**do **vehr**der	potatoes, cabbage and garlic soup
canja	**kahng**zher	soup of rice, chicken and onions
sopa de peixe	**soa**per der **pay**sher	fish and vegetable soup

NUMBERS, see page 78

Meat *Carnes*

I'd like some ...	**Queria ...**	ker**ree**er
beef	**carne de vaca**	**kahr**ner der **vah**ker
chicken	**frango**	**frahng**goo
goat	**cabrito**	ker**bree**too
lamb	**borrego**	boo**rreh**goo
pork	**carne de porco**	**kahr**ner der **por**koo
veal	**vitelo**	vi**teh**loo

bifes com batatas fritas	**bee**fersh kawng ber**tah**tersh **free**tersh	steak, french fries and rice
caldeirada de cabrito	kahlday**rah**der der ker**bree**too	stewed goat with vegetables and rice

feijoada (fayjoo**ah**der) stewed pork, beef, vegetables and beans in a sauce, served with rice

muamba de galinha (moo**wahng**ber der gher**lee**nyer) stewed chicken in palm oil sauce and *fufu* (a pasta of ground dried cassava or maize)

boiled/fried	**cozido/frito**	koo**zee**doo/**free**too
grilled	**grelhado**	gri**llyah**doo
roast	**assado**	er**ssah**doo
stewed	**guisado**	gi**zzah**doo
underdone (rare)	**mal passado**	mahl per**ssah**doo
medium	**meio passado**	**may**oo per**ssah**doo
well-done	**bem passado**	bayng^{y} per**ssah**doo

Fish and seafood *Peixes e mariscos*

bacalhau com grao	berker**llyahoo** kawng grahng^{w}	boiled cod and chick-pea
caldeirada de choco	kahldey**rah**der der **shoh**koo	stewed squid in sauce
choco frito	**shoh**koo **free**too	fried squid and potatoes
cozido de bacalhau	koo**zee**doo der berker**llyahoo**	boiled cod, vegetables and eggs
gambas grelhadas	**gahng**bersh gri**llyah**dersh	grilled king prawns and vegetables

mufete (moo**feh**ter) grilled fish and boiled cassava or sweet potato, with chilli and onion sauce

Vegetables *Legumes*

beans (green)	**feijão verde**	fay**zhahng^{w} vehr**der
cabbage	**repolho**	rer**poh**llyoo
onion	**cebolas**	ser**boa**lersh
potatoes	**batatas**	ber**tah**tersh
rice/tomatoes	**arroz/tomates**	er**rohzh**/too**mah**tersh

Fruit–Dessert *Frutas–Sobremesa*

apple	**maçã**	mers**sahng**
cherries	**cerejas**	ser**ray**zhersh
lemon/orange	**limão/laranja**	li**mahng^{w}**/ler**rahng**zher
plum	**ameixas**	er**may**shersh
cake	**bolo**	**boh**loo
ice-cream	**gelado**	zher**lah**doo

Drinks *Bebidas*

beer	**cerveja**	ser**vay**zher
coffee	**um café**	oong ker**feh**
with/without milk	**com/sem leite**	kawng/sayhng^{y} **lay**ter
fruit juice	**um sumo de fruta**	oong **soo**moo der **froo**ter
(glass of) milk	**(um copo de) leite**	(oong **ko**ppoo der) **lay**ter
mineral water	**uma água mineral**	**oo**mer **ahg**wer minner**rahl**
tea	**um chá**	oong shah
wine	**vinho**	**vee**nyoo
red/white	**tinto/branco**	**teeng**too/**brahng**koo

kissangua (kee**ssahng**gwer) a non-alcoholic homemade pineapple drink; traditionally goes with chewed ginger root

maruvo (mer**roo**voo) alcoholic drink made with fermented palm tree ingredients

Paying *A conta*

I'd like to pay.	**Queria pagar.**	ker**ree**er per**gahr**
I think there's a mistake in the bill.	**Creio que se enganou na conta.**	**kray**oo ker ser aynggerr**noa** ner **kawng**ter
We enjoyed it, thank you.	**Gostámos muito, obrigado(-a).**	goosh**tah**moosh **moong^{y}**too oabrig**gah**doo(-er)

Travelling around *Excursões*

Plane *Avião*

Is there a flight to Luanda?	**Há vôo para Luanda?**	ah **voa**oo **per**rer **l^{w}an**der
What time do I check in?	**A que horas e o check-in?**	er ker **or**rersh eh oo sherking
I'd like to… my reservation.	**Queria… uma reserva.**	ker**reeer**… **oo**merr rez**zehr**ver
cancel/change	**cancelar/mudar**	kahngsser**lahr**/moo**dahr**
confirm	**confirmar**	kawngfirr**mahr**

Train *Comboio*

I want a ticket to Maputo.	**Quero um bilhete para Maputo.**	**keh**roo oong bill**yay**ter **per**rer mah**poo**too
single (one-way)	**ida**	**ee**der
return (roundtrip)	**ida e volta**	**ee**der ee **voll**ter
first/second class	**primeira/segunda classe**	prim**may**rer/ ser**goong**der **klah**sser
How long does the journey (trip) take?	**Quanto tempo demora a viagem?**	**kwahng**too **tayng**poo der**mor**rer er **vyah**zhahng^{y}
When is the … train to Beira?	**Quando é o … comboio para Beira?**	**kwahng**doo eh oo … kawng**boy**oo **per**rer **bey**rer
next	**próximo**	**proa**ssimmoo
last	**último**	**ool**timmoo

Bus–Coach *Autocarro*

Is there a bus today.	**Ha autocarros hoje?**	ah awto**kkah**rroosh **oh**zher
What bus do I take to …?	**Qual é o autocarro que vai para o …?**	kwahl eh oo owto**kkah**-rroo ker vigh **per**rer oo
How much is the fare to…?	**Quanto e o bilhete para…?**	**kwahng**too eh oo bill**yay**ter **per**rer
Will you tell me when to get off?	**Pode avisar-me quando devo descer?**	**po**dder ervi**zzahr** mer **kwahng**doo **day**voo dish**sayr**

TELLING THE TIME, see page 77

Taxi *Táxi*

How much is it to …?	**Qual é o preço do percurso para …?**	kwahl eh oo **pray**ssoo doo perr**koor**soo **per**rer
Take me to this address.	**Leve-me a este endereço.**	**leh**ver mer er **aysh**ter ayngder**ray**ssoo
Please stop here.	**Páre aqui, por favor.**	**pah**rer er**kee** poor fer**voar**

Car hire (rental) *Aluguer de viaturas*

I'd like to hire (rent) a car.	**Queria alugar um carro.**	ker**ree**er erloo**gahr** oong **kah**rroo
I'd like it for …	**Queria-o por …**	ker**ree**er oo poor
a day	**um dia**	oong **dee**er
a week	**uma semana**	**oo**mer ser**mer**ner
Where's the nearest filling station?	**Qual é a bomba de gasolina mais próxima?**	kwahl eh er **bohng**ber der gerzo**lee**ner mighsh **proa**ssimmer
Give me… litres of petrol (gasoline).	**Dê-me … litros de gasolina.**	day mer … **lee**troosh der gerzoo**lee**ner
How do I get to …?	**Como se vai para …?**	**koa**moo ser vigh **per**rer
I've had a breakdown at …	**Tive uma avaria em …**	**tee**ver **oo**mer erver**ree**er ahng[w]
Can you send a mechanic/break-down truck?	**Pode enviar-me um mecanico/reboque?**	**po**dder ing**vyahr**mer oong mer**kah**nikoo/ rer**boh**ker
Can you mend it?	**Consegue conserta-lo?**	kawngs**seh**ger kawngsser**tah**loo

☞ You're on the wrong road.	**Enganou-se na estrada.** ☜
Go straight ahead.	**Vá sempre em frente.**
It's down there	**É ali**
on the left/right.	**à esquerda/à direita.**
opposite/behind …	**em frente de/atrás de …**
next to/after …	**ao lado de/depois de …**
north/south/east/west	**norte/sul/(l)este/oeste**

NUMBERS, see page 78

Sightseeing *Visitas turisticas*

Where's the tourist office?	**Onde fica a agencia de turismo?**	**awng**der **fee**ker er er**zhehng**ssyer der too**reezh**moo
Is there an English-speaking guide?	**Há algum guia que fale inglês?**	ah ahl**goong ghee**er ker **fah**ler eeng**glaysh**
Where is/are the…?	**Onde fica …?**	**awng**der **fee**ker
botanical gardens	**o jardim botânico**	oo zherr**deeng** boo**ter**nikkoo
church	**a igreja**	er **iggray**zher
city centre	**o centro da cidade**	oo **sehng**troo der sid**dah**der
harbour/harbor	**o porto**	oo **poar**too
library	**a biblioteca**	er bibblyoo**teh**ker
market	**o mercado**	oo merr**kah**doo
museum	**o museu**	oo moo**zeh**oo
President's palace	**o palacio presidencial**	oo per**lah**ssio prezideng**ssiahl**
shops	**a zona comercial**	er **zoa**ner koomerr**syahl**
square	**a praça**	er **prah**sser
What are the opening hours?	**Quais são as horas de abertura?**	kwighsh sahng[w] ersh **o**rrersh der erber**too**rer
How much is the entrance fee?	**Quanto custa a entrada?**	**kwahng**too **koosh**ter er ayng**trah**der

Relaxing *Distracções*

What's playing at the theatre/theater?	**Qual e a peca que esta no teatro?**	kwahl eh er **peh**sser ker ish**tah** noo **tyah**troo
How much are the seats?	**Qual é o preço dos lugares?**	kwahl eh oo **pray**ssoo doosh loo**gah**rersh
Would you like to go out with me tonight?	**Quer sair comigo hoje à noite?**	kehr sereer koo**mee**goo **oa**zher ah **noy**ter
Would you like to dance?	**Quer dançar?**	kehr dahng**sahr**
Thank you. It's been a wonderful evening.	**Obrigado(-a), passei uma noite maravilhosa.**	oabrig**gah**doo(-er) per**ssay oo**mer **noy**ter merrervi**llyo**zzer

TELLING THE TIME, see page 77

Shops, stores and services *Lojas e serviços*

Where's the nearest ...?	**Onde é ... mais próximo(-a)?**	**awng**der eh ... mighsh **proa**ssimmoo(-er)
baker's	**o padaria**	er pahder**reeer**
bookshop	**a livraria**	er livvrer**reeer**
butcher's	**o talho**	oo **tahl**yoo
chemist's/drugstore	**a farmácia**	er ferr**mahs**syer
dentist	**o dentista**	oo dayng**teesh**ter
department store	**a zona comercial**	er **zoh**ner kawmmers**syahl**
grocery	**a mercearia**	er merrsier**reeer**
hospital	**o hospital**	oo oshpi**ttahl**
newsagent	**tabacarias**	terberker**ree**yer
post office	**os correios**	oosh koo**rray**oosh
supermarket	**o supermercado**	oo soopehrmerr**kah**doo
toilets	**as casas de banho**	ersh **kah**zersh der **ber**nyoo

General expressions *Expressões gerais*

Where's the main shopping area?	**Onde é a zona comercial?**	**awng**der eh er **zoa**ner koomerr**syahl**
Do you have any ...?	**Tem ...?**	tahng^y
Do you have anything ...?	**Não tem nada ...?**	nahng^w tahng^y **nah**der
better	**melhor**	mill**yor**
cheaper	**mais barato**	mighsh ber**rah**to
larger	**maior**	mah**yor**
smaller	**mais pequeno**	mighsh per**kay**noo
Can I try it on?	**Posso experimentar?**	possoo ishperimeng**tahr**
How much is this?	**Quanto custa isto?**	**kwahng**too **koosh**ter **eesh**too
Please write it down.	**Pode escrever num papel?**	**po**dder ishkrer**vayr** noong per**pehl**
That's too much.	**Esta muito caro.**	ishtah **moong**^{y}too **kah**roo.
How about ... kwanza?	**Faz por ... kwanza?**	**fahzh** poor ... **kwahn**zer
No, I don't like it.	**Não, não gosto.**	nahng^w nahng^w **gosh**too
I'll take it.	**Fico com ele.**	**fee**koo kawng **ay**ler

NUMBERS, see page 78

Do you accept credit cards?	**Aceitam cartões de crédito?**	er**ssay**tahng^{w} kerrtawng^{y}sh der **kreh**dittoo

black	**preto**	**preh**too
blue	**azul**	er**zool**
brown	**castanho**	kersh**tah**nyoo
green	**verde**	**vehr**der
orange	**cor-de-laranja**	koar der ler**rahng**zher
red	**vermelho**	verr**meh**llyoo
white	**branco**	**brahng**koo
yellow	**amarelo**	ermer**reh**loo

I want to buy…	**Quero comprar…**	**keh**roo kawng**prahr**
anti-malaria tablets	**comprimidos anti-malaria**	kawngpri**mee**doosh angtee mer**lah**ryer
aspirin	**aspirinas**	ershpi**rree**nersh
newspaper	**um jornal**	oong zhoor**nahl**
American	**americano**	ermerri**kker**noo
English	**inglês**	eeng**glaysh**
shampoo	**um shampoo/xampu**	oong shahng**poa**/ shahng**poo**
soap	**um sabonete**	oong serboo**nay**ter
sun-tan cream	**creme bronzeador**	**kreh**mer brawngzyerdoar
toothpaste	**uma pasta de dentes**	**oo**mer **pahsh**ter der **dayng**tish
a half-kilo of tomatoes	**meio-quilo de tomate**	**may**oo **kee**loo der too**mah**ter
a litre of milk	**um litro de leite**	oong **lee**troo der **lay**ter
I'd like film for this camera.	**Queria um rolo para esta máquina.**	ker**ree**er oong **roa**loo perrer **ehsh**ter **mah**kinner

Souvenirs *Lembranças*

panos do Congo	**pah**noosh doo **kohng**goo	large printed cloth (worn by women)
pecas de artesanato	**peh**ssersh der erterzer**nah**too	handmade statues portraying local history
postais	poesh**tah**eesh	postcards
quadros	**kwah**droosh	painting by local artist

At the bank *Banco*

Where's the nearest bank/currency exchange office?	**Onde é o banco/a agência de câmbio mais próximo/-a?**	**awng**der eh oo **bahng**koo/er er**zhayng**syer der **kahng**byoo mighsh **proa**ssimmoo/-er
I want to change some dollars/pounds.	**Quero trocar dólares/libras.**	**keh**roo troo**kahr** **do**llersh/**lee**brersh
What's the exchange rate?	**A como (Quanto) está o câmbio?**	er **koa**moo (**kwahng**toa) ish**tah** oo **kahng**byoo
I want to cash a traveller's cheque.	**Quero levantar um travel cheque.**	**keh**roo lervahng**tahr** oong **trah**vel **sheh**ker

At the post office *Nos Correios*

I want to send this by airmail/express.	**Quero enviar isto por avião/ por expresso.**	**keh**roo ingvi**ahr** **eesh**too poor er**vyahng**ʷ/ poor ish**preh**ssoo
I want …-kwanza stamps.	**Um selo de … kwanza, por favor.**	oong **say**loo der … **kwahn**zer poor fer**voar**
What's the postage for a letter/postcard to America?	**Qual é a franquia de um postal para os Estados Unidos?**	kwahl eh er frahng**keeer** der oong poosh**tahl** **per**rer oosh ish**tah**doosh oo**nee**doosh
Is there any mail for me? My name is …	**Há correio para mim? O meu nome é …**	ah koo**rrayoo** **per**rer meeng. oo **me**hoo **noa**mer eh

Telephoning *Telefones*

Where's the nearest public phone?	**Onde fica e cabine telefónica mais próxima?**	**awng**der **fee**ker er kah**bee**ner terler**fo**nnikker mighsh **pro**ssimmer
May I use your phone?	**Posso utilizar o seu telefone?**	**po**ssoo ootilli**zzahr** oo **se**hoo terle**fo**nner
Hello. This is … speaking.	**Está (Alô)? Aqui fala…**	ish**tah** (ahl**oa**). er**kee** **fah**ler
I want to speak to …	**Queria falar com …**	ker**reeer** fer**lahr** kawng

NUMBERS, see page 78

When will he/she be back?	**Quando é que ele/ela voltara?**	**kwahng**doo eh ker **ay**ler/**eh**ler vohlter**rah**
Will you tell him/her that I called?	**Pode dizer-lhe que eu telefonei?**	**po**dder diz**zayr** lyer ker **eh**oo terlerfoo**nay**

Time and date *Horas e data*

It's one o'clock.	**É uma hora.**	eh **oo**mer **o**rrer
It's two o'clock.	**São duas horas.**	sahng^{w} **doo**ersh **o**rrersh
five past …	**… e cinco**	… ee **seeng**koo
quarter after …	**… e um quarto**	… ee oong **kwahr**too
twenty after …	**… e vinte**	… ee **veeng**ter
half-past …	**… e meia**	… ee **may**er
twenty-five to …	**vinte e cinco para as …**	**veeng**ter ee **seeng**koo **per**rer ersh
ten to …	**dez para as …**	dehsh **per**rer ersh
noon/midnight	**meio-dia/meia-noite**	**may**oo **dee**yer/**may**er **noy**ter
in the morning	**da manhã**	der mer**nyahng**
in the afternoon	**da tarde**	der **tahr**der
in the evening	**da noite**	der **noy**ter
yesterday/today	**ontem/hoje**	**awng**tayhng^{y}/**oa**zher
tomorrow	**amanhã**	ahmer**nyahng**
spring	**a Primavera**	er primmer**veh**rer
summer	**o Verão**	oo ver**rahng**^{w}
autumn (fall)	**o Outono**	oo oa**toa**noo
winter	**o Inverno**	oo eeng**vehr**noo

January	**Janeiro**	zher**nay**roo
February	**Fevereiro**	ferver**ray**roo
March	**Março**	**mahr**soo
April	**Abril**	er**breel**
May	**Maio**	**migh**oo
June	**Junho**	**zhoo**nyoo
July	**Julho**	**zhoo**llyoo
August	**Agosto**	er**goash**too
September	**Setembro**	ser**tehng**broo
October	**Outubro**	oa**too**broo
November	**Novembro**	noo**vehng**broo
December	**Dezembro**	der**zehng**broo

Sunday	**domingo**	doo**meeng**goo
Monday	**segunda-feira**	ser**goong**der **fayrer**
Tuesday	**terça-feira**	**tehr**ser **fayrer**
Wednesday	**quarta-feira**	**kwahr**ter **fayrer**
Thursday	**quinta-feira**	**keeng**ter **fayrer**
Friday	**sexta-feira**	**saysh**ter **fayrer**
Saturday	**sábado**	**sah**berdoo

Numbers *Números*

0	**zero**	**zeh**roo	11	**onze**	**awng**zer
1	**um (uma)**	oong (**oo**mer)	12	**doze**	**doa**zer
2	**dois (duas)**	doysh (**doo**ersh)	13	**treze**	**tray**zer
3	**três**	traysh	14	**catorze**	ker**toar**zer
4	**quatro**	**kwah**troo	15	**quinze**	**keeng**zer
5	**cinco**	**seeng**koo	16	**dezasseis**	derzer**ssaysh**
6	**seis**	saysh	17	**dezassete**	derzer**sseh**ter
7	**sete**	**seh**ter	18	**dezoito**	der**zoy**too
8	**oito**	**oy**too	19	**dezanove**	derzer**no**vver
9	**nove**	**no**vver	20	**vinte**	**veeng**ter
10	**dez**	dehsh	21	**vinte e um**	**veeng**ter ee oong

30	**trinta**	**treeng**ter
40	**quarenta**	kwer**rehng**ter
50	**cinquenta**	seeng**kwehng**ter
60	**sessenta**	ser**ssehng**ter
70	**setenta**	ser**tehng**ter
80	**oitenta**	oy**tehng**ter
90	**noventa**	noo**vehng**ter
100/1,000	**cem/mil**	sayng^{y}/meel
first	**primeiro(-a)**	prim**may**roo(-er)
second	**segundo(-a)**	ser**goong**doo(-er)
a half	**uma metade**	**oo**mer mer**tah**der

Emergency *Urgências*

Call the police	**Chame a polícia**	**sher**mer er poo**lee**ssyer
Get a doctor	**Chame um médico**	**sher**mer oong **meh**dikkoo
Go away	**Vá-se embora**	vah ser ayng**bo**rrer
HELP	**SOCORRO**	soo**koa**rroo
I'm ill/sick	**Estou doente**	ish**toa dwayng**ter

I'm lost	**Perdi-me**	perr**dee** mer
STOP THIEF	**AGARRA GATUNO**	er**gah**rrer ger**too**noo
My… has been taken.	**Roubaram-me …**	roa**bah**rahng^w mer
I've lost my …	**Perdi …**	perr**dee**
handbag	**a pasta de mão**	er **pash**ter der mahng^w
passport	**o passaporte**	o persser**porr**ter
wallet	**a minha carteira**	er **mee**nyer kerr**tay**rer

Guide to Portuguese pronunciation

Consonants

Letter	Approximate pronunciation	Symbol	Example	
b, d, f, l, p, r, t, v		as in English		
c	1) like **k** in **k**ill	k	**casa**	**kah**zer
	2) like **s** in **s**it	s	**cedo**	**say**doo
ç	like **s** in **s**it	s	**maçã**	mer**ssahng**
ch	like **sh** in **sh**ut	sh	**chamar**	sher**mahr**
g	1) like **g** in **g**o	g/gh	**garfo**	**gahr**foo
	2) like **s** in plea**s**ure	zh	**gelo**	**zhay**loo
h	always silent		**homem**	ommahng^y
j	like **s** in plea**s**ure	zh	**já**	zhah
lh	like **lli** in mi**lli**on	ly	**olho**	oalyoo
m	1) like **m** in **m**et	m	**mais**	mighsh
	2) nasalizes preceeding vowel; generally silent	ng	**tempo**	**tayng**poo
		ng^y	**tem**	tayng^y
n	1) like **n** in **n**o	n	**novo**	**noa**voo
	2) nasalizes preceeding vowel; generally silent	ng^y	**homens**	omm-ahng^{y}sh
nh	like **ni** in o**ni**on	ny	**vinho**	**vee**nyoo
q	like **k** in **k**ill	k	**querer**	kerr**ayr**
s	1) like **s** in **s**it	s/ss	**saber**	ser**bayr**
	2) like **z** in ra**z**or	z	**casa**	**kah**zer
	3) like **sh** in **sh**ut	sh	**país**	per**eesh**
	4) like **s** in plea**s**ure	zh	**cisne**	**seezh**ner
x	1) like **sh** in **sh**ut	sh	**baixo**	**bigh**shoo
	2) like **z** in ra**z**or	z	**exacto**	iz**zah**too
	3) like **x** in e**x**it	ks	**táxi**	**tah**ksi

TELEPHONING, see page 76

z	1) like **z** in razor	z	**zero**	**zeh**ro
	2) like **sh** in **sh**ut	sh	**feliz**	fer**leesh**
	3) like s in pleasure	zh	**luz da**	loozh der

Vowels

a	1) between c**u**t and p**a**rty	ah	**nado**	**nah**doo
	2) like **a** in **a**bout	er	**porta**	**por**ter
e	1) like **e** in g**e**t	eh	**perto**	**pehr**too
	2) like **a** in l**a**te	ay	**cabelo**	ker**bay**loo
	3) like **er** in oth**er**	er	**pesado**	per**zah**doo
	4) like **i** in h**i**t	i	**exacto**	i**zzah**too
é	like **e** in g**e**t	eh	**café**	ker**feh**
ê	like **a** in l**a**te	ay	**mês**	maysh
i	1) like **ee** in s**ee**d	ee	**riso**	**ree**zoo
	2) like **i** in com**i**ng	i	**final**	fi**nnahl**
o	1) like **o** in r**o**d	o	**fora**	**for**rer
	2) like **o** in n**o**te	oa	**voltar**	voal**tahr**
	3) like **oo** in f**oo**t	oo	**caso**	**kah**zoo
ô, ou	like **o** in n**o**te	oa	**pôs**	poash
u	1) like **oo** in s**oo**n	oo	**número**	**noo**merroo
	2) silent in **gu**, **qu** before **e**, **i**		**querer**	ker**rayr**

Nasal vowels

ã, am, an	like **ung** in l**ung** or **an** in French d**an**s	ahng	**maçã**	mer**ssahng**
em, en	a mixture of **a** in l**a**te and **ing** in s**ing**	ayng	**cento**	**sayng**too
im, in	nasalized **ee** as in f**ee**t	eeng	**cinco**	**seeng**koo
om, on	like **orn** in c**orn**cob	awng	**bom**	bawng
um, un	nasalized **oo** in f**oo**t	oong	**um**	oong

Semi-nasalized diphthongs

ãe, ãi, em, final **en(s)**, usually final **em**	as **ã** followed by **y** in **y**et	ahng^y	**mãe**	mahng^y
ão, final unstressed **am**	as **ã** followed by **w** in **w**as	ahng^w	**mão**	mahng^w
õe	like **orn** in c**orn**cob, followed by **y** in **y**et	awng^y	**põe**	pawng^y

Shona

Basic expressions *Mazwi emazuva ese*

Yes.	**Ehe [Hongu].**	**eh**eh [**hon**goo]
No.	**Aiwa [Kwete].**	**igh**wa [**kwet**eh]
Thank you.	**Ndatenda.**	^{n}da**ten**da
I beg your pardon?	**Pamusoroi?**	pamooso**roy**

Introductions *Kwaziso*

Good morning.	**Mangwanani.**	mangwa**na**nee
Good afternoon.	**Masikati.**	mas**ka**tee
Good night.	**Manheru.**	mane**ro**o
Good-bye.	**Chisarai/Fambai zvakanaka.**	**chee**sarigh/**fam**bigh zhaka**na**ka
This is …	**Ava ndi …**	**a**va ^{n}dee
My name is …	**Zita rangu ndi …**	**zee**ta **ran**goo ^{n}dee
Pleased to meet you.	**Ndinofara kukuzivai.**	^{n}deeno**fa**ra koo**koo**zivigh
What's your name?	**Munonzi ani?**	moo**non**zi **a**nee
How are you?	**Makadii?**	maka**dee**
Fine thanks. And you?	**Ndiripo makadiwo?**	^{n}dee**ree**po maka**dee**wo
Where do you come from?	**Munobva kupi?**	moo**no**bva **koo**pee
I'm from …	**Ndinobva ku …**	^{n}dee**no**bva koo
I'm with my …	**Ndiri no …**	^{n}**dee**ree no
wife/girlfriend	**mukadzi wangu**	moo**ka**dzee **wan**goo
husband/boyfriend	**murume wangu**	moo**roo**may **wan**goo
children	**vana vangu**	**va**na **van**goo
parents	**vabereki vangu**	**va**berekee **van**goo
I'm married.	**Ndakaroora (Ndakaroorwa).**	^{n}dakaro-**ora** (^{n}dakaro-**or**wa)
I'm not yet married.	**Handisati kuroor(w)a.**	handee**sa**tee kooro**or**(w)a
I'm on my own.	**Ndiri ndega.**	^{n}**dee**ree ^{n}**day**ga
I'm on holiday/on business.	**Ndiri pahoriday/ pabasa.**	^{n}**dee**ree pa**ho**reeday/ pabasa

GUIDE TO PRONUNCIATION, see page 95/EMERGENCIES, see page 94

Questions *Mibvunzo*

How…?/When…?	**… sei?/… rini?**	… **se**yee/… **ree**nee
Why…?/Which…?	**… sei?/… chipi?**	… **se**yee/… **chee**pee
Who is this/that?	**Ndiani?**	^{n}dee**a**nee
What is this/that?	**Chii?**	chee
Where is/are …?	**… iri kupi?**	… eeree **koo**pee
Where can I get/ find …?	**Ndinozviwana … kupi?**	^{n}deenozhee**wa**na … **koo**pee
How far?	**Kure zvakadii?**	**koo**ray zhaka**dee**
How long?	**Kunotora yakadii?**	koono**to**ra yaka**dee**
How much?	**Imarii?**	eema**ree**
Can I have …?	**Ndipeiwo …?**	^{n}dee**pe**yiwo
Can you help me?	**Ndibatsirewo?**	^{n}deebatsee**ray**wo
What does this mean?	**Zvinoreva chii?**	zheeno**re**va chee
I understand.	**Ndazvinzwa.**	^{n}da**zhin**zwa
I don't understand.	**Handina kuzvinzwa.**	handeena ku**zhin**zwa
Please speak slowly.	**Tauraiwo zvishoma.**	ta^{oo}**righ**wo zhi**sho**ma
Can you translate this for me?	**Munogona kunditurikira here?**	moono**go**na koondee-too**ree**keera **he**reh
Do you speak English?	**Munogona kutaura chiRungu here?**	moono**go**na koo**ta**^{oo}ra chee**roon**goo **he**reh
I don't speak Shona.	**Handigoni kutaura chiShona**	handee**go**nee koo**ta**^{oo}ra chee**sho**na

A few useful words *Ma mwe ma zwi*

better/worse	**chirinani/ chakashatisa**	cheeree**na**nee/ chakasha**tee**sa
big/small	**chikuru/chidiki**	chee**koo**roo/chee**dee**kee
cheap/expensive	**chakachipa/ chinodhura**	chaka**chee**pa/ cheeno**Doo**ra
good/bad	**zvakanaka/zvakashata**	zhaka**na**ka/zhaka**sha**ta
hot/cold	**chinopisa/ chinotonhora**	cheeno**pee**sa/ cheenoto**no**ra
old/young	**chikuru/chidiki**	chee**koo**roo/chee**dee**kee
right/wrong	**chakanaka/chakashata**	chaka**na**ka/chaka**sha**ta

Hotel–Accommodation *Kurara muhotera*

We've reserved two rooms.	**Takareserva maroomi maviri.**	takareserva maroomee maveeree
Do you have any vacancies?	**Mune zvimbo here?**	**moo**nay **zhim**bo **he**reh
I'd like a … room.	**Ndinoda room …**	^{n}dee**no**da room
single	**imwe**	**im**weh
double	**hombe**	**hom**beh
with twin beds	**nemibhedha miviri**	nemiBeDa mee**vee**ree
with a double bed	**nomubhedha mukuru**	nomooBeDa moo**koo**roo
with a bath	**nebhavhu**	ne**Ba**voo
with a shower	**neshawa**	ne**sha**wa
We'll be staying overnight only.	**Ticharara chete.**	teecha**ra**ra cheteh
We'll be staying …	**Tichagara …**	teecha**ga**ra
a few days	**mamwe kwazuva akati kuti**	**mam**weh kwa**zoo**va a**ka**tee **koo**tee
a week	**kwevhiki**	kwe**vee**kee

Decision *Kufunga*

May I see the room?	**Tingaonawo room here?**	tinga**on**awo room **he**reh
That's fine. I'll take it.	**Room yakanaka. Ndinoida.**	room yaka**na**ka. ^{n}dee**noy**da
No. I don't like it.	**Aiwa. Handidi.**	**igh**wa. han**dee**dee
It's too cold/hot.	**Inotonhoresa/ Inopisisa.**	eenotono**re**sa/ eenopees**ee**sa
It's too dark/small.	**Haina raiti./Idikisa.**	hae**en**a rightee/ ee**dee**keesa
Do you have a … room?	**Mune imwe room … here?**	**moo**nay **im**way room … **he**reh
better/bigger	**irinani/huru**	eeree**na**nee/**hoo**roo
cheaper	**yakachipa**	yaka**chee**pa
quieter	**yakanyarara**	yaka**nya**rara
May I please have my bill?	**Ndipewo biri?**	^{n}dee**pay**wo **bee**ree
It's been a very enjoyable stay.	**Ndakafadzwa chaizvo.**	^{n}daka**fad**zwa chighzho

NUMBERS, see page 94

Eating out *Kudya*

I'd like to reserve a table for 4.	**Ndinoda kureserva table evanhu vana.**	^{n}dee**no**da koore**ser**va table eva**noo va**na
We'll come at 8.	**Tichasvika na 8.**	teecha**shee**ka na 8
I'd like breakfast/ lunch/dinner.	**Ndipewo breakfast/ lunch/dinner.**	^{n}dee**pay**wo "breakfast"/ "lunch"/"dinner"
Do you have a set menu/local dishes?	**Mune set menu/ sadza here?**	**moo**nay "set menu"/ **sad**za **he**reh
What do you recommend?	**Dishi ramunoreko-menda nderipi?**	deeshee ramoono**reko**-menda ^{n}de**ree**pee
Do you have vegetarian dishes?	**Mune mavegetarian dishes here?**	**moo**nay ma "vegetarian dishes" **he**reh

Breakfast *Chisvusvuro*

May I have some ...?	**Ndipewo ...**	^{n}dee**pay**wo
bread	**chingwa**	**ching**wa
butter	**bata**	bata
eggs	**mazai**	ma**zigh**
jam	**jamu**	**ja**moo
peanut butter	**dovi**	**do**vee
rolls	**mabuns**	ma**buns**

Starters *Kutanga*

chibbage	chee**ba**gee	maize cobs
machipisi	ma**chee**peesee	chips/(*US*) fries
makripisi	ma**kree**peesee	crisps/(*US*) chips
nzungu dzakakangwa	**nzoo**ngoo dzaka**kang**wa	roasted peanuts
samusa	sa**moo**sa	samosa

Meat *Nyama*

I'd like some ...	**Ndipewo nyama ...**	^{n}dee**pay**wo **nya**ma
beef	**yemombe**	ye**mom**beh
chicken	**yehuku**	ye**hoo**koo
goat	**yembudzi**	yem**boo**dzi
lamb	**yehwai**	ye**wigh**
pork	**yenguruve**	yengoo**roo**vay
veal	**yemhuru**	ye**moo**roo

NUMBERS, see page 94

kari	ka**ree**	curry
nyama yemuto	**ny**ama ye**moo**to	meat cooked in a sauce
sichu	see**choo**	stew
usave (oo**sa**vee)	a dish, usually meat or, sometimes, vegetables, to accompany *sadza* (staple diet of corn/maize)	

boiled	**yakabikwa**	yaka**bee**kwa
fried	**yakakangwa**	yaka**kang**wa
grilled	**yakagrila**	yaka**gree**la
roast	**yakagochwa**	yaka**goch**wa
underdone (rare)	**haisati yabikwa**	high**sa**tee ya**bee**kwa
medium	**yakagochwa ezviviri pakati napakati**	yaka**goch**wa ezhee**vee**ree pa**ka**tee napa**ka**tee
well-done	**yakagochwa zvikuru**	yaka**goch**wa zhee**koo**roo

Fish and seafood *Hove*

brimi	**bree**mi	bream
kapenta matemba	ka**pen**ta ma**tem**ba	dried whitebait
makwaya	ma**kwa**ya	bass
trauti	**tra**^{oo}tee	trout

Vegetables *Muriwo*

beans	**nyemba**	**nyem**ba
cabbage	**kabichi**	ka**bee**chee
carrots	**makaroti**	ma**ka**rot
onion	**maonioni**	mao**ny**on
peas	**mapisi**	ma**pee**si
potatoes	**mabatatisi**	maba**ta**tees
rice	**mpunga**	m**poo**nga
spinach/rape	**repu**	**re**poo
manhanga	ma**na**nga	pumpkin, usually boiled
mbambaira	m**bam**bighra	sweet potatoes
muriwo nedovi isina nyama	moo**ree**wo ne**do**vee eeseena **nyama**	vegetable dish with peanut butter
muriwo usina nyama	moo**ree**wo oo**seena** nyama	side dish to accompany *sadza*, without meat

Fruit–Dessert *Michero nemakeki*

apple	**apuro**	a**poo**ro
banana	**bhanana**	Ba**na**na
guava	**gwavha**	gwava
lemon	**limoni**	lee**mo**nee
orange	**ranjisi**	ran**jee**see
papaya	**popo**	pawpaw
biscuits	**mabisikitsi**	ma**bi**sikitsee
cake	**keki**	kekee
fruit	**muchero**	moo**che**ro
ice-cream	**ice cream**	"ice cream"

Drinks *Madhiringi*

beer	**dhoro [whawha]**	Doro [**wa**wa]
coffee	**kofi**	**ko**fee
black	**isina mukaka**	ees**ee**na moo**ka**ka
with milk	**ine mukaka**	**een**nay moo**ka**ka
drinking water	**mvura yekunwa**	mv**oo**ra ye**koon**wa
mineral water	**mvura yekunwa yebotoro**	mv**oo**ra ye**koon**wa yebo**to**ro
tea	**tii**	tee
wine	**waini**	**wigh**ni
chibuku	chee**boo**koo	traditional beer, available in local taverns
mazoe	mazowee	orange squash

Complaints and paying *Kupopota–Kubhadara*

This is too bitter.	**Inovavisa.**	eenova**vee**sa.
This is too sweet.	**Inotapirisa.**	eenotapee**ree**sa
That's not what I ordered.	**Handizvo zvandaodha.**	han**dee**zho zhandaoDa
I'd like to pay.	**Ndinoda kubhadara.**	^{n}dee**no**da kooBaDara
I think you made a mistake in the bill.	**Ndinofunga makanganisa biri**	^{n}deeno**foo**nga ma**kan**ganeesa beeree
I don't have enough change.	**Chenji yangu hainakukwana.**	chenjee **yan**goo highnaku**kwa**na

NUMBERS, see page 94

Can I pay with this credit card?	**Ndinogona kubhadara nekrediti kadhi here?**	^{n}deeno**go**na kooBaDara nekredit kaD **here**h
We only accept cash.	**Tinotambira [Tinogashira] kashi chete.**	teenotam**bee**ra [teenoga**shee**ra] kash **che**teh
Is service included?	**Mainkludha servici here?**	mighn**kloo**Da serveesee **here**h
I'm full.	**Ndaguta.**	^{n}da**goo**ta
We enjoyed it, thank you.	**Tafadzwa chaizvo, tatenda.**	ta**fad**zwa chighzho ta**ten**da
Our compliments to the cook/our host.	**Tinotendai vabiki/ vashanyirwi.**	teenoten**digh** va**bee**kee/ vashan**yeer**wee

Travelling around *Kufamba*

Plane *Ndege*

Is there a flight to Kariba?	**Pane ndege kuKariba here?**	**pa**nay **^{n}de**geh kooka**ree**ba **here**h
What time do I check in?	**Ndosvika nguvai?**	^{n}do**shee**ka in**goo**vigh
I'd like to … my reservation on flight no. …	**Ndinoda ku … reservation yangu paflaiti nhamba …**	^{n}dee**no**da koo … reservation **yan**goo pa**flight**ee **nam**ba …
cancel	**kanzera**	kan**ze**ra
change	**chenja**	**chen**ja
confirm	**konfirma**	kon**fir**ma

Train *Chitima*

I want a ticket to Bulawayo.	**Ndinoda tikiti yokuenda kuBulawayo.**	^{n}dee**no**da te**kee**ti yokoo**en**da kooboola**wa**yo
single (one-way)	**kuenda chete**	koo**en**da **che**teh
return (roundtrip)	**kuenda nokudzoka**	koo**en**da nokoo**dzo**ka
first/second class	**first/second kirasi**	"first/second" kee**ra**see
How long does the journey (trip) take?	**Tinotora nguvai yakareba zvakadii?**	teeno**to**ra in**goo**vigh yaka**ray**ba zhaka**dee**

TELLING THE TIME, see page 93

When is the … train to Harare?	**Chitima … chinoenda kuHarare chinouya rini?**	chee**tee**ma … cheeno-**en**da koo-ha**ra**ree cheeno-**oo**ya **ree**nee
first	**chakatanga**	chaka**ta**nga
next	**chinotevera**	cheenote**ve**ra
last	**chokupedzisira**	chokoo**pe**dzee**see**ra
Is this the right train to Gweru?	**Ndicho chitima chekuGweru here?**	^{n}deecho chee**tee**ma chekoo**gwe**roo **he**reh
There's no train today.	**Hakuna chitima nhasi.**	hak**oo**na chee**tee**ma **na**see

Bus–Coach *Bhazi*

Is there a bus today?	**Pane bhazi nhasi?**	paneh Bazee **na**see
What bus do I take to the centre?	**Ndinotora bhazi ripi kuenda kutaundi?**	^{n}deeno**to**ra Bazee reepee koo**en**da koo**ta**^{oo}nd
How much is the fare to …?	**Rinoita marii kuenda ku …?**	reeno**y**ta ma**ree** koo**en**da koo
Please will you tell me when to get off?	**Ndiudzewo kana ndasvika?**	^{n}deeyoo**dzay**wo kana ^{n}da**shee**ka

Taxi *Tekisi*

How much is it to…?	**Imarii kuenda ku …?**	**ee**ma**ree** koo**en**da koo
Please take me to this address.	**Nditakureiwo kuenda kuadhiresi iyo.**	^{n}deetakoo**ray**wo koo**en**da kooaDi**re**see **ee**yo
Please stop here.	**Ndiburutseiwo pano.**	^{n}deeboorootsaywo **pa**no
Please wait for me. I'll be 10 minutes.	**Ndimirirewo pano kure 10 minitsi.**	^{n}deemeeree**ray**wo **pa**no kooray 10 mee**nee**tsee
Please wait for me. I'll be a short time.	**Ndimirirewo pano kwechinguva shoma-shoma.**	^{n}deemeeree**ray**wo **pa**no kwe**chee**ngoova **sho**ma **sho**ma

Car hire–Automobile rental *Kuhaya motokari*

I'd like to hire (rent) a car.	**Ndinoda kuhaya motokari.**	^{n}dee**no**da koo**ha**ya moto**ka**ree
I'd like it for a day/week.	**Ndinoida kwezuva rimwe/kwevhiki.**	^{n}dee**no**weeda kwe**zoo**va **rim**way/kwe**vee**kee

NUMBERS, see page 94

Where's the nearest filling station?	**Garaji riri kupi?**	**ga**rajee **ree**ree **koo**pee
Full tank, please.	**Zadzaiwo.**	zad**zigh**wo
Give me … litres of petrol (gasoline).	**Ndipewo malita … yepeturu.**	ndee**pay**wo ma**lee**ta … yepe**too**roo
How do I get to …?	**Nzira yekuenda ku… ndeipi?**	n**zee**ra yekoo**en**da koo … nde**yee**pee
I've had a breakdown at …	**Motokari yanjomba [yafa] pa …**	moto**ka**ri yan**jom**ba [**ya**fa] pa
Please send a mechanic.	**Nditumirewo makanika.**	ndeetoomee**ray**wo makaneeka
Can you mend it?	**Munogona kuigadzira here?**	moono**go**na kooweega**dzeera he**reh

☞ You're on the wrong road for …	**Haisi riyo mugwagwa [nzira] yokuenda ku …** ☜
Go straight ahead.	**Endai nepapa.**
It's down there on the left/right.	**Endai neroad iyi iri kuruboshwe/kurudji kwenyu.**
It's opposite/behind …	**Iri opositi/paseri [pashure] …**
It's next to/after …	**Iri padhuze [pedyo]/ mapfuura …**
north/south	**chamhembe/maodzanyemba**
east/west	**mabvazuva/madokero**

Sightseeing *Kuona masights*

Where's the tourist office?	**Turisti hofisi iri kupi?**	tooreestee hofeesee eeree **koo**pee
Is there an English-speaking guide?	**Pane guide vanogona chiRhungu here?**	**pa**nay "guide" vano**go**na chee**roo**ngoo **he**reh
Where is/are the …?	**… iri kupi?**	… eeree **koo**pee
botanical gardens	**Mabotanical gardens**	ma "botanical gardens"
chief's house	**Imba yamambo**	**eem**ba ya**mam**bo
church	**Chechi**	**che**chee
city centre	**Taundi [dhorobha]**	**ta**^oo^nd [DOROBA]
Great Zimbabwe	**Great Zimbabwe**	"great" zeembabweh
shops	**Zvitoro**	zhi**to**ro

When does it open/close?	**Inovhura/Inovhara nguvai?**	eeno**voo**ra/eeno**va**ra in**goo**vigh
How much is the entrance fee?	**Imarii yokupinda?**	ee**ma**ree yokoo**pin**da

Countryside *Nyika*

farm	**famu [purazi]**	**fa**moo [poo**ra**zee]
footpath	**nzira**	nzeera
game reserve	**game park**	"game park"
hill	**kopi**	**ko**pee
lake	**nyanza**	**nyan**za
mountain	**gomo**	**go**mo
river	**rwizi**	roo**wee**zee
savannah	**mapane**	ma**pa**nee
well	**tsime**	**tsee**may

Animals *Mhuka*

baboon	**gudo**	**goo**do
elephant	**nzou**	**zo**-oo
hyena(s)	**bere (mapere)**	**be**reh (ma**pe**reh)
lion	**shumba**	**shoom**ba
snake	**nyoka**	**nyo**ka

Entertainment *Kutamba*

What's playing at the theatre?	**Kune chii kutheatre?**	**koo**nay chee koo theatre
How much are the seats?	**Siti imarii?**	seetee ee**ma**ree
I want to reserve 2 tickets for the show on Friday evening.	**Ndinoda kureserva matikiti maviri neChishanu manheru**	^{n}dee**no**da koore**ser**va matikiti ma**vee**ree nechee**sha**noo ma**ne**roo
Would you like to go with me to … tonight?	**Mungandiperekedza kuenda ku … manheru ano?**	moongandipere**ke**dza koo**en**da koo … ma**ne**roo **a**no
Is there a discoteque in town?	**Kune disiko kutaundi here?**	**koo**nay deeseeko koo**ta**^{oo}nd **he**reh
Thank you. I have had a great time.	**Ndatenda. Ndafadzwa chaizvo.**	^{n}da**ten**da. ^{n}da**fad**zoowa chighzho

DAYS OF THE WEEK/NUMBERS, see page 94

Shops, stores and services *Zvitotoro*

Where's the nearest …?	**… iri kupi?**	eeree **koo**pee
baker's	**Bekari**	bekaree
bookshop	**Chitoro chinotengesa mabhuku**	chee**to**ro cheeno**ten**gesa maBookoo
butcher's	**Bucheri**	boocheree
chemist's	**Chemist**	"chemist"
dentist	**Dentist**	"dentist"
department store	**Chitoro chikuru**	chee**to**ro chee**koo**roo
grocery	**Grosari**	**gro**saree
post office	**Post office**	"post office"
toilets	**Chimbuzi**	chim**boo**zee

General expressions *Zvirevo*

Where's the main shopping area?	**Zvitoro zviri kupi?**	zhee**to**ro zheeree **koo**pee
Do you have any …?	**Mune …?**	moonay
Do you have anything …?	**Mune chinhu …?**	moonay **chee**noo
better	**chirinan**	cheeree**na**nee
cheaper	**chakachipai**	chaka**chee**pa
larger/smaller	**chakakura/chadiki**	chaka**koo**ra/ch**dee**kee
Can I try it on?	**Ndingaedza here?**	^{n}deenga**e**dza **he**reh
How much is this?	**Icho chinoita marii?**	eecho chee**no**yta **ma**ree
Please write it down.	**Ndinyorarewo pasi.**	^{n}deenyora**ray**wo **pa**see
That's too much.	**Inodhura**	eenoDoora
No, I don't like it.	**Aiwa. Handidi.**	**igh**wa han**dee**dee
I'll take it.	**Ndinoida.**	^{n}dee**noy**da
Do you accept credit cards?	**Munotambira macredit kadhi here?**	moonotam**bee**ra makredit kaD **he**reh

black	**tema**	**te**ma
red	**tsvuku**	**choo**koo
white	**chena**	**chay**na

Note that most other colours are as in English.

I want to buy …	**Ndinoda kutenga …**	^{n}deeno**da** koo**te**nga
batteries	**mabateri [macells]**	ma**ba**teree [**masels**]
newspaper	**bhepa nhau**	Bepa **na**^{oo}
soap	**sipo**	seepo
a half-kilo of apples	**hafu kiro yemaapuro**	hafoo keero yemaa**poo**ro
a litre of milk	**rita remukaka**	reeta remoo**ka**ka
I'd like film for this camera.	**Ndinoda firimu rekamera iyi.**	^{n}dee**no**da feereemoo rekamera eeyee
I'd like a hair-cut.	**Ndinoda kugerwa.**	^{n}**dee**noda koo**ger**wa

Souvenirs *Masuvenir*

carvings	**macarving**	macarving
chess set	**machess set**	machess set
flat basket	**rusero**	roo**se**ro
patterned fabric	**mucheka**	moo**che**ka

At the bank *Pabhengi*

Where's the nearest bank/currency exchange office?	**Bhengi riri kupi?**	**Ben**gee reeree **koo**pee
I want to change some money.	**Ndinoda kuchenja mari.**	^{n}dee**no**da koo**chen**ja **ma**ree
What's the exchange rate?	**Exchange rati ichii?**	"exchange rate" eechee

At the post office *PaPositi Hofisi*

I want to send this by …	**Ndinoda kuituma pa …**	^{n}dee**no**da kooee**too**ma pa
airmail	**airmail**	"airmail"
express	**express**	"express"
registered mail	**registered mail**	"registered mail"
I want a … cent stamp.	**Ndinoda mastambi e … cents.**	^{n}dee**no**da mas**tam**bee ay … sents
What's the postage for a letter/postcard to America?	**Inoita marii kutuma tsamba/postcard kuAmerica?**	**ee**noyta **ma**ree koo**too**ma **tsam**ba/"postcard" koo-amerika

NUMBERS, see page 94

Is there any mail for me? My name is …	**Ndine tsamba here? Zita rangu ndi …**	**^{n}dee**nay **tsam**ba **he**reh. **zee**ta **ran**goo dee

Telephoning *Kufona*

Where's the nearest public phone?	**Foni iri kupi?**	fonee eeree **koo**pee
May I use your phone?	**Ndingashandisawo foni yenyu here?**	**^{n}dee**ngashandee**sa**wo fonee **yay**nyoo **he**reh
I want to make an international call to …	**Ndinoda kufonera kunze kwenyika ku …**	^{n}dee**no**da koofo**ne**ra **koo**nzay kwe**nyee**ka koo
Hello. This is … speaking.	**Mhoroi. Ndini …**	mo**roy**. **^{n}dee**nee
I want to speak to …	**Ndinoda kutaura na …**	^{n}dee**no**da koo**ta^{oo}**ra na
When will he/she be back?	**Vanodzoka rini?**	vano**dzo**ka **ree**nee
Please will you tell him/her that I called?	**Vaudzewo kuti ndafona?**	va^{oo}**dzay**wo **koo**tee ^{n}da**fo**na

Time and date *Nguva ne madheti*

English expressions of time are used by Shona-speakers. The English names of the months are also often used, though the Shona alternatives are provided below.

What's the time?	**Nguvai?**	**in**goovigh
noon/midnight	**masikati/pakati pousiku**	masee**ka**tee/pa**ke**tee powoo**see**koo
in the morning	**mangwanani**	mangwa**na**nee
during the day	**pazuva**	pa**zoo**va
in the evening	**manheru**	ma**ne**roo
at night	**pausiku**	pa^{oo}**see**koo
yesterday	**nezuro**	ne**zoo**ro
today	**nhasi**	**na**see
tomorrow	**mangwana**	mang**wa**na
summer (September–May)	**zhizha**	**zee**za
winter (June–August)	**chando**	**chan**do

DAYS OF THE WEEK/MONTHS, see page 94

Sunday	**Svondo**	**shon**do
Monday	**Muvhuro**	moo**voo**ro
Tuesday	**Chipiri**	chee**pee**ree
Wednesday	**Chitatu**	cheetatoo
Thursday	**China**	**chee**na
Friday	**Chishanu**	chee**sha**noo
Saturday	**Mugovera**	moogo**ve**ra
January	**Ndira**	ⁿ**dee**ra
February	**Kukadzi**	koo**kad**zee
March	**Kurume**	koo**roo**me
April	**Kubvumi**	koob**voo**mee
May	**Chivabvu**	chee**vab**voo
June	**Chikumi**	chee**koo**mee
July	**Chikunguru**	cheekoong**goo**roo
August	**Nyamavhuvhu**	nyama**voo**voo
September	**Gunyana**	goon**ya**na
October	**Gumiguru**	goomee**goo**roo
November	**Mbudzi**	**bood**zee
December	**Zvita**	**zhee**ta

Numbers *Manhamba*

Note that English numbers are often used by Shona-speakers.

0	**zero**	**ze**ro
1	**poshi**	**po**shee
2	**piri**	**pee**ree
3	**tatu**	**ta**too
4	**china**	**chee**na
5	**shanu**	**sha**nu
6	**tanhatu**	tan**a**too
7	**chinomwe**	chee**nom**weh
8	**rusere**	roo**se**reh
9	**pfumbamwe**	pfoom**bam**weh
10	**gumi**	**goo**mee
11	**gumi neimwe**	**goo**mee nei**m**weh
12	**gumi nembiri**	**goo**mee nem**bee**ree
13	**gumi nenhatu**	**goo**mee nen**a**too
14	**gumi nechina**	**goo**mee ne**chee**na
15	**gumi neshanu**	**goo**mee ne**sha**noo

16	**gumi netanhatu**	**goo**mee neta**na**too
17	**gumi nenomwe**	**goo**mee ne**nom**weh
18	**gumi nesere**	**goo**mee ne**se**reh
19	**gumi nepfumbamwe**	**goo**mee nepfoom**bam**weh
20	**makumi maviri**	ma**koo**mee ma**vee**ree
21	**makumi maviri neimwe**	ma**koo**mee ma**vee**ree ne**im**weh
30	**makumi matatu**	ma**koo**mee ma**ta**too
40	**makumi mana**	ma**koo**mee **ma**na
50	**makumi mashanu**	ma**koo**mee ma**sha**noo
60	**makumi matanhatu**	ma**koo**mee mata**na**too
70	**makumi manomwe**	ma**koo**mee ma**nom**weh
80	**makumi masere**	ma**koo**mee ma**se**reh
90	**makumi mapfumbamwe**	ma**koo**mee mapfoom**bam**weh
100	**zana**	**za**na
101	**zana neimwe**	**za**na ne**im**weh
200	**mazana maviri**	ma**za**na ma**vee**ree
500	**mazana mashanu**	ma**za**na ma**sha**noo
1,000	**churu**	**choo**roo
100,000	**zana ezvuru**	**za**na e**zhoo**roo
1,000,000	**churu chezvuru**	**choo**roo che**zhoo**roo
first	**chiposhi**	chee**po**shee
second	**chipiri**	chee**pee**ree
once	**kamwe chete**	**kam**weh **che**teh
twice	**kaviri**	ka**vee**re
a half	**hafu**	**ha**foo

Emergency *Emegensi*

Please call the police	**Shevedzaiwo maporisa**	shevedz**igh**wo mapo**ree**sa
Go away	**Ibvapo**	ib**va**po
HELP	**Ndibatsirewo**	^{n}deebatsee**ray**wo
I'm ill	**Ndinorwara**	^{n}deenor**wa**ra
I'm lost	**Ndarasika**	^{n}dara**see**ka
Leave me alone	**Ndisiyawo ndiri ndega**	^{n}deesee**ya**wo **^{n}dee**ree **^{n}day**ga
STOP THIEF	**Tsotsi [Mabhava]! Mira!**	**tso**tsee [ma**ba**va] **mee**ra
Where can I find a doctor?	**Ndingawana dokita kupi?**	^{n}deenga**wa**na **do**keeta **koo**pee

TELEPHONING, see page 93

My … have been stolen.	**… yangu yakabiwa.**	… yangoo yakabeewa
I've lost …	**Ndarasa …**	^{n}darasa …
my handbag	**bhegi rangu**	Begee **ran**goo
my passport	**pasiporti yangu**	**pa**seeportee **yan**goo
my luggage	**nhumbi dzangu**	**noom**bee dzangoo
my money	**mari yangu**	**ma**ree **yan**goo

Guide to Shona pronunciation

Consonants

Letter	Approximate pronunciation	Symbol	Example	
b, ch, d, f, h, j, k, m, n, p, r, s, sh, t, v, w, y, z	as in English			
bh	harder-sounding than **b**	B	**bhanana**	Banana
dh	harder-sounding than **d**	D	**dhoro**	Doro
g	like **g** in **g**ate	g	**gwavha**	gwava
nd	like **nd** in e**nd**	d	**ndiani**	^{n}deeanee
ng	like **ng** in si**ng**	ng	**vangu**	**van**goo
nw	like **nw** in u**nw**orn	ng	**kunwa**	**koon**wa
sv	like **sh** in **sh**oe	sh	**svondo**	shondo
zv	like **s** in plea**s**ure	zh	**zvimbo**	**zhim**bo

Vowels

a	like **a** in **a**t	a	**ani**	anee
e	1) like **e** in **e**gg	e/eh	**kwete**	**kwe**teh
	2) closer to **ay** in m**ay**be	ay	**ndega**	**^{n}day**ga
i	like **ee** in kn**ee**	ee	**chipi**	**chee**pee
o	like **o** in p**o**t	o	**dovi**	**do**vee
u	like **oo** in sh**oo**t	oo	**kupi**	**koo**pee

Diphthongs

ai	like **igh** in s**igh**	igh	**aiwa**	**igh**wa
oi	like **oi** in b**oi**l	oy	**inoita**	eenoyta
au	like **ou** in **ou**t	a^{oo}	**taundi**	ta^{oo}nd

Swahili

Some basic expressions *Maneno ya tumiwayo kila siku*

Yes.	**Ndiyo [Sawa].**	**ndee**yo [**sa**wa]
No.	**A-a [Hapana].**	**a**-a [ha**pa**na]
Please.	**Tafadhali.**	tafaðalee
Thank you.	**Asante [Nashukuru].**	a**san**teh [nashoo**koo**roo]

Introductions *Kujulishana*

Good morning.	**Habari ya [za] asubuhi?**	ha**ba**ree ya [za] asoo**boo**hee
Good afternoon.	**Habari ya mchana.**	ha**ba**ree ya m**cha**na
Good evening.	**Habari za jioni.**	ha**ba**ree za jeeonee
Good-bye.	**Kwaheri.**	kwa**he**ree
My name is …	**Jina langu ni [Naitwa] …**	**jee**na **la**ngoo nee [naeetwa]
Pleased to meet you!	**Nimefurahi kukutana nawe!**	neemefoo**ra**hee kookoo**ta**na **na**weh
What's your name?	**Jina lako nani? [Unaitwaje?]**	**jee**na **la**ko **na**nee [oonaee**twa**jeh]
How are you?	**Hujambo? [Habari gani?]**	hoo**ja**mbo [ha**ba**ree **ga**nee]
Fine, thanks. And you?	**Sijambo, wewe? [Nzuri, habari zako/yako?]**	see**ja**mbo **we**weh [nzooree ha**ba**ree **za**ko/**ya**ko]
Where do you come from?	**Unatoka wapi [nchi gani]?**	oona**to**ka **wa**pee [nchee **ga**nee]
I'm from …	**Natoka …**	na**to**ka
Australia	**Australia**	aoostra**lee**ya
Britain/England	**Uingereza**	ooweenge**re**za
Canada	**Kanada**	ka**na**da
South Africa	**Afrika kusini**	af**ree**ka koo**see**nee
United States	**Marekani**	mare**ka**nee
I'm with my …	**Niko pamoja na … wangu/yangu.**	**nee**ko pamo**ja** na … **wa**ngoo/**ya**ngoo
wife	**mke [bibi]**	**m**keh [**bee**bee]
husband	**mume [bwana]**	**moo**meh [**bwa**na]
family	**familia**	famee**lee**ya
boyfriend/girlfriend	**rafiki yangu**	ra**fee**kee **ya**ngoo

GUIDE TO PRONUNCIATION, see page 112/EMERGENCIES, see page 111

Questions *Masuala*

How?/When?	**Vipi?/Lini?**	veepee/**lee**nee
What?/Why?	**Nini?/Kwa nini?**	**nee**nee/kwa **nee**nee
Who?	**Nani?**	**na**nee
Which?	**Gani/Ipi?**	ganee/**ee**pee
Where is …?	**Iko wapi …?**	**ee**ko **wa**pee
Where are …?	**Ziko wapi …?**	**zee**ko **wa**pee
Where can I find/ get …?	**Wapi naweza [Ninaweza] kupata …?**	**wa**pee naweza [neena**we**za] koo**pa**ta
How far?	**Umbali gani?**	oom**ba**lee **ga**nee
How long?	**Muda gani?**	**moo**da **ga**nee
How much does this cost?	**Hii ni bei gani?**	hee-ee nee **be**-ee **ga**nee
Can I have …?	**Nipatie … tafadhali? [Naweza kupata …?]**	neepa**tee**-eh **…** tafa∂**a**lee [naweza koo**pa**ta]
What does this/that mean?	**Hii/ile ina maana gani?**	hee-ee/**ee**leh **ee**na ma-ana **ga**nee
Can you translate this for me?	**Nifasirie hii, tafadhali.**	neefasee**ree**-eh hee-ee tafa∂alee
Do you speak English?	**Unasema Kiingereza [Kizungu]?**	oona**se**ma kee-eenge**re**za [kee**zoo**ngoo]
I don't speak Swahili.	**Sisemi Kiswahili sana.**	see**se**mee keeswa**hee**lee **sa**na

It's … *Ni* …

better/worse	**bora [afadhali]/ mbaya**	**bo**ra [afa∂alee]/ ^{m}**ba**ya
big/small	**kubwa/ndogo**	**koo**bwa/**ndo**go
cheap/expensive	**rahisi/ghali**	ra**hee**see/**RH**alee
early/late	**mapema/chelewa**	ma**pe**ma/che**le**wa
good/bad	**nzuri/mbaya**	nzooree/^{m}**ba**ya
here/there	**hapa/pale**	**ha**pa/**pa**leh
hot/cold	**joto/baridi**	**jo**to/ba**ree**dee
near/far	**karibu/mbali**	ka**ree**boo/^{m}**ba**lee
next/last	**ya pili/ya mwisho**	ya **pee**lee/ya ^{m}**wee**sho
old/new	**ya zamani/mpya**	ya za**ma**nee/**m**pya
open/shut	**fungua/funga**	foon**goo**wa/**foo**nga
right/wrong	**sawa/si sawa**	**sa**wa/see **sa**wa

Hotel reservation *Hoteli*

I have a reservation.	**Nimeekesha chumba.**	neemeekesha choomba
Do you have any vacancies?	**Kuna vyumba vitupu?**	koona vyoomba veetoopoo
I'd like a …	**Ningependa …**	neengependa
single room	**chumba cha mtu mmoja**	choomba cha mtoo ^{m}moja
double room	**chumba cha watu wawili**	choomba cha watoo waweelee
room with twin beds	**chumba chenye vitanda viwili**	choomba chen^{y}eh veetanda veeweelee
with a bath/shower	**chenye bafu/shawa**	chen^{y}eh bafoo/shawa
We'll be staying …	**Tutakaa kwa …**	tootaka-a kwa
overnight only	**usiku mmoja tu**	ooseekoo mmoja too
a few days	**siku chache**	seekoo chacheh
a week	**wiki moja**	weekee moja

Decision *Uamuzi*

May I see the room?	**Naweza kukiona chumba?**	naweza kookeeona choomba
That's fine. I'll take it.	**Sawa. Nimekikubali.**	sawa. neemekeekoobalee
No. I don't like it.	**Hapana. Sikipendi.**	hapana. seekeependee
It's too…	**Ni … sana.**	nee … sana
dark/small	**giza/kidogo**	geeza/keedogo
noisy	**kelele**	keleleh
Do you have anything …?	**Una chumba …?**	oona choomba
better	**bora zaidi**	bora zaeedee
bigger	**kikubwa zaidi**	keekoobwa zaeedee
cheaper	**rahisi zaidi**	raheesee zaeedee
quieter	**kimya zaidi**	keemya zaeedee
May I have my bill, please?	**Nipatie hesabu yangu, tafadhali?**	neepatee-eh hesaboo yangoo tafaðalee
It's been a very enjoyable stay.	**Kwa kweli tumestarehe sana na makaazi yetu.**	kwa kwelee toomestareheh sana na maka-azee yetoo

NUMBERS, see page 110

Eating out *Kulanje*

I'd like to reserve a table for 4.	**Nataka kuekesha meza kwa watu wanne, tafadhali.**	nataka kooe**ke**sha **me**za kwa **wa**too **wan**neh tafa∂alee
We'll come at 8.	**Tutakuja saa mbili usiku.**	toota**koo**ja sa-a ^{m}**bee**lee oo**see**koo
I'd like …, please.	**Nataka … tafadhali.**	nataka … tafa∂alee
breakfast	**chakula cha asubuhi**	cha**koo**la cha asoo**boo**hee
lunch	**chakula cha mchana**	cha**koo**la cha m**cha**na
dinner	**chakula cha usiku**	cha**koo**la cha oo**see**koo
What do you recommend?	**Chakula gani unakiona kizuri, niambie?**	cha**koo**la **ga**nee oonakeeona kee**zoo**ree neeyam**bee**-eh
Do you have any vegetarian dishes?	**Kuna vyakula vya mboga mboga?**	**koo**na vya**koo**la vya ^{m}**bo**ga ^{m}**bo**ga

Breakfast *Chakula cha asubuhi*

bread/butter	**mkate/siagi**	m**ka**teh/see**ya**gee
fruit juice	**maji ya matunda**	**ma**jee ya ma**too**nda
honey	**asali**	a**sa**lee
milk	**maziwa**	ma**zee**wa
rolls/toast	**mikate/tosti**	mee**ka**teh/**to**stee

Snacks *Vitafunio*

bajia	ba**jee**ya	spiced bean flour balls
chipsi za muhogo	**chee**psee za moo**ho**go	cassava chips
kaa	ka-a	crab meat
kamba	**ka**mba	prawns/shrimp/cray fish
korosho	ko**ro**sho	cashew nuts
nyama baridi	n^{y}ama ba**ree**dee	cold meat
paja la nguruwe	**pa**ja la ngoo**roo**weh	pig's thigh

Meat *Nyama*

beef	**nyama ya ngombe**	**n^{y}a**ma ya **ngo**mbeh
chicken/duck	**kuku/bata**	**koo**koo/**ba**ta
lamb	**nyama ya kondoo**	**n^{y}a**ma ya **ko**ndo-o
pork	**nyama ya nguruwe**	**n^{y}a**ma ya ngoo**roo**weh
veal	**nyama ya ndama**	**n^{y}a**ma ya **nda**ma

matumbo	mat**oo**mbo	tripe with seasonings
mchuzi wa kima	mch**oo**zee wa **kee**ma	curried minced meat
mchuzi wa kondoo	mch**oo**zee wa **ko**ndoo	lamb curry
pavu la paa	**pa**voo la paa	venison tenderloin
steki ya mbuzi	**ste**kee ya ^{m}**boo**zee	goat steak

baked	**iliyookwa**	eeleeyo-**ok**wa
boiled	**iliyochemshwa**	eeleeyo**chem**shwa
fried	**iliyokaangwa**	eeleeyoka-**an**gwa
grilled	**iliyochomwa**	eeleeyo**chom**wa
roast	**iliyokaushwa**	eeleeyoka**oo**shwa
underdone (rare)	**iliyoiva kidogo**	eeleeyo**ee**va kee**do**go
medium	**ya kuiva kiasi**	ya koo**ee**va kee**ya**see
well-done	**iliyoiva sawa sawa**	eeleeyo**ee**va **sa**wa **sa**wa

kuku aliyepakwa (**koo**koo aleeye**pa**kwa)	roast chicken with a sauce of coconut milk, often served with pancakes
mchicha na nyama (m**chee**cha na **n**^{y}ama)	beef and spinach, flavoured with ginger and sweet peppers, served with *ugali*
viazi vya nyama (vee**a**zee vya **n**^{y}ama)	sweet potatoes cooked in coconut milk and served with chunks of beef

Fish and seafood *Samaki wa aina mbali mbali*

dagaa	**da**ga-a	sardines
kombe	**ko**mbeh	shellfish
mkunga	mkoonga	eel
nguru	**ngoo**roo	king fish
pweza wa kuchoma	**pwe**za wa koo**cho**ma	roast octopus
sumbururu	soomboo**roo**roo	tunny (tuna)
tasi	**ta**see	herring

papa mbichi (**pa**pa ^{m}**bee**chee)	sun-dried trout, marinated and served with lemon, raw onions and tomatoes

Vegetables–Salads *Mboga–Saladi*

aubergine (eggplant)	**biringani**	beereen**ga**nee
lentils	**hadesi**	ha**de**see
rice	**nyanya**	**n**^{y}an^{y}a
tomatoes	**mbaazi**	^{m}**ba-a**zee
vegetable marrow	**mumunye**	moo**moon**^{y}eh

dodoki la sukari	dodo**kee** la soo**ka**ree	pumpkin cooked in coconut milk
iriyo	ee**ree**yo	potato, cabbage and bean mash
makopa ya tangawizi	ma**ko**pa ya tanga**wee**zee	sun-dried cassava cooked with ginger
matoke na achari	ma**to**keh na a**cha**ree	cooked green bananas with pickles
mchicha	m**chee**cha	spinach-like vegetable
ugali	oo**ga**lee	stiff porridge or maize
vitambua	veetam**booa**	ground rice fritters
wali	**wa**lee	sweet potatoes (yams)

Fruit–Desserts *Matunda–Vitamu tamu*

chungwa	**choo**ngwa	orange
embe	embeh	mango
komamanga	koma**ma**nga	pomegranate
mapera	ma**pe**ra	guavas
matufaha	matoo**fa**ha	Swahili apples
mzuzu	m**zoo**zoo	plantain (type of banana)
nazi	**na**zee	coconut
ndimu	**ndee**moo	lemon
ndizi	**ndee**zee	banana
tikiti	tee**kee**tee	watermelon
aiskrimu	aee**skree**moo	ice cream
chapati ya ndizi	cha**pa**tee ya **ndee**zee	hot, mashed banana
kashata	ka**sha**ta	fudge made of nuts, almonds or coconut
tamu	**ta**moo	fritters

dafu (**da**foo)	unripe coconut; often sold in streets on the coast, its sweet juice is refreshing
ubuyu (oo**boo**yoo)	baobab fruit; gourd-like with an edible pulp called monkey bread

Drinks *Vinywaji*

beer	**biya**	**bee**ya
coffee	**kahawa**	ka**ha**wa
black	**bila maziwa**	**bee**la ma**zee**wa
with milk	**na maziwa**	na ma**zee**wa
hot ginger drink	**tangawizi**	tanga**wee**zee

lemonade	**soda ya ndimu**	**so**da ya **ndee**moo
milk	**maziwa**	ma**zee**wa
soft drink/soda	**soda**	**so**da
tea	**chai**	**cha**ee
with milk/lemon	**na maziwa/ndim**	na ma**zee**wa/**ndee**moo
wine	**mvinyo [divai]**	^{m}**veen**^{y}o [dee**va**ee]
red/white	**nyeupe/nyekundu**	n^{y}**eoo**peh/n^{y}**ekoon**doo

The bill (check) *Hesabu*

I'd like to pay.	**Nataka kulipa.**	na**ta**ka koo**lee**pa
I think there's a mistake in this bill.	**Nafikiri umefanya makosa katika hesabu hii.**	nafee**kee**ree oome**fan**^{y}a ma**ko**sa ka**tee**ka hes**sa**boo hee-ee
Do you accept credit cards?	**Unapokea kadi za benki?**	oonapo**ke**a **ka**dee za **ben**kee
We enjoyed it, thanks.	**Tumefurahi, asante.**	toomefoo**ra**hee a**san**teh

Travelling around *Kutembea [Kusafiri]*

Plane *Ndege*

Is there a flight to Mombasa?	**Kuna [Iko] ndege ya kwenda Mombasa?**	**koo**na [**ee**ko] **nde**geh ya **kwe**nda mom**ba**sa
What time should I check in?	**Saa ngapi nifike uwanja wa ndege? [Saa ngapi kufika kiwanjani?]**	saa **nga**pee nee**fee**keh oo**wa**nja wa **nde**geh [saa **nga**pee koo**fee**ka keewan**ja**nee]
I'd like to … my reservation.	**Nataka ku … safari yangu.**	na**ta**ka koo … sa**fa**ree **ya**ngoo
cancel	**kukensel [kuvunja safari]**	koo**ke**nsel [koo**voo**nja sa**fa**ree]
change	**kubadilisha**	koobadee**lee**sha
confirm	**kuhakikisha [kuthibitisha]**	koohakee**kee**sha [kootheebee**tee**sha]

Train *Treni*

I'd like a ticket to Tabora.	**Nataka tikti ya kwenda Tabora.**	na**ta**ka **tee**ktee ya **kwe**nda ta**bo**ra
single (one-way)	**ya kwenda tu**	ya **kwe**nda too
return (round trip)	**kwenda na kurudi**	**kwe**nda na koo**roo**dee

NUMBERS, see page 110/TELLING THE TIME, see page 109

When is the … train to Nairobi?	**Saa ngapi [Wakati gani] … treni ya Nairobi?**	saa **nga**pee [waka**tee** ganee] … **tre**nee ya naee**ro**bee
first/last/next	**ya kwanza/ya mwisho/nyengine**	ya **kwan**za/ya **mwee**sho/n^yen**gee**neh
Is this the right train to Kampala?	**Hii ndiyo treni inayokwenda Kampala?**	hee-ee **ndee**yo **tre**nee eenayo**kwe**nda kam**pa**la

Bus–Mini vans *Basi–Matutu*

When's the next coach/minivan to …?	**Wakati gani kuna basi jengine/matatu nyengine …?**	waka**tee** ga**nee** **koo**na **ba**see jen**gee**neh/ma**ta**too n^yen**gee**neh
How much is the fare to …?	**Shilingi ngapi [Kiasi gani] nauli …?**	shee**leen**gee **nga**pee [kee**ya**see **ga**nee] na**oo**lee
Will you tell me when to get off?	**Utaniambia wapi niteremke?**	ootaneeya**mbee**ya **wa**pee neete**rem**keh

Taxi *Teksi*

What's the fare to …?	**Nauli ni kiasi gani kwenda …?**	na**oo**lee nee kee**ya**see **ga**nee **kwe**nda
Take me to … this address	**Nipeleke… tafadhali. anuwani hii [mahali hapa]**	neepe**le**keh … tafa∂alee anoo**wa**nee hee-ee [ma**ha**lee **ha**pa]
Please stop here.	**Simama hapa, tafadhali.**	see**ma**ma **ha**pa tafa∂alee

Car hire–Automobile rental *Kukodi [Gari za kukodi]*

I'd like to hire (rent) a car.	**Nitapenda kukodi gari.**	neeta**pe**nda koo**ko**dee **ga**ree
I'd like it for a day/ a week.	**Naitaka kwa siku moja/wiki moja.**	naee**ta**ka kwa **see**koo **mo**ja/**wee**kee **mo**ja
Where's the nearest filling station?	**Kiko wapi kituo cha karibu cha petroli?**	**kee**ko **wa**pee kee**too**-o cha ka**ree**boo cha pe**tro**lee
Give me … litres of petrol (gasoline).	**Nipatie … lita za petroli.**	neepa**tee**-eh … **lee**ta za pe**tro**lee

How do I get to …?	**Vipi unafika …?**	**vee**pee oona**fee**ka
I've had a break-down at …	**Gari langu limeharibika …**	ga**ree lan**goo leemeharee**bee**ka
Can you send a mechanic?	**Tafadhali nipatie fundi [makenika]?**	tafaðalee neepa**tee**-eh **foon**dee [make**nee**ka]
How long will you be?	**Muda gani utachukua kufika?**	**moo**da **ga**nee ootachoo-**koo**wa koo**fee**ka

☞ You're on the wrong road.	**Uko kwenye barabara siyo.** ☜
Go straight ahead.	**Nenda moja kwa moja.**
It's down there on the left/right.	**Iko kule chini kushoto/kulia.**
opposite/behind …	**mbele yako/nyuma yako …**
next to/after …	**karibu na/baada ya …**
north/south	**kaskazini/kusini**
east/west	**mashariki/magharibi**

Sightseeing *Kutazama mji*

Where's the tourist office?	**Ofisiya watalii iko wapi?**	o**fee**seeya wa**ta**lee-ee **ee**ko **wa**pee
Is there an English-speaking guide?	**Yuko mtu wa kutuongoza anayesema Kizungu [Kiingereza]?**	**yoo**ko mtoo wa kootoo-**ongo**za anaye**se**ma kee**zoon**goo [kee-eenge**re**za]
Where is/are the …?	**Iko/Ziko wapi …?**	**ee**ko/**zee**ko **wa**pee
church	**kanisa**	ka**nee**sa
city centre	**mjini**	mj**ee**nee
cultural centre	**jumba la utamaduni**	**joo**mba la ootama**doo**nee
game sanctuary	**mahali pa kutunza wanyama**	ma**ha**lee pa koo**toon**za wan^y^ama
market	**soko**	**so**ko
museum	**makumbusho**	makoo**mboo**sho
waterfall	**mporomoko wa maji**	mporo**mo**ko wa **ma**jee
What are the opening hours?	**Saa gani hufunguliwa?**	sa-a **ga**nee hoofoongoo**lee**wa
How much is the entrance fee?	**Kiingilio kiasi gani?**	kee-eengee**lee**-o kee**ya**see **ga**nee

TELLING THE TIME, see page 109

Relaxing *Burudani*

What's on at the cinema tonight?	**Leo wanaonyesha filam [mchezo] gani snema?**	leo wanaon^{y}esha fee**lam** [m**che**zo] **ga**nee **sne**ma
How much are the seats?	**Kiasi tikiti?**	kee**ya**see tee**kee**tee
Would you like to go out with me tonight?	**Utapenda tutoke pamoja leo usiku?**	oota**pe**nda too**to**keh pa**mo**ja **leo** oo**see**koo
Would you like to dance?	**Utapenda kudansi?**	oota**pe**nda koo**dan**see
Thank you, it's been a wonderful evening.	**Asante, nimefurahi sana jioni hii.**	a**san**teh neemefoo**ra**hee sana jee-**o**nee hee-ee

Shopping *Maslezo juu ya maduka*

Where's the nearest…?	**… ya [la] karibu liko [iko] wapi?**	… ya [la] ka**ree**boo **lee**ko [**ee**ko] **wa**pee
baker's	**Duka la mikate**	**doo**ka la mee**ka**teh
bookshop	**Duka la vitabu**	**doo**ka la vee**ta**boo
butcher's	**Duka la nyama**	**doo**ka la **n^{y}a**ma
chemist's/drugstore	**Duka la dawa**	**doo**ka la **da**wa
department store	**Duka kubwa [Dipatment stoo]**	**doo**ka **koo**bwa [dee**pat**ment sto-o]
grocer's	**Duka la chakula**	**doo**ka la cha**koo**la
market	**Soko**	**so**ko
post office	**Posta**	**pos**ta
souvenir shop	**Duka la kitalii**	**doo**ka la kee**ta**lee-ee
supermarket	**Supamaket**	soopama**ket**

General expressions *Masuala ya kawaida [kufaa]*

Where's the main shopping area?	**Madukani ni wapi?**	madoo**ka**nee nee **wa**pee
Do you have any …?	**Kuna …?**	**koo**na
Don't you have anything …?	**Unayo …?**	oo**na**yo
better	**bora zaidi**	**bo**ra za**ee**dee
cheaper	**ya rahisi**	ya ra**hee**see
larger	**kubwa zaidi**	**koo**bwa za**ee**dee
smaller	**ndogo zaidi**	**ndo**go za**ee**dee
Can I try it on?	**Niijaribu?**	nee-eeja**ree**boo

TELLING THE TIME, see page 109

How much is this?	**Hii bei gani?**	hee-ee **be**-ee **ga**nee
Please write it down.	**Tafadhali niandikie.**	tafa∂**a**lee neeyandee**kee**-eh
I don't want to spend more than… shillings.	**Sitaki kutumia zaidi ya shilingi …**	see**ta**kee kootoo**mee**ya za**ee**dee ya shee**leen**gee
No, I don't like it.	**A-a, siipendi hii.**	**a**-a see-ee**pen**dee hee-ee
I'll take it.	**Nitainunua.**	neetaeenoo**noo**wa
Do you accept dollars/pounds?	**Unapokea dala/ pauni?**	oonapo**kea da**la/ pa**oo**nee
Do you accept credit cards?	**Unapokea kadi za benki?**	oonapo**kea ka**dee za **ben**kee

black	**nyeusi**	n^{y}e**oo**see
blue	**bluu**	bloo-oo
brown	**kahawiya**	kaha**wee**ya
green	**kijani**	kee**ja**nee
red	**nyekundu**	n^{y}e**koon**doo
white	**nyeupe**	n^{y}e**oo**peh
yellow	**manjano**	man**ja**no
light …	**rangi isiyokoza …**	**ran**gee eeseeyo**ko**za
dark …	**rangi iliyokoza …**	**ran**gee eeleeyo**ko**za

I'd like to buy …	**Nataka kununua …**	na**ta**ka koonoo**noo**wa
aspirin	**aspirini**	aspee**ree**nee
condoms	**makondom**	ma**kon**dom
insect repellent/spray	**dawa ya kujikinga na vidudu**	**da**wa ya koojee**keen**ga na vee**doo**doo
newspaper	**gazeti**	ga**ze**tee
American	**la kimarekani**	la keemare**ka**nee
English	**la kiingereza**	la kee-eenge**re**za
shampoo	**shampuu**	**sham**poo-oo
soap	**sabuni**	sa**boo**nee
sun-tan cream	**dawa ya ngozi**	**da**wa ya **ngo**zee
toothpaste	**dawa ya meno**	**da**wa ya **me**no
I'd like a film for this camera.	**Nataka filam ya kamera hii.**	na**ta**ka fee**lam** ya ka**me**ra hee-ee
black and white	**isiyokuwa ya rangi**	eeseeyo**koo**wa ya **ran**gee
colour	**ya rangi**	ya **ran**gee

NUMBERS, see page 110

Souvenirs *Vikumbusho*

chetezo cha udongo	chete**zo** cha oo**do**ngo	earthenware incense burner
kanga	**ka**nga	East African fabrics
kiyondo	kee**yo**ndo	Kenyan baskets
kofia ya mkono	kof**ee**ya ya mk**o**no	handmade caps
kombe	**ko**mbeh	sea shells
mashanuo	masha**noo**wo	Swahili combs
mkeka	mk**e**ka	straw mat
mkoba wa ukili	mk**o**ba wa oo**kee**lee	straw basket
tembo wa mti	**te**mbo wa mtee	wooden elephant
vinyago	vee**nʸa**go	*makonde* carvings

Bank *Benki*

Where's the nearest bank?	**Iko wapi benki ya karibu?**	eeko **wa**pee **ben**kee ya ka**ree**boo
I want to change some dollars/pounds.	**Nataka kubadilisha dala/paun, tafadhali.**	nataka koobadee**lee**sha **da**la/**pa**oon tafa∂**a**lee
What's the exchange rate?	**Kubadilisha pesa ni kiasi gani?**	koobadee**lee**sha **pe**sa nee kee**ya**see **ga**nee

Post Office *Posta*

I'd like to send this (by) …	**Nataka kupeleka … kwa.**	nataka koope**le**ka … kwa
airmail	**ndege**	**nde**geh
registered mail	**rejesta**	**re**jesta
A …-shilling stamp, please.	**Ya shilingi …, tafadhali.**	ya shee**leen**gee… tafa∂alee
What's the postage for a letter to London?	**Stempu ya London bei gani?**	**stem**poo ya **lon**don **be**-ee **ga**nee
Is there any mail for me? My name is …	**Kuna baruwa zangu? Jina langu ni …**	**koo**na ba**roo**wa **zan**goo. **jee**na **lan**goo nee
I'd like to send a telegram/fax.	**Nataka kupeleka simu/feksi.**	nataka koopeleka **see**moo/**fek**see

Telephoning *Kupiga simu*

Where's the nearest telephone booth?	**Simu ya karibu iko wapi?**	**see**moo ya ka**ree**boo **ee**ko **wa**pee

NUMBERS, see page 110

I'd like a telephone token.	**Nataka kadi ya kupigia simu.**	nata**ka** **ka**dee ya koopeegee**ya** **see**moo
May I use your phone?	**Naweza kutumia simu yako tafadhali?**	naweza kootoo**mee**ya **see**moo **ya**ko tafaðalee
I'd like to call… in England.	**Nataka kupiga simu … Uingereza.**	nataka koo**pee**ga **see**moo… ooweengere**za**
Hello. This is …	**Halo, ni mimi …**	**hal**o nee **mee**mee …
I'd like to speak to …	**Nataka kusema na … tafadhali.**	nata**ka** koo**se**ma na … tafað**a**lee
When will he/she be back?	**Wakati gani [Lini] atarudi?**	waka**tee** **ga**nee [**lee**nee] ata**roo**dee
Will you tell him/her I called?	**Mwambie kwamba nimepiga simu, tafadhali.**	mwam**bee**-eh **kwa**mba neeme**pee**ga **see**moo tafað**a**lee

Date and time — *Tarehe na saa [wakati]*

Time is counted in two 12-hour cycles in East Africa. The daytime cycle (*asubuhi*) begins at sunrise – 6 a.m. – and ends with sunset. The night-time cycle (*jioni*) stretches from approximately 6 p.m. to dawn.

What time is it?	**Saa ngapi?**	saa **nga**pee
It's …	**Ni …**	nee
five past one	**saa saba na dakika tano**	sa-a **sa**ba na da**kee**ka **ta**no
a quarter past three	**saa tisa na robo**	sa-a **tee**sa na **ro**bo
twenty past four	**saa kumi na dakika ishirini**	sa-a **koo**mee na da**kee**ka eeshee**ree**nee
half past six	**saa kumi na mbili na nusu**	sa-a **koo**mee na ^{m}**bee**lee na **noo**soo
twenty-five to seven	**saa moja kasoro dakika ishirini na tano**	sa-a **mo**ja kas**o**ro dakeeka eeshee**ree**nee na **ta**no
a quarter to nine	**saa tatu kasorobo**	sa-a **ta**too kaso**ro**bo
ten to ten	**saa nne kasoro dakika kumi**	sa-a **n**neh kas**o**ro dakeeka **koo**mee
twelve o'clock noon/ midnight	**saa sita mchana/ usiku**	sa-a **see**ta m**cha**na/ oo**see**koo
in the morning	**asubuhi**	asoo**boo**hee
in the afternoon	**mchana**	m**cha**na
in the evening	**jioni**	jee**o**nee

Sunday	**Jumapili**	jooma**pee**lee
Monday	**Jumatatu**	jooma**ta**too
Tuesday	**Jumanne**	joo**man**neh
Wednesday	**Jumatano**	jooma**ta**no
Thursday	**Alhamisi**	alha**mee**see
Friday	**Ijumaa**	ee**joo**ma-a
Saturday	**Jumamosi**	jooma**mo**see
January	**Januari**	janoo**wa**ree
February	**Febuari**	feboo**wa**ree
March	**Machi**	**ma**chee
April	**Aprili**	ap**ree**lee
May	**Mei**	me-ee
June	**Juni**	**joo**nee
July	**Julai**	joo**la**ee
August	**Agosti**	a**gos**tee
September	**Septemba**	sep**tem**ba
October	**Oktoba**	ok**to**ba
November	**Novemba**	no**vem**ba
December	**Disemba**	dee**sem**ba

yesterday	**jana**	**ja**na
today	**leo**	**le**o
tomorrow	**kesho**	**ke**sho

Numbers *Nambari*

0	**sufuri/ziro**	soof**oo**ree/**zee**ro
1	**moja**	**mo**ja
2	**mbili**	**^{m}bee**lee
3	**tatu**	**ta**too
4	**nne**	**n**neh
5	**tano**	**ta**no
6	**sita**	**see**ta
7	**saba**	**sa**ba
8	**nane**	**na**neh
9	**tisa [kenda]**	**tee**sa [**ken**da]
10	**kumi**	**koo**mee
11	**kumi na moja**	koomee na **mo**ja
12	**kumi na mbili**	koomee na **^{m}bee**lee

13	**kumi na tatu**	**koo**mee na **ta**too
14	**kumi na nne**	**koo**mee na **n**neh
15	**kumi na tano**	**koo**mee na **ta**no
16	**kumi na sita**	**koo**mee na **see**ta
17	**kumi na saba**	**koo**mee na **sa**ba
18	**kumi na nane**	**koo**mee na **na**neh
19	**kumi na tisa**	**koo**mee na **tee**sa
20	**ishirini na moja**	eeshee**ree**nee na **mo**ja
30	**thalathini**	thala**thee**nee
40	**arbaini [arobaini]**	arba**ee**nee [aroba**ee**nee]
50	**hamsini**	ham**see**nee
60	**sitini**	see**tee**nee
70	**sabiini**	sabee-**ee**nee
80	**thamanini**	thama**nee**nee
90	**tisiini**	teesee-**ee**nee
100	**mia**	**mee**ya
1000	**elfu moja**	**el**foo **mo**ja
first	**kwanza**	**kwan**za
second	**pili**	**pee**lee
once	**mara moja**	**ma**ra **mo**ja
twice	**mara mbili**	**ma**ra ^{m}**bee**lee
a half	**nusu**	**noo**soo
a quarter/one third	**robo/thuluthi**	**ro**bo/thoo**loo**thee

Emergency *Dharura*

Call the police	**Mwite polisi**	m**wee**teh po**lee**see
Get a doctor	**Daktari**	dak**ta**ree
HELP	**MSAADA [KUSAIDIA]**	msa-ada [koosaee**dee**ya]
I'm ill	**Naumwa**	na**oo**mwa
I'm lost	**Nimepotea**	neemepo**te**a
Leave me alone	**Usinisumbue/ Niache**	ooseeneesoo**mboo**weh/ neeyacheh
STOP THIEF	**MKAMATE MWIZI**	mka**ma**teh m**wee**zee
My … has been stolen.	**… yangu imeibiwa.**	… **yan**goo eeme-ee**bee**wa
I've lost my …	**Nimepoteza …**	neemepo**te**za
handbag	**mkoba/mfuko**	m**ko**ba/m**foo**ko
passport	**paspoti**	pas**po**tee
wallet	**kikoba cha pesa**	kee**ko**ba cha **pe**sa

TELEPHONING, see page 108

Guide to Swahili pronunciation

Consonants

These are pronounced as in English, but the following points should be noted:

Letter	Approximate pronunciation	Symbol		Example
f	always like **f** in few	f	**afya**	**af**ya
g	always as in **go**, never as in **gin**	g	**giza**	**gee**za
m	1) when it occurs as a prefix for nouns, it sounds like a separate syllable, as if it has a short **oo** sound in front	m	**mpunga**	mpoonga
	2) when followed by **b** or **v**, it is not a separate syllable and should be elided with the following letter;	^{m}	**mbali**	^{m}**ba**lee
	however, in words containing only one vowel, sounds like 1) above		**mbu**	**m**boo
s	always like **s** in so	s	**hesabu**	hesa**b**oo

Groups of consonants

dh	like **th** in **th**is	∂	**dhuru**	∂**oo**roo
gh	like the **ch** of Scottish lo**ch**	RH	**ghafula**	RHa**foola**
ny	before a vowel, like **ni** in o**ni**on	n^y	**nyasa**	**n^y**asa
th	always like **th** in **th**in	th	**thelathini**	thela**thee**nee

Vowels

a	like **a** in f**a**ther	a	**paka**	**pa**ka
e	like **e** in f**e**tch	e/eh	**enda**	**en**da
i	like **ee** in m**ee**t	ee	**fisi**	**fee**see
o	like **o** in **o**strich	o	**toka**	**to**ka
u	like **oo** in s**oo**t	oo	**rudi**	**roo**dee

Tswana

Basic expressions *Kakaretso*

Yes.	**Ee.**	**ee**-ee
No.	**Nnyaa.**	**nya**-a
Please.	**Tswee tswee.**	**tswee**-ee **tswee**-ee
Thank you.	**Ke a leboga.**	**kee a** lee-bo-**gah**
I beg your pardon?	**Ke kopa gore o bue gape?**	**kee ko**-pah **go-ree** oa **boo**-ee **ga**-pee

Introductions *Dikitsiso*

Good morning.	**Dumela.**	**doo**-mee-lah
Good afternoon.	**Dumela.**	**doo**-mee-lah
Good night.	**Robala sentle.**	**ro**-bah-lah see-**nclee**
Good-bye.	**Sala sentle.**	sah-lah see-**nclee**
May I introduce …?	**Ke le itsese …?**	kee lee i-**tsee**-see
My name is …	**Leina lame ke …**	lee-**i**-nah la-mee kee
Pleased to meet you.	**Ke itumelela go go itse.**	kee **i-too**-me-lee-lah **goa-goa i-tsee**
What's your name?	**Leina la gago ke mang?**	lee-**i**-nah lah **ga**-goa kee ma-**ng**
How are you?	**Le kae?**	lee **ka-ee**
Fine thanks. And you?	**Ke teng, wena o kae?**	kee **tee-ng** wee-na oa **ka-ee**
Where do you come from?	**Ko gae ke kae?**	**ko ga-ee** kee **ka-ee**
I'm from …	**Ke tswa ko …**	kee **tswah koa**
Australia	**Australia**	aoo-stra-li-a
Britain	**Ennyelane**	ee-**nnyee-la**-nee
Canada	**Canada**	ka-na-da
USA	**Amerika**	a-mee-ri-**ka**
I'm with my …	**Ke nale … wame.**	**kee** nah lee … **wa**-mee
wife	**mosadi**	moa-**sa**-di
husband	**monna**	moa-**nn-ah**
children	**mana**	ma-nah
parents	**matsadi**	ma-**tsa-di**
boyfriend/girlfriend	**tsala**	**tsa**-lah
I'm on my own.	**Ke nosi.**	kee noa-**si**
I'm on holiday (vacation).	**Ke mo bo itapolosong.**	kee moa boa **i**-ta-poa-loa-soa-ng

Questions *Dipotso*

When?	**Leng?**	lee-**ng**
How?	**Jang?**	ja-**ng**
Why?	**Ka go reng?**	ka **goa ree-ng**
Which?	**Efe/Sefe?**	**ee**-fee/**see**-fee
What is this/that?	**Ke eng mo/mole?**	kee ee-**ng** moa/moa-lee
Who is this/that?	**Motho yo/yole ke mang?**	moa-**thoa** yoa/yoa-lee kee ma-**ng**
Where is/are …?	**O/Ba kae …?**	o/ba ka-**ee**
Where can I find …?	**Ke ka bona kae …?**	kee ka **boa-na** ka-ee
How far?	**Go bokgakala bo bo kae?**	**goa** bo-**kha**-kala boa boa **ka-ee**
How long?	**Ke boleele bo bo kae?**	**kee** boa-lee-**ee**-lee boa boa **ka-ee**
How much?	**Ke bokae?**	kee boa-**ka-ee**
Can you help me?	**Ke kopa thuso?**	kee koa-pa **too**-saw
What does this mean?	**Golo mo go raya eng?**	**goa**-law moa goa **ra-ya ee-ng**
I understand.	**Ke a tlhaloganya.**	kee **a** cla-loa-**ga**-nya
I don't understand.	**Ga ke tlhaloganye.**	**ga** kee **cla**-loa-ga-**nyee**
Please speak slowly.	**Ke kopa gore o bue ka bonya.**	kee koa-pa **goa**-ree oa boo-ee ka boa-nya
Can you translate this for me?	**Ke kopa gore o ntolokele?**	kee koa-pa **goa**-ree oa **n-to**-law-**kee-lee**
Can I have …?	**Ke kopa…?**	kee **koa**-pa
Do you speak English?	**A o bua sekgoa?**	**ah** oa **boo-a** see-**khoa-a**
I don't speak Tswana.	**Ga ke bue setswana.**	**ga** kee boo-ee see-**tswa**-na

It's … *E …*

beautiful/ugly	**ntle/maswe**	**n-clee**/ma-**swee**
better/worse	**botoka/ga e botoka**	boa-**toa-ka**/ga ee boa-**toa-ka**
big/small	**tona/nnye**	**toa-na/n-nyee**
cheap/expensive	**ga e ture/e a tura**	ga **ee too-ree/ee ah too-rah**
good/bad	**siame/senyega**	**si-a**-mee/**see-nyee-ga**
hot/cold	**tsididi/bolelo**	**tsi-di-di**/boa-**lee**-law
near/far	**gaufi/kgakala**	**ga-oo-fi/kha-ka**-lah
right/wrong	**siame/fosa**	**si-ah**-mee/**foa**-sah

Hotel–Accommodation *Boroko*

We've reserved two rooms.	**Re beeleditse.**	**ree** bee-ee-lee-**di-tsee**
Here's the confirmation.	**Bosupi ke bo.**	boo-**soo-pi** kee **boa**
Do you have any vacancies?	**A le nale tiro?**	ah lee na-lee **ti**-roa
I'd like a … room.	**Ke batla phapose …**	kee ba-**cla pah-poa**-see
single	**ya motho a le mongwe**	yah moa-**thoa** a lee moa-**ng-wee**
double	**ya batho baba bedi**	ya ba-**thoa** ba-ba **bee-di**
with twin beds	**e nale malao a mabedi**	**ee** na-lee ma-la-oa a ma-**bee-di**
with a double bed	**boloao jo bo botona**	bo-la-oa jaw boa boa-toa-na
with a bath	**e nale bata**	ee na-lee ba-**tah**
with a view	**e nale pono**	ee na-lee poa-noa
We'll be staying …	**Re tlile go nna …**	ree **cli**-lee goa n-nah
overnight only	**bosigo bole bongwe**	boa-si-**goa** boa-lee boa-ng-wee
a few days	**malatsi a se kae**	ma-la-**tsi** a see ka-ee
a week	**beke**	bee-kee
Is there a campsite near here?	**A go nale kampa gaufi?**	a **goa** na-lee ka-**mpa** **ga**-oo-fi

Decision *Phetso*

May I see the room?	**A ke ka bona rumu?**	**ah** kee-**ka boa**-na **roo-moo**
That's fine. I'll take it.	**Go siame. Ke tla e tsaya.**	**goa** si-**ah**-mee. kee **clah ee tsa-ya**
No. I don't like it.	**Nnyaa ga ke e rate.**	**n-nyaa ga** kee ee **rah-tee**
It's too …	**E … thata.**	ee … **tha-ta**
cold	**tsididi**	**tsi-di-di**
dark	**lefifi**	lee-fi-fi
hot	**bolelo**	boa-lee-law
small	**nnye**	**n-nyee**
noisy	**modumo**	moa-**doo**-moa

NUMBERS, see page 126

Do you have anything …?	**A o nale sepe sese …?**	ah oa na-lee see-**pee** **see**-see
better	**botoka**	boa-**toa**-ka
bigger	**golwane**	**goa**-lwa-nee
cheaper	**botoka**	boa-**toa-ka**
quieter	**didimetse**	**di-di**-mee-**tsee**
May I please have my bill?	**Ke kopa tlhwatlhwa.**	kee koa-pa cloa-cloa
It's been a very enjoyable stay.	**Re itumeletse go nna fa.**	**ree i-too-mee**-lee-**tsee** goa **n**-na fa

Eating out *Resetshurente*

I'd like to reserve a table for 4.	**Ke kopa go beeletsa tafole tse 4.**	kee koa-**pa goa** bee-**ee**-lee-**tsa** ta-foa-**lee** tsee **n**-nee
We'll come at 8.	**Re tla tla ka 8.**	**ree cla cla** ka boa-**roa**-ba-boa-bee-**di**
I'm hungry/thirsty.	**Ke tshwerwe ke tlala/lenyora.**	kee **tshwee**-rwee kee cla-la/lee-n-nyoa-rah
I'd like …	**Ke batla …**	kee ba-**cla**
breakfast	**sefitlholo**	see-fi-cloa-loa
lunch	**dijo tsa motshegare**	di-joa tsa moa-tshee-ga-ree
dinner	**dijo tsa maitseboa**	di-jo tsa may-tse-boa-ah
Do you have local dishes?	**A le nale dijo tsa setswana?**	ah lee na-lee **di-jaw tsa** see-**tswa**-na
What do you recommend?	**Tse di monate ke dife?**	**tsee** di moa-na-**tee** kee **di-fee**
Do you have vegetarian dishes?	**A le nale tse di senang nama?**	ah lee na-lee **tsee di see**-na-**ng** nah-mah

Breakfast *Sefitlholo*

May I have some …?	**Ke kopa …?**	kee ko-**pa**
bread	**borotho**	boa-**roa-thoa**
butter	**botoro**	boa-**toa-roa**
eggs	**mae**	mah-ee
jam	**jeme**	**jee-mee**
milk	**mashi**	ma-**shi**
porridge	**motogo**	moa-**toa**-goa

sour milk	**madila**	ma-**di**-la
sugar	**sukiri**	soo-**ki-ri**

Starters *Dijonnye*

legapu	lee-**ga-poo**	water melon
manoko	mah-**naw-koa**	peanuts
mmidi o o besitsweng	**m-mi-di** oa oa bee-**si-tswee-ng**	roasted corn on the cob
ntshe	**n-chee**	sweet reed

Meat *Nama*

I'd like some …	**Ke batla …**	kee ba-**clah**
beef	**nama ya kgomo**	nah-mah yah **khoa-moa**
chicken	**koko**	**koa-koa**
goat	**pudi**	**poo-di**
lamb	**nku**	**n-koo**
pork	**kolobe**	koa-loa-**bee**

nama	nah-mah	stew
segwapa	see-**gwa-pa**	biltong
serobe	see-**roa-bee**	tripe
seswaa	see-**swa-ah**	boiled shredded meat

baked	**e bakilweng**	**ee** bah-**kee-lwen**
boiled/stewed	**e bedisitswe**	**ee** beh-**di-si-tswee**
fried	**e gadikilwe**	**ee** ga-**di-ki**-lweh
grilled/roast	**e besitweng**	**ee** bee-**si-tswen**
medium	**e sa butswa thata**	**ee** sa **boo-tswa tha-ta**
well-done	**e budule**	**ee boo-doo**-lee

Vegetables *Merogo*

beans	**dinawa**	di-na-**wa**
cabbage	**khabeche**	**kha**-bee-**chee**
carrots	**digwete**	di-**gwee**-tee
lentils	**ditlhodi**	di-**cloa**-di
onion	**kwii**	**kwi**-i
peas	**dinawa**	di-na-**wa**
potatoes	**ditapole**	di-**ta-poa-lee**
rice	**reise**	**ree-i**-see
spinach	**sepinichi**	see-**pi**-ni-**chi**

Fruit *Leungo*

apple	**apole**	**a**-poa-lee
banana	**panana**	pa-na-na
grapes	**moretlwa**	mo-**ree-cloa**
orange	**namune**	na-moo-nee
water melon	**legapu**	lee-**ga-poo**

Drinks *Dino*

beer	**biri**	**bi-ri**
coffee	**kofi**	koa-fi
black	**e ntsho**	ee **n-tsho**
with milk	**e nale mashi**	ee **nah**-lee ma-**shi**
tea	**tee**	tee-ee
chibuku	**chi**-boo-koo	sorghum beer
khadi	**kha**-di	wild berry beer

Paying *Tuelo*

This is too …	**Golo mo go …**	**goa-loa** moa **goa**
bitter	**botlhoko**	boa-**cloa-koa**
sweet	**sukiri**	**soo-ki-ri**
That's not what I ordered.	**Ga se se ke se kopileng.**	**ga** see see **kee** see koa-**pi**-lee-**ng**
I'd like to pay.	**Ke batla go duela.**	kee ba-**cla goa doo-ee**-la
I think you made a mistake in the bill.	**Ke akanya gore o dirile phoso mo biling.**	kee **a**-ka-**nya** goa-**ree** oa **di-ri**-lee **phoa-soa** moa **bi-li-ng**
Can I pay with this credit card?	**A ke ka duela ka karata ya banka?**	**a** kee **ka doo-ee**-la ka **ka-rah-tah** yah bah-**n-ka**
We only accept cash.	**Re tsaya madi fela.**	ree **tsa-ya** mah-di **fee-lah**
Is service included?	**A le tsentse service?**	a lee **tseen**-tsee see-vi-si
I'm full.	**Ke kgotshe.**	kee **kho-tshee**
We enjoyed it, thank you.	**Re itumeletse dijo, re a leboga.**	ree **i-too**-mee-lee-**tsee di**-joa **ree a** lee-**boa-ga**
Our compliments to the cook/our host.	**Re lebogela moapei.**	**ree** lee-**boa-gee**-la moa-**a**-pee-**i**

Travelling around *Go etela mafelo*

Plane *Sefofane*

Is there a flight to Maun?	**A go nale sefofane goya Maun?**	ah **goa** na-lee see-foa-**fa**-nee **goa-ya** ma-**oo-ng**
What time do I check in?	**Ke cheka-in leng?**	kee chee-ka-in lee-**ng**
I'd like to … my reservation on flight no. …	**Ke batla go duelela sepagamo sa sefofane sa …**	kee ba-**cla goa doo-ee-lee-la** see-**pa-ga**-moa sa see-foa-fa-nee sa
cancel	**tlosolosa**	**cloa**-soa-**loa**-sa
change	**chencha**	**chee-n-cha**
confirm	**go siame**	**goa** si-**ah**-mee

Train *Terena*

I want a ticket to Maun.	**Ke batla thekethe ke ya Maun.**	kee ba-**cla thee-kee-thee** kee ya ma-**oo-ng**
single (one-way)	**go ya fela**	**goa** ya fee-**lah**
return (roundtrip)	**go ya le go boa**	**goa** ya lee **goa** boa-**a**
How long does the journey (trip) take?	**Go tsatya lobaka lolo kae?**	**goa tsa-ya** loa-ba-**ka** loa-loa **ka**-ee
When is the … train to Palapye?	**Terena … ee yang ko Palapye e tsamaya leng?**	**tee-ree**-na … ee-**ee** ya-**ng** koa **pa-la**-p-yee ee **tsa**-ma-**ya** lee-**ng**
first	**ya ntlha**	yah n-**cla**
next	**e e latelang**	ee **ee** la-**tee**-la-**ng**
last	**ya bofelo**	ya boa-**fee**-loa
Is this the right train to Lobatse?	**A terena e ke yone ya Lobatse?**	ah **tee-ree-na ee** kee **yoa**-nee ya loa-ba-**tsee**
There's no train today.	**Ga gona terena gompieno.**	**ga goa**-na **tee-ree**-na **goa**-mpi-ee-no

Bus–Coach *Bese*

Is there a bus today.	**A go nale bese gompieno?**	**ah goa** na-lee **bee-see goa-mpi-ee**-no
What bus do I take to the centre?	**Ke tsamaya ka bese efe go ya toropong?**	kee **tsa**-ma-ya ka **bee-see ee**-fee **goa** ya **toa-roa-poa-ng**

NUMBERS, see page 126/TELLING THE TIME, see page 125

How much is the fare to town?	**Ke bokae go ya toropong?**	kee boa-**ka-ee goa** ya **toa-roa-poa-ng**
Will you tell me when to get off?	**Ke kopa gore o mpolelele fa ke fologa?**	kee **koa**-pa **goa-ree** oa **m-poa-lee-lee-lee** fa kee **foa**-loa-**ga**

Taxi *Taxi*

How much is it to …?	**Ke bokae go ya ko …?**	kee boa-**ka-ee goa** ya koa
Take me to this address.	**Ke ya ko …**	kee ya koa
Please stop here.	**Ke kopa gore o eme fa.**	kee **koa**-pa **goa**-ree oa ee-mee **fa**
Please wait for me. I'll be 10 minutes.	**Ke kopa gore o nkemele metsatso ee lesome.**	kee **koa-pa goa-ree** oa **n-kee**-mee-lee mee-**tsa-tsoa ee** lee-**soa**-mee

Car hire (rental) *Ko go hirwang dikoloi*

I'd like to hire (rent) a car.	**Ke batla go renta koloi.**	kee ba-**cla** goa ree-n-ta koa-loy
I'd like it for …	**Ke e batla …**	kee ee ba-**cla**
a day	**letsatsi**	lee-tsa-tsi
a week	**beke**	bee-kee
Where's the nearest filling station?	**Ko go tshelwang dipeterole ke kae?**	koa **goa tshee**-lwa-**ng** di-pee-tee-roa-lee kee **ka-ee**
Full tank, please.	**Ke kopa gore o e tlatse.**	kee **koa-pa goa-ree** oa **ee cla-tsee**
Give me … litres of petrol (gasoline).	**Ntshela … di litara leokwane.**	n-tshee-la … **di** li-ta-ra lee-**o-kwa**-nee
I've had a breakdown at …	**Koloi ya me e senyegetse ko …**	koa-loy ya-mee ee see-**nyee-gee-tsee** koa
Can you send a break-down truck?	**Ke kopa gore o romele koloi e tle go e goga?**	kee **koa-pa goa-ree** oa **roa-mee-lee** koa-loy **ee** clee **goa ee goa-ga**
Can you mend it?	**A o ka e baakanya?**	**a** oa ka ee **baa**-ka-**nya**

NUMBERS, see page 126

How do I get to …?	**Ke tsamaya jang go ya ko …?**	kee **tsa**-mah-yah jah-**ng goa** ya koa

☞ You're on the wrong road.	**O mo tseleng ee seng yone.** ☜
Go straight ahead.	**Tswelela fela jaana.**
It's down there on the left/ right.	**Go ko pele mo molemeng/ mojena.**
It's opposite/behind …	**Go lebagana/Ko morago ga …**
It's next to/after …	**Go bapa le/morago …**
north/south	**bokone/borwa**
east/west	**botlhaba/bophirima**

Sightseeing *Go bona*

Where's the tourist office?	**Ofisi ya tlholego e kae?**	o-**fi-si** yah **clo-lee-go** ee **ka-ee**
Is there an English-speaking guide?	**A go nale buka ya Sekgowa?**	**ah goa** na-lee **boo-ka** ya see-**kgoa-wa**
Where is/are the …?	**… e/di kae?**	… ee/**di ka-ee**
chief's house	**Ko ga kgosi**	koa **ga kgoa-si**
church	**Kereke**	kee-**ree**-kee
city centre	**Ko toropong**	koa toa-**roa-poa-ng**
market	**Mmaraka**	m-**ma-rah**-ka
President's palace	**Ko ga tautona**	koa **ga** ta-oo-toa-na
shops	**Dishopo**	di-shoa-poa
When does it open?	**Go bulwa?**	**kho boo**-lwa
When does it close?	**Tswala leng?**	**twah**-lah lee-**ng**
How much is the entrance fee?	**Go tsenwa bokae?**	**goa tsee-nwa** boa-**ka-ee**

Countryside *Ko nageng*

desert	**sekaka**	see-kah-kah
farm	**tshimo**	**tshi**-moa
footpath	**tselana**	tsee-lah-nah
lake	**lekadiba**	lee-ka-di-bah
mountain	**lentswe**	leen-**tswee**
river/well	**noka/sediba**	**noa**-ka/see-**di**-bah

TELLING THE TIME, see page 125

Entertainment *Maitiso*

What's playing at the theatre?	**Go tshameka eng ko holong?**	**goa tsha-mee-ka** ee-ng koa hoa-loa-**ng**
How much are the seats?	**Go tsenwa bokae?**	**goa tsee-nwa** boa-**ka-ee**
I want to reserve 2 tickets for the show on Friday evening.	**Ke batla thekethe tse 2 tsa labotlhano maitseboa.**	kee ba-**cla thee-kee-thee** tsee pee-**di** tsa la-boa-**cla**-noa ma-**i**-tsee-boa-**a**
Would you like to go out with me tonight?	**A ga o batle go tsamaya le nna maitseboa?**	**ah ga** oa ba-**clee go tsa**-ma-ya lee **n-na** mah-**i**-tse-boa-**a**
Is there a discotheque in town?	**A go nale disco mo?**	ah **goa** na-lee di-sco moa
Would you like to dance?	**A ga o batle go bina?**	ah ga oa ba-**clee goa** bi-na
Thank you. It's been a wonderful evening.	**Ke a leboga maitiso a a ne a le monate.**	kee a lee-boa-**ga** ma-**i-ti-soa** a a nee a lee moa-na-**tee**

Shops, stores and services *Dishopo*

Where's the nearest …?	**… e e gaufi e kae?**	… **ee ee ga-oo-fi** ee **ka-ee**
baker's	**lebaka**	lee-ba-ka
bookshop	**shopo ya dibuka**	**shoa-poa** ya **di-boo-ka**
butcher's	**buchara**	**boo-cha-ra**
dentist	**ngaka ya meno**	**ng**-a-ka ya mee-noa
grocery	**supermarket**	"supermarket"
hairdresser/barber	**ko go diriwang meriri**	koa **goa di-rwa-ng** mee-**ri-ri**
post office	**poso**	poa-soa
supermarket	**koporase**	koa-poa-**rah**-see
toilets	**ntlwana ya boithomelo**	n-**clwa**-na yah **boy**-toa-mee-law

General expressions *Kakaretso*

Where's the main shopping area?	**Ko toropong ke kae?**	koa **toa-roa-poa-ng** kee **ka-ee**

NUMBERS/DAYS OF THE WEEK, see page 126

Do you have any …?	**A ga o na …?**	**ah gah oa** nah
Do you have anything …?	**A o nale …?**	**ah oa** nah-lee
cheaper better larger smaller	**chipi** **botoka** **tona** **nnye**	**chi-pi** boa-**toa-kah** **toa**-na **n-nyee**
Can I try it on?	**A ke ka itekanya?**	ah kee ka **i-tee**-ka-**nya**
How much is this?	**Go lo mo ke bokae?**	**goa** loa moa kee boa-ka-ee
Please write it down.	**Ke kopa gore o kwale.**	kee koa-pa **goa**-ree oa kwa-lee
That's too much.	**E a tura.**	**ee** yah **too-rah**
No, I don't like it.	**Nnyaa ga ke e batle.**	**n-nyaa ga** kee ee ba-**clee**
I'll take it.	**Ke tla e tsaya.**	kee **cla** ee **tsa**-ya
Do you accept credit cards?	**A le tsaya di karata tsa banka?**	**ah** lee **tsa**-ya **di** ka-**ra-tah tsah** ba-**n-kah**
Can you order it for me?	**Ke kopa gore le e kope?**	ke **koa-pa goa-ree** lee ee **koa-pee**

black	**ntsho**	n-tsho
blue	**tala**	ta-lah
brown	**thokwa**	**thoa-kwa**
green	**tala**	**ta**-lah
orange	**khibidu**	**ki-bi-doo**
red	**khibidu**	**ki-bi-doo**
yellow	**borobe**	boa-**roa**-beh
white	**tshweu**	tshweh-oo

I want to buy …	**Ke batla go reka …**	kee ba-**cla goa ree-ka**
anti-malaria tablets	**dipilisi tsa malaria**	di-**pi-li-si tsa** ma-la-**ri-a**
aspirin	**dipilisi tsa tlhogo**	di-**pi-li-si tsa cloa-goa**
batteries	**malatlha**	ma-la-**cla**
newspaper	**pampiri**	pa-**m-pi-ri**
soap	**sesepa**	see-see-pah
toothpaste	**colgate®**	"colgate"

a half-kilo of apples	**kgetsana ya diapole**	khee-tsa-nah yah di-a-poa-lee
a litre of milk	**litara ya mashi**	li-ta-ra ya ma-shi
I'd like… film for this camera.	**Ke batla filimi ya khamera ya me.**	kee ba-cla fi-li-mi ya **kha-mee-ra** ya-mee
black and white	**bontsho le bosweu**	boa-**n-tshoa** lee boa-**swee-oo**
colour	**mmala**	m-ma-lah
I'd like a hair-cut.	**Ke batla go kgaola moriri.**	kee ba-**cla goa kha**-oa-la moa-**ri-ri**

Souvenirs *Segopotsi*

lefeelo	le-**fee-law**	dried-grass broom
mae a ntshe	ma-ee a n-**chee**	ostrich egg shells
matlalo	ma-**cla-loa**	small game skins
sego	see-**goa**	fruit shell cup
stenge	ste-n-gee	African print cloth
tlatlana	**cla-cla**-na	fruit basket

At the bank *Ko bankeng*

Where's the nearest bank/currency exchange office?	**Banka e e gaufi e kae?**	ba-n-ka ee ee **ga-oo-fi** ee ka-ee
I want to change some dollars/pounds into Pula.	**Ke batla go fetola madi ame mo dipontong go isa ko dipuleng.**	kee ba-**clah goa fee-to**-la ma-**di** a-mee moa **di**-poa-**n**-toa-**ng** goa **i**-sa koa **di-poo-lee-ng**
What's the exchange rate?	**'Exchange rate' ya lona ke bokae?**	"exchange rate" yah lo-nah kee boa-**ka-ee**

At the post office *Ko posong*

I want to send this by …	**Ke batla go romela ka …**	kee ba-**cla goa roa**-mee-lah ka
airmail	**sefofane**	see-**fo-fa**-nee
What's the postage for a letter/postcard to America?	**Ke bokae go romela lekwalo/postcard ko Amerika?**	kee bo-**ka-ee goa roa**-mee-**la** lee-**kwa**-loa/ "postcard" koa a-mee-ri-**ka**

NUMBERS, see page 126

I want …-Pula stamps.	**Ke batla ditempe tsa … Pula.**	kee ba-**cla** di-tee-mpee tsa … poo-la
Is there any mail for me? My name is …	**A ga kena lekwalo? Ke nna …**	**ah ga** kee-na lee-**kwa**-loa. kee **n-na**
Can I send a telegram/fax?	**A ke ka romela mogala/fax?**	**ah** kee ka **roa**-mee-**la** moa-**ga-la/**faks

Telephoning *Go bua ka mogala*

Where's the nearest public phone?	**Mogala e e gaufi o kae?**	moa-**ga-la** ee ee **ga-oo-fi** oa **ka-ee**
May I use your phone?	**Ke kopa go dirisa mogala wa gago?**	kee **koa-pa goa** di-**ri-sa** moa-**ga-la** wa **ga-goa**
I want to make an international call to …	**Ke batla go leletsa ko …**	kee ba-**cla goa** lee-lee-**tsa** koa
Hello. This is … speaking.	**Dumelang. Ke … yo o buang.**	du-mee-la-**ng**. kee … yoa **oa boo-a-ng**
I want to speak to …	**Ke batla go bua le …**	kee ba-**cla goa** **boo-ah** lee
When will he/she be back?	**O ya go boa leng?**	oa ya goa boa-ah lee-ng
Will you tell him/her that I called?	**Ke kopa gore o mmolelele gore ke ne ke leditse?**	kee **koa-pa goa-ree oa m**-moa-loa-lee-lee-lee **goa-ree** kee nee kee lee-**di-tsee**

Time and date *Nako le letsatsi*

Usually the time of day rather than the actual hour is used in Tswana, e.g. **phakela** (morning), **motshera** (afternoon), **maitseboa** (evening).

What's the time?	**Nako ke mang?**	na-**koa** kee ma-**ng**
in the morning	**phakela**	**pha-kee**-la
during the day	**motshegare**	moa-**tshee-ga-ree**
in the evening	**maitseboa**	ma-**i-tsee**-boa-**a**
at night	**bosigo**	boa-**si-goa**

Sunday	**Tshipi**	**tsee**-pee
Monday	**Mosupologo**	mo-**soo**-**poa**-loa-**goa**
Tuesday	**Labobedi**	la-boa-beh-**dee**
Wednesday	**Laboraro**	la-boa-**ra**-**roa**
Thursday	**Lbone**	la-boa-**neh**
Friday	**Labotlhano**	la-boa-**cla**-**noa**
Saturday	**Matlhatso**	ma-**cla**-**tsoa**
January	**Firikgong**	fi-**ri**-**khoa**-**ng**
February	**Tlhakole**	**cla**-**koa**-lee
March	**Mopipi**	moa-**pi**-**pi**
April	**Moranang**	moa-**ra**-na-**ng**
May	**Motsheganong**	moa-**tshee**-**ga**-noa-**ng**
June	**Seetebosigo**	see-ee-tee-boa-**si**-**goa**
July	**Phukwi**	**poo**-kwi
August	**Phatwe**	**pha**-twee
September	**Lwetse**	lo-**eh**-**tsee**
October	**Diphalane**	dee-**pha**-lan-ee
November	**Ngwanatsele**	**ng**-**wa**-na-**tseh**-**lee**
December	**Sedimonthole**	see-di-moa-n-**thoa**-lee

yesterday	**maabane**	ma-**a**-ba-nee
today	**gompieno**	**goa**-**m**-**pi**-**ee**-noa
tomorrow	**ka moso**	kah moa-soa
summer	**selemo**	see-lee-mo
autumn (fall)	**letlhafula**	lee-**cla**-**foo**-la
winter	**mariga**	ma-**ri**-**gah**

Numbers *Palo*

0	**nnoto**	**n**-naw-**toa**
1	**nngwe**	**n**-**ng**-**wee**
2	**pedi**	**pee**-**di**
3	**tharo**	**tha**-**roa**
4	**nne**	n-nee
5	**tlhano**	**cla**-**noa**
6	**thataro**	**tha**-**ta**-**roa**
7	**supa**	**su**-**pa**
8	**robedi**	**roa**-bee-**di**
9	**robongwe**	**roa**-boa-**ng**-**wee**
10	**lesome**	lee-**soa**-mee

11	**lesome le bongwe**	lee-**soa**-mee lee boa-**ng-wee**
12	**lesome le bobedi**	lee-**soa**-mee lee boa-bee-**di**
13	**lesome le boraro**	lee-**soa**-mee lee boa-**ra-roa**
14	**lesome le bone**	lee-**soa**-mee lee boa-**nee**
15	**lesome le botlhano**	lee-**soa**-mee lee boa-**cla-noa**
16	**lesome le borataro**	lee-**soa**-mee lee boa-**ra-ta-roa**
17	**lesome le bosupa**	lee-**soa**-mee lee boa-**su-pa**
18	**lesome le borobedi**	lee-**soa**-mee lee boa-**roa-bee-di**
19	**lesome le borobongwe**	lee-**soa**-mee lee boa-**roa**-boa-**ng-wee**
20	**masome mabedi**	ma-**soa**-mee ma-bee-**di**
21	**masome mabedi le bongwe**	ma-**soa**-mee ma-bee-**di** lee boa-**ng-wee**
30	**masome a mararo**	ma-**soa**-mee **ah** ma-**ra**-roa
40	**masome a mane**	ma-**soa**-mee **ah** ma-**nee**
50	**masome a matlhano**	ma-**soa**-mee **ah** ma-**cla-noa**
60	**masome a marataro**	ma-**soa**-mee **ah** ma-**ra-ta-roa**
70	**masome a supa**	ma-**soa**-mee **ah su-pa**
80	**masome a robedi**	ma-**soa**-mee **ah roa**-bee-**di**
90	**masome a robongwe**	ma-**soa**-mee **ah roa**-boa-**ng-wee**
100	**lekgolo**	lee-**khoa**-loa
101	**lekgolo le motso o le mongwe**	lee-**khoa**-loa lee **moa-tsoa oa** lee moa-**ng-wee**
200	**makgolo a mabedi**	ma-**khoa**-loa **ah** ma-bee-**di**
1,000	**tousane**	**toa-oo**-sa-nee

first	**ntlha**	**n-cla**
second	**sephatlo sa motsotso**	see-**pha**-cloa sa moa-**tsoa-tsoa**
once/twice	**gangwe/gabedi**	**ga-ng-wee/ga**-bee-**di**
a half	**sephatlo**	see-**pha-cloa**

Emergency *Tshoganyetso*

Call the police	**Bitsa mapodisi**	**bi-tsa** ma-poa-**di-si**
Get a doctor	**Bitsa ngaka**	**bi-tsa ng**-a-ka
Go away	**Tswaa o tsamaya**	**tswa-a** oa **tsa**-may-ee
HELP	**Thusang**	**too**-sa-**ng**
I'm ill	**Ke a lwala**	kee **ah** l-**wah**-lah
I'm lost	**Ke latlhegile**	kee la-**clee-gi**-lee
Leave me alone	**Ntlogele**	n-**cloa**-gee-lee
Stop thief	**Tshwarang legodu ke leo**	**tshwa**-ra-ng lee-goa-doo kee lee-oa

TELEPHONING, see page 125

My … have been stolen.	**… yame e utswilwe.**	ya-mee **ee oo-tswi-lwee**
I've lost my …	**Ke latlhile … yame.**	kee la-**cli**-lee… ya-mee
handbag/luggage	**beke/dithoto**	bee-kee/di-**thoa-toa**
passport/wallet	**pasa/sepache**	pa-sa/see-pal-**chee**
Where can I find a doctor who speaks English?	**Ke ka bona ngaka e e buang sekgoa kae?**	kee kah boa-na **n**-ga-ka ee **ee** boo-a-**ng** see-**khoa-a** ka-ee

Guide to Tswana pronunciation

Vowels

Letter	Approximate pronunciation	Symbol	Example	
a	1) like **a** in hat	a	**mosadi**	moa-**sa**-di
	2) like **a** in **a**fternoon	ah	**nama**	nah-mah
e	like **e** in we	ee	**le**	lee
i	like **i** in kick	i	**itse**	**itsee**
o	1) like **oa** in cocoa	oa	**koko**	koa-koa
	2) like **a** in **a**ll	aw	**bolelo**	boa-**lee**-law
u	1) like **oo** in boot	oo	**pudi**	poo-di
	2) like **u** in put	u	**supa**	su-pa

Consonants

b, d, f, h, j, k, l, m, n, w, y are pronounced as in English

g	always throaty	g	**gago**	**ga**-goa
p	softer than in English when followed by a vowel	p	**apole**	a-poa-lee
r	strongly pronounced as in ve**r**y	r	**reng**	reeng
s	like **s** in set	s	**sentle**	seen-**tlee**
t	softer than in English when followed by a vowel	t	**tee**	tee-ee
tl/thl	like **cl** in **cl**imb	cl	**tlhogo**	**cloa**-goa

Wolof

Basic expressions *Deggeral*

Yes/No.	**Waaw/Deedeet.**	wahw/**day**dayt
Please.	**Baal ma.**	bahl ma
Thank you.	**Jerejef.**	**jehreh**jehf
Excuse me (sorry).	**Baal ma.**	bahl ma
I beg your pardon?	**Ngane.**	**ngah**neh

Introductions *Wonnalee*

Good morning.	**Jama nga fanaan.**	**ja**ma nga fa**nahn**
Good afternoon.	**Jama nga yendoo.**	**ja**ma nga yehn-doo
Good night.	**Fanaanal ag jamm.**	fa**nah**nal ak **ja**ma
Good-bye.	**Ba beneen yon.**	ba beh**nayn** yon
My name is …	**Maangi tudd …**	**mahn**gi **tū**da
Pleased to meet you.	**Beg naa tase ag yow.**	bek nah **ta**seh ak yoh
What's your name?	**Na nga tudd?**	na nga **tū**da
How are you?	**Na nga def?**	na nga deh
Fine thanks. And you?	**Ci jamm rekk. Yow nag?**	chi **ja**ma rek. yoh nak
Where do you come from?	**Fan nga joge?**	fan nga **jo**geh
I'm from…	**Maangi joge …**	**mahn**gi **jo**geh
Australia	**Ostaraali**	**ostarah**li
Britain	**Angalteer**	**angal**tayr
Canada	**Kanada**	**ka**nada
South Africa	**Afrik Sud**	**af**rik sūd
USA	**Amerig**	**ameh**rik
I'm with my …	**Maa ngi ag sama …**	mah ngi ak **sa**ma
wife	**jabar**	jab-ar
husband	**jekker**	**jehk**-ehr
children	**doom**	dom
parents	**waajur**	**wah**jūr
boyfriend/girlfriend	**far/coro**	far/**cho**ro
I'm on my own.	**Man rekk la.**	man rek la
I'm on vacation.	**Da ma noopaloo.**	da ma **noo**paloo

GUIDE TO PRONUNCIATION, see page 143/EMERGENCIES, see page 143

Questions *Laajteh*

When?	**Kanch?**	kanch
Why?	**Lu tax?**	lū taKH
How?	**Naka?**	**na**ka
Who is this/that?	**Kii/Kee kan la?**	kee/kay kan la
What is this/that?	**Lii/Lee lan la?**	lee/lay lan lah
Where is/are …?	**Ana …?**	a-na
Where can I get/find …?	**Fan laay amee/gis?**	fan ligh **am**-eh/giss
How far?	**Soreena?**	**so**reena
How long?	**Kan?**	kan
How much?	**Naata?**	**nah**ta
Can you help me?	**Men nga ma dimbale?**	mehn nga ma **dimb**aleh
What does this mean?	**Lii lu muy tekki?**	lee lū myoo **teh**-ki
I understand.	**Xam naa?**	KHam nah
I don't understand.	**Xamuma.**	**KHa-mū**-ma
Please speak slowly.	**Baal ma, waxal ndank.**	bahl ma waKH-al ndank
Can you translate this for me?	**Men nga ma tekkil lii?**	mehn nga ma **teh**-kil lee
Can I have …?	**Men naa am …?**	mehn nah am
Do you speak English?	**Degg nga Angale?**	**dehg** nga **anga**leh
I don't speak Wolof.	**Degguma Wolof.**	dehg**ū**ma wollof

It's… *… na*

better/worse	**gen/gen bon**	gehn/gehn bon
big/small	**rey/tuuti**	ray/**too**ti
cheap/expensive	**yomb/bare**	yom-b/**bar**-eh
early/late	**teel/yeex**	tayl/yayKH
good/bad	**bax/bon**	baKH/bon
hot/cold	**tang/sedd**	tang/sehd
near/far	**jage/sore**	**ja**-geh/**so**reh
next/last	**topp/mujj**	top/mūj
old/young	**mag/ndaw**	mak/ndaw
right/wrong	**jub/jubadi**	jūp/**jūb**-ad-i

Hotel–Accommodation *Daluwaye*

We've reserved two rooms.	**Ber nanu naari neeg.**	behr nanū **nah**ri nayk
Here's the confirmation.	**Firnde bi a ngi.**	**fir**-ndeh bi a ngi
Do you have any vacancies?	**Ndax am nga neeg?**	ndaKH am nga nayk
I'd like a … room.	**Da ma beg ab… neeg.**	**da**-ma behg ab … nayk
single	**benn**	ben
double	**naar [seex]**	nahr [sayKH]
with twin beds	**naari lal**	nah-ri lal
with a double bed	**laal bu mag**	lahl bū mak
with a bath	**ag sangukaay**	ak **sangū**-kigh
with a shower	**ag sangukaay**	ak **sangū**-kigh
with a balcony	**ag peroy**	ak **peh**-rong
with a view	**ag gis**	ak giss
We'll be staying …	**Dinanu fanaan …**	di-nanū fan**ahn**
overnight only	**guddi gireckk**	gū-**di** gi-rehk
a few days	**ay fan [aybes]**	igh fan [ay-behs]
a week	**bes bu ayi**	behss dū igh

Decision *Terral*

May I see the room?	**Mennaa gis neeg bi?**	**mehn**-nah giss nayk bi
That's fine. I'll take it.	**Baax na. Dina kojel.**	bah-KH na. **dina ko**-jehl
No. I don't like it.	**Deedeet. Neexuma [Beggumako].**	day**dayt**. **nay**KHūma [**behg**-ū-ma-ko]
It's …	**Dafa …**	da-fa
too cold/hot	**sedd/tang lool**	sehda/tang lol
dark/small	**lendem/tuuti**	**lehn**dehm/tooti
noisy	**bare coow**	**ba**-reh chow
Do you have anything …?	**Am nga lu …?**	am nga lū
better/bigger	**gen li/gen rey**	gehn li/gehn ray
cheaper/quieter	**gen yomb/lu teey**	gehn yom-b/lū tay
May I please have my bill?	**Baal ma wa ma njegli?**	bahl ma wa ma **njehg**-li
It's been a very enjoyable stay.	**Beg naa lool ci ndal mi.**	bek nah lol chi ndal mi

NUMBERS, see page 142

Eating out *Lekk ci biti*

I'd like to reserve a table for 4.	**Da ma buga ab taabal ngir nent.**	**da**-ma **bū**-ga ap **tah**bal ngir nehnt
We'll come at 8.	**Dinanu agsi si juroom-nyetti waxtu.**	**di-na**nū **ag**si si **jū**room neht **waKHtū**
I'm hungry.	**Da ma xiif.**	**da**-ma KHeef
I'm thirsty.	**Da ma mar.**	**da**-ma mar
I'd like …	**Da ma buga …**	**da**-ma **bū**-ga
breakfast	**ndekki**	**ndeh**ki
lunch/dinner	**anch/reer**	anch/rayr
Do you have local dishes?	**Am nga togi reew mi?**	am nga **tog**-i rayw mi
What do you recommend?	**Lan nga fook ne** moo gen.	lan nga fook ne moo gen
Do you have vegetarian dishes?	**Am nga togg bu dul yapp?**	am nga tog bū dul **yap**a

Breakfast *Ndekki*

In Senegal and Gambia, breakfast generally consists of little more than porridge.

Starters *Ubeeku*

caakiri	**chahk**ri	couscous with milk
cere	**cheh**-reh	couscous
laax	lah-KH	millet with curdled milk
mboq	mbo-k	maize

Meat *Yapp*

I'd like some …	**Da ma buga …**	**da**-ma **bū**-ga
beef	**yappu nag**	**yap**pu nak
chicken	**yappu ginaar**	**yap**pu gi**nahr**
goat	**yappu bey**	**yap**pu bay
lamb	**yappu xar**	**yap**pu KHar
pork	**yappu mbaam**	**yap**pu mbahm
veal	**yappu sallu**	**yap**pu **sa**-lū
ceebu yapp	**chay**bū **yap**pa	rice dish with meat
ceebu ganaar	**chay**bū **gan**ahr	rice dish with chicken

NUMBERS, see page 142/TELLING THE TIME, see page 141

baked	**lakk**	**lak**-ka
boiled	**baxal**	baKHal
fried	**fiirir**	**fay**reer
grilled	**saaf**	sahf
roast	**afara**	afara
stewed	**suusal**	**soo**sal
underdone (rare)	**bum nyor lol**	būm nyor lol
medium	**mu eem**	mū aym
well-done	**na nyor bu bah**	na nyor bū bah

Fish and seafood *Ceebu jen*

ceebu jan	**chay**bū jan	pilaf rice with fish
coxolaan	**choKHo**lahn	sea crab
junxoob	**jūnKH**-oop	land crab
nankar	**nan**kar	crab
paan	pahn	mussels
sipax	**si**paKH	shrimps/prawns
sumb	sūm-b	lobster
yoxos	**yoKH**os	oysters

Vegetables *Leguum*

aubergine (eggplant)	**batase/jaxatu**	batanseh/jaKHatū
beans	**nebbe**	**neh**-beh
cabbage	**su**	choop
carrots	**karoot**	ka-rot
okra	**kanj**	ka-nja
onion	**soble**	**sob**leh
peas	**puwaa**	**pū**wah
potatoes	**pombiteer**	**pom-pi**-tayr
rice	**ceeb**	chehb
spinach	**begej**	**beh**gehj

Fruit *Kojomtu*

apple	**pom**	pom
banana	**banaana**	ba-nahn-na
ginger	**ginjeer**	**gin**-jayr
lemon	**limon**	**li**-mon
orange	**soraas**	**so**-rahss
sorel	**bisaab**	**bi**-shahp

tamarind	**daxxaar**	**da**KH-KHahr
ice-cream	**radi galaas**	ra-di **ga**lahs

Drinks *Naan*

beer	**berr**	behr
coffee	**kafe**	**ka**feh
black	**rekk**	rehka
with milk	**ag meew**	ak mayw
fruit juice	**njar**	njar
mineral water	**ndoxu samsam**	**ndo**KH-ū **sam**sam
tea	**attaaya**	**at**ah-ya
wine	**bun**	būn
red	**bu xong**	bū KHong
white	**bu weex**	bū weh-KH
vodka	**wodka**	**wod**ka
dagaar	**da**-gahr	tamarind juice
dute/kinkille ba	**dū**-teh/kin-ki-leh ba	herbal "bush" tea

Complaints–Paying *Jambat–Fey*

This is too …	**Lii dafa … lool.**	lee dafa … lol
bitter	**wegh**	weh
sour	**forox**	**fo**-roKH
sweet	**negh**	neh
That's not what I ordered.	**Li ma laaj du li.**	li ma lahj doo li
I'd like to pay.	**Da ma buga fay.**	**da**-ma **bū**-ga fay
I think you made a mistake in the bill.	**Yaakaar naa ni danga juum ci njegli.**	**yah**-kahr nah ni da-nga joom chi **njehg**-li
Can I pay with this credit card?	**Munaa fay ag karta?**	**moo**nah fay ak kar-ta
We only accept cash.	**Haalis rekk lanuy jeel.**	**hah**-lis rehk la-nyoo jeel
Is service included?	**Weexal ci la bokk?**	**way**KHal chi la **bo**ka
I'm full.	**Man fees na.**	man fays na
We enjoyed it, thank you.	**Beg nanu, jerejef.**	behk **na**nū **jehreh**jehf
Our compliments to the cook/our host.	**Jerejef si togagi.**	**jehreh**jehf si **toga**gi

NUMBERS, see page 142

Travelling around *Worr di tukki*

Plane *Fefel naaw [Roplan/Abiyon]*

Is there a flight to Banjul?	**Am na abiyon buydem Banjul?**	am na **abi**-yon **byoo**dem **ban**jūl
What time do I check in?	**Ben waxtu laa war dugg?**	behn **waKHtū** lah war **dū**-ga
I'd like to … my reservation on flight no. …	**Da ma buga … ber sama toogu ci abiyon number …**	**da**-ma **bū**-ga … behr sama **too**gū chi **abi**-yon **num**ber
cancel	**fomm**	fom
change	**soppi**	sopi
confirm	**daganal**	**daga**nal

Train *Ottorai*

I want to buy a ticket to Dakar.	**Da ma buga jend biye ba Dakar.**	**da**-ma **bu**-ga jehnd biyeh ba da-kar
single (one-way)	**dem rekk**	dem rek
return (roundtrip)	**dem ag dellusi**	dem ak **dehl**ūsi
first/second class	**toogu kanam/toogoo ginnaaw**	**too**gu ka-nam/**too**goo **gi**nahw
How long does the journey (trip) take?	**Naata waxtu la tukki bi?**	**nah**ta **waKHtū** la **tu**-ki bi
When is the… train to Ziguinchor?	**Kanch la ottorai bu jekk pur Zinganchor?**	kanch la **otto**-righ bū jek pūr zi-ngan-chor
first/next	**jekk/topp**	jehk/**top**a
last	**mujj**	mūja
Is this the right train to Kaolack?	**Bii, ottorai Kaolack la?**	bee **otto**-righ **kao**-lak la
There's no train today.	**Tey saxaar amul.**	tay **saKH**ahr amūd

Bus–Coach *Rapid*

Is there a bus today.	**Kaar rapid am na tey?**	kahr ra-pid am na tay
What bus do I take to the centre?	**Ban kaar laay jel pur dekk ba?**	ban kahr ligh jehl pūr dek ba
How much is the fare to …?	**Naata ngay fay ba …?**	**nah**ta ngay fay ba

TELLING THE TIME, see page 142

Will you tell me when to get off?	**Men nga ma wax fan laay wace?**	mehn nga ma waKH fan ligh wa-cheh

Taxi *Wotto [Taxi]*

How much is it to …?	**Naata la ba …?**	**nah**ta la ba
Take me to this address.	**Yobbu ma ci dekkuwaay bii.**	yobū ma chi **deh**kūwigh bee
Please stop here.	**Baal ma tayamal fii.**	**bahl** ma ta-ya-mal fee
Please wait for me. I'll be 10 minutes/ a short while.	**Baal ma, xaar ma 10 minit/tuuti.**	bahl ma KHahr ma 10 **mi**nit/**too**ti

Car hire–Automobile rental *Luwee motto*

I'd like to hire (rent) a car.	**Dama buga luwe motto.**	**da**ma **bū**ga loo-weh **mo**to
I'd like it for a day/week.	**Dama buga pur benn fan/besbu aye.**	**da**ma **bū**ga pūr behn fan/**behs**bū igh
Where's the nearest filling station?	**Ban garaas a gen jage?**	ban **ga**rahs a gehn **ja**geh
Full tank, please.	**Feesal ko, jerejef.**	**fay**sal ko **jehreh**jehf
Give me… litres of petrol (gasoline).	**May ma … walaati peterol.**	may ma … **wal**ahti **peh-teh**-rol
How do I get to …?	**Nu may deme … ?**	nū may **deh**-meh
I've had a breakdown at …	**Sama woto dafa paan …**	**sa**ma **wo**to **da**fa pahn
Can you send a mechanic?	**Men nga ma yonneel mekanisen bi?**	mehn nga ma yon-ayl **meh**-ka-ni-sehn bi
Can you mend it?	**Men nga ko dafarr?**	mehn nga ko dafar

Go straight ahead.	**Tallalal.**
It's down there on the left/right.	**Fee la ci sa cammon/ndeyjoor.**
opposite/behind …	**jakkarlo/ci ginnaaw …**
next to/after …	**dend ag/so rombe …**
north/south	**bej gannaar/bej ganjool**
east/west	**penku/sowu**

NUMBERS, see page 142

Sightseeing *Gissukai*

Where's the tourist office?	**Fan la biro turist yi?**	fan la **biro tū**-rist yi
Is there an English-speaking guide?	**Amna ku fi degg Angale?**	**am**-na kū fi deg **a-nga**-leh
Where is/are the …?	**Ana …?**	a-na
botanical gardens	**tooli toortoor**	**tooli toor**-toor
castle	**taata**	**tah**ta
chief's house	**ker buur**	kehr boor
church	**jakka/egiliis**	**jaka/egi**-leess
city centre	**bir dekk**	bir dehk
harbour	**takk**	**taka**
market	**jaba**	jaba
museum	**ker xarala**	kehr **KHa**rala
President's palace	**ker buur**	kehr boor
shops	**butig**	**boo**-tik
When does it open?	**Kan laye ubbi?**	kan la-yeh ūbb-i
When does it close?	**Kan laye tej?**	kan la-yeh teh-j
How much is the entrance fee?	**Nduggu mi naata la?**	**ndoog**-ū mi **nah**-ta la

Countryside *All bi*

desert	**jati**	jat-i
farm	**tool**	tool
footpath	**nall/yoon**	nal/yoon
game reserve	**park**	park
lake	**deeg**	dayk
mountain	**doj/xeer**	doj/KHayr
oasis	**teen**	tayn
river	**dex**	dehKH
savannah	**degjoor**	**dek**joor
well	**teen**	tayn

Entertainment *Beegal*

What's playing at the theatre?	**Ban foh mo am si teyaator?**	ban foh mo am si tay-**ah**-tor
How much are the seats?	**Naata la toogu yi?**	nah-ta la **to**-gū yi

DAYS OF THE WEEK, see page 142

I want to reserve 2 tickets for the show on Friday evening.	**Da ma buga ber naari biye ajjuma ci guddi.**	**da**-ma **bū**-ga behr na-ahri **bih**-yeh **a-jū**-ma chi **gū**-di
Would you like to go out with me tonight?	**Buga nga genna man tey ci guddi?**	**bū**-ga nga gehn-na man tay chi gudi
Is there a discoteque in town?	**Feccukaay am na ci bir dekk bi?**	fe-jū-kigh am na chi bir dehka bi
Would you like to dance?	**Buga nga fecc?**	**bū**-ga nga feh-cha
Thank you. It's been a wonderful evening.	**Jerejef. Guddi gi neexoon na.**	**jehreh**jehf. **gū**-di gi **nay**-KHoon na

Look out for the following forms of popular entertainment.

sabarr	**sa**barr	drumming/dancing
lamb	lam-b	wrestling match

Shops, stores and services *Buutig*

Where's the nearest …?	**Ana … bi gen jage?**	a-na … bi gehn **ja**geh
baker's	**mbulanse**	**mbūlan**seh
bookshop	**libereri**	**librehri**
butcher's	**teflekatbi**	**tef**leh**kat**bi
chemist's	**farmasi**	**far**masi
dentist	**doktor**	**dok**-tor
department store	**mangasin**	man-ga-sin
grocery	**jaba**	**ja**ba
hairdresser/barber	**lettkatbi/watkatbi**	**letkat**bi/**watkat**bi
newsagent	**xibaarukaay**	**KHi**bahrūkigh
post office	**post**	post
supermarket	**mangasin bu mag**	man-ga-sin bū mak
toilets	**wanag**	**wa**-nak

General expressions *Deggeral*

Where's the main shopping area?	**Fan la jaba ju mag ji nekk?**	fan la **ja**ba jū mak ji nehk
Do you have anything …?	**Am nga lu gen …?**	am nga lū gehn
cheaper/better	**yomb/baah**	yom-b/ba-ah
larger/smaller	**rey/tuuti**	ray/**too**ti

NUMBERS, see page 142

Do you have any …?	**Am nga ay …?**	am nga ay
Can I try it on?	**Men naa ko jeem?**	mehn nah ko jaym
How much is this?	**Lii naata la?**	lee **nah**ta la
Please write it down.	**Baal ma, bind ko.**	bahl ma **bin**da ko
That's too much. How about… derem?	**Loolu dafa bare. … derem nak?**	loolū dafa bareh. … deh-rehm nak
No, I don't like it.	**Deedeet. Neexuma.**	**day**dayt. **nay**KHūma
OK, I'll take it.	**Baaxna. Di naa ko jel.**	bah-KH-na. dee nah ko jehl
Do you accept credit cards?	**Di nga jel credit card?**	dee nga jehl **kre**dit kard
Can you order it for me?	**Men nga ma ko wutal?**	mehn nga ma ko **wū**tal

black	**nuul**	nool	blue	**bulo**	**bū**loo
brown	**xeereer**	**KHay**rayr	green	**ngeel**	ngayl
orange	**mbaasan**	**mbah**san	red	**xonxx**	KHonKH
yellow	**puur**	poor	white	**weex**	wayKH

I want to buy …	**Dama buga jend …**	**da**ma **bū**-ga jehnd
anti-malaria tablets	**tobbi sibiru**	**to**bi **sibi**-rū
aspirin	**asporo**	**ass-po**-ro
bottle opener	**ubbikaayu buteel**	**ubi**-kigh-ū **bū**-tayl
newspaper	**xibaaruwaay**	**KHi-bah-rū**-wigh
English/American	**Angale/Ameriken**	**a-nga**-leh/**amehr**ikehn
shampoo	**shampoo**	sham**poo**
soap	**saabu**	**sah**-bū
toothpaste	**dentifiriis**	dehntifirees
a half-kilo of apples	**genn wallu kilo pom**	gehn **wall**oo **ki**lo pom
a litre of milk	**bena liitarr meew**	behna lee-tarr mayw
I'd like … film for this camera.	**Da ma buga … pelikiil.**	**da**-ma **bū**-ga **…** **peli**keel
black and white	**nuul ag weex**	nool ak **wayKH**
colour	**kuloor/cuub**	kūloor/koob
I'd like a hair-cut.	**Da ma buga wannee suma kawarrgi.**	da ma **bū**-ga wan-nee **sū**ma kawarr-gee

TELLING THE TIME, see page 141

Souvenirs *Sarice [Yobbal]*

anaango	**anah**-ngo	two-piece suit
carax	**char**aKH	sandals
ceemis	chee-mees	shirt
jaaro	**jah**rū	ring
lam	lam	bracelet
mbaxane	**mbaKHa**neh	hat
sabarr	sabar	drum
yatt	yat	sculpture, mask

At the bank *Bank*

Where's the nearest bank?	**Fan la bank bi gen jage nekk?**	fan la bank bi gehn **ja**geh nek
I want to change some dollars/pounds into Dalasi.	**Da ma buga wecci ay dollar/pound si dalasi.**	**da**-ma **bū**-ga wee-chi ay **doll**ar/"pound" si **dala**si
What's the exchange rate?	**Naata la wecci wi?**	**nah**ta la wee-chi wi

At the post office *Post*

I want to send this by …	**Da ma buga yonnee lii ci …**	da-**ma bū**-ga **yon**-ay lee chee
airmail	**abiyon**	**abi**-yon
express	**saasi**	sahssi
I want …-derem stamps.	**Dama buga … derem stamp.**	**da**ma **bū**-ga… **deh**rehm stamp
What's the postage for a letter/postcard to America?	**Naata la leetar/kart ba Amerig?**	**nah**ta la **lay**tar/kart ba **ameh**rik
Is there any mail for me? My name is …	**Am na fi leetar? … ma ngi tudd.**	am na fi **lay**tar. … ma ngi tūd
Can I send a telegram/fax.	**Men naa yonnee telegaram/faks.**	mehn nah **yon**-ay teh-leh-garam/faks

Telephoning *Telefonee*

Where's the nearest public phone.	**Ana telefon ni mbedd bu gen jageh?**	a-na teh-leh-fon ni mbehd bū gehn **ja**geh

NUMBERS, see page 142

May I use your phone?	**Men naa abb sa telefonbi?**	mehn nah ab sa **tehleh**fonbi
I want to make an international call.	**Da ma buga woote bitim reew.**	da ma **bū**-ga **wooteh bi**tim rayw
Hello. This is … speaking.	**Jama-ngam. Man la …**	**ja**ma ngam. man la
I want to speak to …	**Da ma buga wax ag …**	da ma **bū**-ga WAKH ak
When will he/she be back?	**Kan lay dellusi?**	kan lay **dehl**-lūsi
Will you tell him/her that I called?	**Waxal mako ne woote naa?**	**wa**KHal **ma**-ko neh **woo**teh nah

Time and date *Wahtu ak bes*

What's the time/hour?	**Ba waxtu o jot?**	ba **wa**KHtū o jot
five past one	**benn waxtu tegal na juroomi minit**	behn **wa**KHtū **teh**-gal na **jū**roomi **mi**nit
quarter after three	**nett waxtu tegal na fukki minit ag juroom**	neht **wa**KHtū **teh**-gal na fū-ki **mi**nit ak **jū**room
twenty after five	**juroomi waxtu tegal na naar fukki minit**	**jū**roomi **wa**KHtū **teh**gal na nahr fū-ki **mi**nit
half-past seven	**juroom naar waxtu ag genewala**	**jū**room nahr **wa**KHtū ak geh-na-wala
twenty-five to nine	**juroom nenti waxtu dese na naar fukk ag juroomi miniti**	**jū**room nehnti **wa**KHtū dehseh na nahr fook ak **jū-roo**mi **mi**nit
ten to ten	**fukki waxtu dese na fukki minit**	**fū**-ki **wa**KHtū dehseh na **fu**-ki **mi**nit
noon	**njolloor**	**njo**loor
midnight	**xaaju guddi**	**khah**jū **gū**-di
in the morning	**ci suba**	chi **sū**-ba
during the day	**ci becceq**	chi beh-chehk
in the evening	**ci ngoon**	chi ngoon
at night	**ci guddi**	chi **gū**-di
yesterday	**demb**	dem-ba
today	**tey**	tay
tomorrow	**elleg/suba**	eh-lehk/**sū**-ba
winter-spring	**noor**	nor
summer-autumn (fall)	**nawet**	**na**weht

Sunday	**dibeer**	dibayr
Monday	**altine**	al-ti-neh
Tuesday	**talaata**	ta-lah-ta
Wednesday	**allarba**	**al**-ar-ba
Thursday	**al xames**	**al**-KHa-mehs
Friday	**aljuma**	al-jū-ma
Saturday	**gaaw**	gahw

For months, it is easiest to use either English or French names; in Wolof they are linked to variable religious festivals.

Numbers *Cont*

0	**dara/neen**	**da**ra/nayn
1	**benn**	ben
2	**naar**	nahr
3	**nett**	net
4	**nent**	nent
5	**juroom**	**jū**room
6	**juroom benn**	**jū**room behn
7	**juroom naar**	**jū**room nahr
8	**juroom nett**	**jū**room neht
9	**juroom nent**	**jū**room nehnt
10	**fukk**	fūk
11	**fukk ag benn**	fūk ak behn
12	**fukk ag naar**	fūk ak nahr
13	**fukk ag nett**	fūk ak neht
14	**fukk ag nent**	fūk ak nent
15	**fukk ag juroom**	fūk ak **jū**room
16	**fukk ag juroom ben**	fūk ak **jū**room ben
17	**fukk ag juroom nar**	fūk ak **jū**room nahr
18	**fukk ag juroom net**	fūk ak **jū**room neht
19	**fukk ag juroom nent**	fūk ak **jū**room nehnt
20	**naar fukk**	nahr fūk
21	**naar fukk ag benn**	nahr fūk ak behn
30	**fan weer**	fan wayr
40	**nent fukk**	nent fūk
50	**juroom fukk**	**jū**room fūk
60	**juroom benn fukk**	**jū**room behn fūk
70	**juroom naar fukk**	**jū**room nahr fūk
80	**juroom nett fukk**	**jū**room neht fūk
90	**juroom nent fukk**	**jū**room nehnt fūk

100	**teemeer**	**tay**-mayr
101	**teemeer ag benn**	**tay**-mayr ak ben
200	**naar teemeer**	nar **tay**-mayr
1,000	**junni**	**jū**-ni
1,000,000	**fukki teemeeri junni**	fū-ki **tay**-may-ri **jū**ni
first	**njekkeel**	**njeh**-kayl
second	**naaral**	**nah**ral
once	**benn yoon**	**behn** yoon
twice	**naari yoon**	**nah**-ri yoon
a half	**genn wall**	gehn wala

Emergency *Jampa*

Call the police	**Woowal alkaati yi**	**woo**wal **al**-kah-ti yi
Get a doctor	**Wuutal Doktor**	**woo**tal **dok**tor
Go away	**Joge fi**	**jo**-geh fi
HELP	**NDIMBAL**	**ndim**bal
I'm ill	**Da ma feebar**	**da**-ma **fay**bar
I'm lost	**Da ma reer**	**da**-ma rayr
Leave me alone	**Bayyi ma**	**bayi** ma
STOP THIEF	**SACC EEY**	sa-chay
My … have been stolen.	**Danu sacc sama …**	danū sach sama
I've lost my …	**Dama reeral sama …**	**da**ma **ray**ral **sama**
handbag/wallet	**saag/kalpe**	sahk/**kal**peh
passport	**paspoor**	**pass**poor
luggage	**bagaas yi**	**ba**gahss yi
Where can I find a doctor who speaks English?	**Fan laa men gise doktoor bu degg Angale?**	fan lah mehn **gi**seh **dok**tor bū **dehg** **a-nga**-leh

Guide to Wolof pronunciation

Consonants

b, d, f, j, k, l, m, n, p, r, s, t, w		like in English		
c	1) like **ch** in **ch**arge	ch	**ci**	chi
	2) like **k** in **k**it	k	**cuub**	koob
cc	like **ch** in **ch**arge	ch	**fecc**	feh-cha
g	like **g** in garb	g	**gis**	giss
j	like **j** in jot	j	**jama**	**ja**ma

TELEPHONING, see page 140

ng	like **ng** in goi**ng**	ng	**ngam**	ngam
q	like **k** in **k**it	k	**mboq**	mbo-k
x	like **ch** in Scottish lo**ch**	KH	**tax**	taKH
y	like **y** in **y**ale	y	**yow**	yoh

Note: Double consonants lengthen the sound.

Vowels

a	like **a** in c**a**t	a	**ngam**	ngam
aa	like **a** in c**a**r	ah	**baal**	bahl
e	usually like **e** in butt**e**r	eh	**jerejef**	**jehreh**jehf
ee	like **ay** in h**ay**	ay	**reer**	rayr
i	like **i** in f**i**t	i	**maangi**	**mahng**i
ii	like **ee** in f**ee**t	ee	**fii**	fee
o	like **o** in c**o**t	o/oh	**joge**	**jo**geh
oo	1) like **oo** in p**oo**l 2) like **o** in c**o**t	oo o	**doom** **lool**	doom lol
u	like **oo** in b**oo**t	ū	**waajur**	**wah**jūr
uu	like long **oo** in w**oo**	oo	**tuuti**	**too**ti

Diphthongs

aay	like **igh** in l**igh**t	igh	**laay**	ligh
aw	like **ow** in n**ow**	a^oo	**ndaw**	nda^oo
ey	like **ay** in d**ay**	ay	**rey**	ray
uy	like **ew** in n**ew**	ooy	**muy**	myoo
ow	1) in Gambia, like **o** in c**o**t 2) in Senegal, like **ow** in n**ow**	o/oh a^oo	**yow** **yow**	yoh ya^oo
oy	like **ong** in l**ong**	ong	**peroy**	**peh**-rong

Notes:

At the end of words, **-g** is pronounced k, **-b** is pronounced p

e.g. **ag** (ak) **jub** (jup)

After double consonants at the end of words, an extra **-a** sometimes appears in pronunciation

e.g. **jamm** (jama) **sedd** (sehda)

Xhosa

Basic expressions *Izisho ezilula*

Yes./No.	**Ewe./Hayi.**	**eh**weh/**hah**yi
Please.	**Nceda.**	**n!c!eh**dah
Thank you.	**Enkosi.**	eh**nkaw**see
I beg your pardon?	**Uxolo andivanga.**	oo!**x!aw**law ahndeev**ah**ngah

Introductions *Ukwazisana*

Good morning/ Good afternoon.	**Molo.**	**maw**law
Good night.	**Ulale kakuhle.**	oo**lah**leh kah**koo**HLeh
Good-bye.	**Uhambe/Usale kakuhle.**	oo**hah**mbeh/oo**sah**leh kah**koo**HLeh
My name is …	**Igama lami wu …**	ee**gah**mah lah**mee** woo
Pleased to meet you.	**Ndiyavuya ukukwazi.**	ndeeyah**voo**yah ookoo**kwah**zee
What's your name?	**Ngubani igama lakho?**	ngoo**bah**nee ee**gah**mah **lah**kaw
How are you?	**Unjani?**	oo**njah**nee
Fine thanks. And you?	**Ndikhona. Enkosi. Kunjani kuwe?**	ndee**kaw**nah. e**nkaw**see. koo**njah**nee **koo**weh
Where do you come from?	**Uvelaphi?**	oovehl**ah**pee
I'm from …	**Ndivela …**	ndee**veh**lah
Australia	**Australia**	oseetreh**lee**yah
Britain	**Brithani**	bree**tah**nee
Canada	**Canada**	kah**nah**dah
USA	**Amelika**	ahmeh**lee**kah
I'm with my …	**Ndino … wami.**	**ndee**naw … **wah**mee
wife	**nkosikazi**	nkawsee**kah**zee
husband	**myeni**	**myeh**nee
children	**bantwana**	bah**ntwah**nah
boyfriend/girlfriend	**umhlobo**	oo**mHLaw**baw
I'm on vacation.	**Ndisekhefini.**	ndeesekeh**fee**nee
I'm on business.	**Ndize ngerhwebo.**	**ndee**zeh ngeh**hweh**baw

Questions *Imibuzo*

When?/How?	**Nini?/Njani?**	**nee**nee/**njah**nee
Why?/Which?	**Ngoba?/Yiphi?**	**ngaw**bah/**yee**pee
What is this/that?	**Yintoni le/lanto?**	yee**ntaw**nee leh/**lah**ntaw
Who is this/that?	**Ngubani lo/lowa?**	ngoo**bah**nee law/**law**wah
Where is/are…?	**Iphi/Ziphi i …?**	**ee**pee/**zee**pee ee
Where can I get/ find …?	**Ndingayifumana phi …?**	ndeengahyeefoomah**nah** pee
How far?	**Kude kangakanani?**	**koo**deh kahngahkah**nah**nee
How long?	**Ixesha elingakanani?**	ee!**x**!**eh**shah ehleengahkah**nah**nee
How much?	**Kangakanani?**	kahngahkah**nah**nee
Can you help me?	**Ungandinceda?**	oongahndee**n**!**c**!**eh**dah
What does this mean?	**Ithetha ntoni lento?**	ee**teh**tah **ntaw**nee **leh**ntaw
I understand.	**Ndiyeva.**	ndee**yeh**vah
I don't understand.	**Andiva.**	ah**ndee**vah
Please speak slowly.	**Khawucothise.**	kahwoo!c!aw**tee**seh
Can you translate this for me?	**Khawundi tolikele lento?**	kah**woon**dee tawlee**keh**leh **leh**ntaw
Can I have …?	**Ndicela i …?**	ndee!**c**!**eh**lah ee
Do you speak English?	**Uyasithetha isingesi na?**	ooyahsee**teh**tah eeseen**geh**see nah
I don't speak Xhosa.	**Andisithethi isiXhosa.**	ahndeesee**teh**tee eesee!**x**!**aw**sah

It's … *I …*

better/worse	**-bhetere/-bi kakumbi**	-beh**teh**reh/-bee kah**koo**mbee
big/small	**nkulu/ncinci**	**nkoo**loo/**n**!**c**!**een**!c!ee
cheap/expensive	**-tshiphu/-duru**	-**tshee**poo/-**doo**roo
good/bad	**-nhle/mbi**	nHLeh/mbee
near/far	**duzane/kude**	doo**zah**neh/**koo**deh
right/wrong	**eyiyo/engasiyiyo**	eh**yee**yaw/ ehngahsee**yee**yaw
vacant/occupied	**ayinamntu/inomntu**	ayee**nah**mntoo/ ee**naw**mntoo

Hotel–Accommodation *Inhotela–Indawo yokuklala*

We've reserved a rooms.	**Sibhukishe amagumbi.**	seebook**ee**sheh ahmah**goo**mbee
Do you have any vacancies?	**Ikhona indawo?**	ee**kaw**nah een**dah**waw
I'd like a … room.	**Ndifuna igumbi …**	ndee**foo**nah ee**goo**mbee
single	**lomntu omnye**	**law**mntoo **aw**mnyeh
double	**labantu ababini**	lah**bah**ntoo ahbah**bee**nee
with twin beds	**elinebhedi ezimbini**	ehleeneh**beh**dee ehzeembeenee
with a bath	**elinebhafu**	ehleeneh**bah**foo
with a shower	**elineshawa**	ehleeneh**shah**wah
We'll be staying …	**Sizohlala …**	seezaw**HLah**lah
overnight only	**lobusuku kuphela**	lawboo**soo**koo koo**peh**lah
a few days	**iintsuku ezimbalwa**	ee**ah**ntsookoo ehzee**mbah**lwah
a week (at least)	**(ngaphezu) kweveki**	(ngah**pe**zoo) kweh**ve**kee
Is there a campsite near here?	**Ikhona ikampu eduze na apha?**	ee**kaw**nah ee**kah**mpoo eh**doo**zeh nah**ah**pah

Decision *Ukukhetha*

May I see the room?	**Ndicela ukubona igumbi elo?**	ndee!**c**!**eh**lah ookoo**baw**nah ee**goo**mbee **eh**law
That's fine. I'll take it.	**Lilungile. Ndizalithatha.**	leeloo**ngee**leh ndeezahlee**tah**tah
No. I don't like it.	**Cha. Andilithandi.**	!**c**!**a**. ahndeelee**tah**ndee
It's too …	**Li … kakhulu.**	lee … kah**koo**loo
dark/small	**mnyama/ncinci**	**mnyah**mah/**n**!c!**een**!c!ee
noisy	**nengxolo**	neh**ng**!**x**!**aw**law
Do you have anything …?	**Ninalo eli … kunaleli?**	nee**nah**law ehlee… koonah**leh**lee
better/bigger	**bhetere/khulu**	beh**teh**reh/**koo**loo
cheaper/quieter	**tshiphile/thulile**	tshee**pee**leh/too**lee**leh
May I please have my bill?	**Ndicela iakhawunti yami?**	ndee!**c**!**eh**lah ee-ahkah**woo**ntee **yah**mi
It's been a very enjoyable stay.	**Sonwabile.**	sawnwah**bee**leh

NUMBERS, see page 158/DAYS OF THE WEEK, see page 157

Eating out *Ukutaya ngaphandle*

I'd like to reserve a table for 4.	**Ndingathanda ukubekelwa itafile yabantu abane.**	ndeengah**tah**ndah ookoobeh**keh**lwah eetahf**ee**leh yah**bah**ntoo ah**bah**neh
We'll come at 8.	**Sizofika ngentsimbi yesibhozo.**	seezaw**fee**kah ngeh**ntsee**mbee yehsee**baw**zaw
I'd like …	**Ndifuna isidlo …**	ndee**foo**nah eesee**DLAW**
breakfast	**sakusasa**	sahkoo**sah**sah
lunch	**sasemini**	sahseh**mee**nee
dinner	**sangokuhlwa**	sahngaw**kooHL**wah
Do you have local dishes?	**Ninako ukutya kwalendawo?**	nee**nah**kaw oo**koo**tyah kwahleh**ndah**waw
What do you recommend?	**Yintoni emnandi?**	yee**ntaw**nee eh**mnah**ndee
Do you have vegetarian dishes?	**Ninako ukutya okungenanyama?**	nee**nah**kaw oo**koo**tyah awkoongehnah**nyah**mah

Breakfast *Ukutya kwakusasa*

May I have some …?	**Ndicela i …?**	ndee!c!**eh**lah ee
bread/butter	**sonka/bhotoro**	**saw**nkah/baw**taw**rah
cereal	**siriyeli**	seeree**yeh**lee
eggs	**qanda**	!**q**!**ah**ndah
jam/rolls	**jemu/amaroli**	**jeh**moo/ahmah**raw**lee

Starters *Ukutya kokuqala*

amadongomane	ahmahdawngaw**mah**neh	peanuts, boiled or roasted
iidumba	ee**doo**mbah	tuber: a type of potato
imfe	**ee**mfeh	type of sweet sugar cane
ugcado	oo!**gc**!**ah**daw	roasted whole corn kernels
umpherhu	oo**mpeh**hoo	maize stalks
iinkobe (ee**nkaw**beh)	boiled kernels of maize or sorghum with salt added to taste	
umqwayito (oom!q!wah**yee**taw)	biltong; strips of dried meat, cured in the sun	

Meat *Inyama*

I'd like some …	**Ndifuna …**	ndee**foo**nah
beef	**inyama yenkomo**	ee**nyah**mah yeh**nkaw**maw
chicken	**inyama yenkukhu**	ee**nyah**mah yeh**nkoo**koo
goat	**inyama yebhokwe**	ee**nyah**mah yeh**baw**kweh
lamb	**inyama yetakane legusha**	ee**nyah**mah yehtah-**kah**neh lehg**oo**shah
pork	**inyama yehagu**	ee**nyah**mah yeh**hah**goo

baked	**ebhakiwe**	ehbah**kee**weh
boiled	**ebilisiwe**	ehbeelee**see**weh
fried	**eqhotsiwe**	eh!q!aw**see**weh
grilled/roast	**eyosiweyo**	ehyawsee**weh**yaw
underdone (rare)	**engavuthwanga**	ehngahvoo**twah**ngah
medium	**engavuthwanga kakhulu**	ehngahvoo**twah**ngah kah**khoo**loo
well-done	**evuthisisiwe**	ehvooteesee**see**weh

In Xhosa, meat dishes are generally described by the way they are cooked. For example:

inyama eyosiweyo	ee**nyah**mah ehyawsee**weh**yaw	roasted meat

Vegetables *Izivuno*

beans	**imbotyi**	ee**mbaw**tyee
cabbage	**ikhaphetshu**	eekah**peh**tshoo
potatoes	**iitapile**	eetah**pee**leh
rice	**irayisi**	eerah**yee**see
spinach	**isipinatshi**	eeseepee**nah**shee
idombolo	eedaw**mbaw**law	maize dumpling
isonka sombona	eesaw**nkah** saw**mbaw**nah	corn bread, normally served with sour milk
umqa	**oo**m!q!ah	pumpkin mixed with sorghum or corn meal
umxhaxha	oo**m**!x!**ah**!xh!ah	corn grains with pumpkin
umfino (oo**mfee**naw)	spinach mixed with stiff corn porridge	
umvubo (oo**mvoo**baw)	sour milk mixed with stiff corn or sorghum porridge	

Fruit & dessert *Iziqhamo*

apple	**iapule**	ee-ah**poo**leh
banana	**ibhanana**	eebah**nah**nah
lemon	**ilamuni**	eelah**moo**nee
orange	**iorenji**	ee-aw**reh**njee
plum	**iplam**	**ee**plahm
cake	**ikeyiki**	eekeh**yee**kee
ice-cream	**iayiskhrim**	ee-ah**yee**skreem

Drinks *Iiselo*

beer	**ibhiri**	ee**bee**ree
(hot) chocolate	**ikoko**	ee**kaw**kaw
coffee	**ikofi**	ee**kaw**fee
black	**elimnyama**	ehlee**mnyah**mah
with milk	**elinobisi**	ehleenaw**bee**see
fruit juice	**ijuzi**	ee**joo**zee
orange	**ye-orenji**	yeh-aw**reh**njee
mineral water	**amanzi anetyuwa yomhlaba**	ah**mah**nzee ahneh**tyoo**wah yaw**mHLah**bah
tea	**iti**	**ee**tee
wine	**iwayine**	eewah**yee**neh
red/white	**ebomvu/emhlophe**	eh**baw**mvoo/ eh**mHLaw**peh

irhemere (ee-heh**meh**reh) a semi-traditional Xhosa drink, similar to ginger beer

umqombhothi (oom!q!aw**mbaw**tee) traditional alcoholic drink made from sorghum

Complaints and paying *Ukulila no kuthatala*

This is too … bitter/sweet	**Lento i … kakhulu. yarharha/nencasa**	**leh**ntaw ee … kah**koo**loo yah-**hah**-ha/nehn**!c!ah**sah
I'd like to pay.	**Ndicela ukubhatala.**	ndee!**c**!elah ookoobah**tah**lah
I think you made a mistake in the bill.	**Ndibona ngathi nenze iphutha kule akhawunti.**	ndee**boaw**nah **ngah**tee **neh**nzeh ee**poo**tah **koo**leh ahkah**woo**ntee
We enjoyed it, thank you.	**Sonwabile. Enkosi.**	sawnwah**bee**leh. eh**nkaw**see

NUMBERS, see page 158

Travelling around *Ukuhamba*

Plane *Inqwelomoya*

Is there a flight to Durban?	**Ikhona inqweolomoya eya eDurban?**	ee**kaw**nah een!q!wehawlaw**maw**yah **eh**yah ehdoorban
What time do I check in?	**Kumele ndifike nini e ephothi?**	koo**meh**leh ndee**fee**keh **nee**nee eh eh**paw**tee
I'd like to … my reservation.	**Ndicela uku … isihlalo endibekelwe.**	ndee!**c**!**eh**lah ookoo … eeseeHLahlaw ehndeebe**kehl**weh
cancel/change	**rhoxisa/tshintsha**	haw!x!**ee**sah/**tshee**ntshah
confirm	**qinisa**	!q!**ee**nee**e**sah

Train *Itreyini*

I want a ticket to Umtata.	**Ndicela itikiti eliya eUmtata.**	ndee!**c**!**eh**lah eetee**kee**tee eh**lee**yah eh-oom**tah**tah
single (one-way)	**eliyayo kuphela**	ehlee**yah**yaw koo**peh**lah
return (roundtrip)	**elibuyayo**	ehleeboo**yah**yaw
first/second class	**ikilasi lokuqala/ lesibini**	eekee**lah**see lawkoo!**q**!**ah**-lah/lehsee**bee**nee
How long does the journey (trip) take?	**Luthatha ixesha elingakanani loluhambo?**	loo**tah**tah ee!**x**!**eh**shah ehleengahkah**nah**nee loloo**hah**mbaw
When is the … train to Indwe?	**Ihamba nini itreyini … eya eIndwe?**	ee**hah**mbah **nee**nee eetreh**yee**nee … ehyah eh**ee**ndweh
first	**eyokuqala**	ehyawkoo!**q**!**ah**lah
next	**ezayo**	eh**zah**yaw
last	**esokugqibela**	ehsawkoog!q!ee**beh**lah

Bus–Coach *Ibhasi*

Is there a bus today?	**Ikho ibhesi namhlanje?**	**ee**kaw ee**be**shee nah**mHLah**njeh
What bus do I take to the centre?	**Ndithatha yiphi ibhasi ukuya embindini?**	ndee**tah**tah **yee**pee ee**bah**see oo**koo**yah ehmbeen**dee**nee
How much is the fare to …?	**Yimalini ukuya e …?**	yeemah**lee**nee oo**koo**yah eh

TELLING THE TIME, see page 156

Taxi *Iteksi*

How much is it to …?	**Yimalini ukuya e …?**	yeemah**lee**nee oo**koo**yah eh
Take me to this address.	**Ndise kule adresi.**	**ndee**seh **koo**leh ah**dreh**see
Please stop here.	**Ima apha.**	**ee**mah **ah**pah

Car hire–Automobile rental *Ukuqesha imoto*

I'd like to hire (rent) a car.	**Ndingathanda ukuqesha imoto.**	ndeengah**tah**ndah ookoo**q**'**eh**shah ee**maw**taw
I'd like it for a week/day.	**Ndizoyisebenzisa iveki/imini ibenye.**	ndeezawyeesehbeh**nzee**sah ee**veh**kee/ee**mee**nee ee**beh**nyeh
Where's the nearest filling station?	**Ikuphi ifilingi steshini eseduzane?**	ee**koo**pee eefee**lee**ngee steh**shee**nee ehsehdoo**zah**neh
Fill it up, please.	**Yizalise.**	yeezah**lee**seh
Give me … litres of petrol (gasoline).	**Ndiphe amalitha awu … epetroli.**	**ndee**peh ahmah**lee**tah **ah**woo … ehpe**traw**lee
How do I get to …?	**Ndiya njani e …?**	**ndee**yah **njah**nee eh
I've had a breakdown at …	**Ndiphukelwe yimoto e …**	ndeepoo**keh**lweh yee**maw**taw eh
Can you send a mechanic?	**Ungathumela umkhandi?**	oongahtoo**meh**lah oo**mkah**ndee
Can you mend it?	**Ungayilungisa?**	oongahy-eeloo**ngee**sah

☞ You're on the wrong road. — **Usendleleni engasiyiyo.** ☜
Go straight ahead. — **Qonda ngqo.**
It's down there on the left/right. — **Ipha ezansi ngasokhohlo/ngasekunene.**
next to/after … — **kufuphi na …/ngemva kwe …**
north/south — **entla/emzantsi**
east/west — **empumalanga/entshonalanga**

NUMBERS, see page 158

Sightseeing *Ukubona indawo*

Where's the tourist office?	**Likuphi iofisi loomcandizwe?**	lee**koo**pee ee-aw**fee**see lawm!c!ah**ndee**zweh
Is there an English-speaking guide?	**Ikho inkokheli ethetha isiNgesi?**	**ee**kaw eenkaw**keh**lee eh**teh**tah eeseen**geh**see
Where is/are the …?	**Iphi i/Ziphi izi …?**	**ee**pee ee/**zee**pee eezee
church	**cawe**	**!c!ah**weh
city centre	**embindini dolophi**	ehmbeen**dee**nee daw**law**pee
market	**makethe**	mah**keh**teh
museum	**imuziyam**	eemoozee**yah**m
shops	**iivenkile**	eeven**kee**leh
zoo	**zu**	zoo
When does it open/close?	**Ivulwa/Ivalwa nini?**	ee**vah**lwah/ee**vool**wah **nee**nee
How much is the entrance fee?	**Yimalini ukungena?**	yeemah**lee**nee ookoo**ngeh**nah

Countryside *Emapulazini*

game reserve	**uthanga lwezilwanyana**	oo**tah**ngah lwehzeelwah**nyah**nah
lake	**ichibi**	ee!**c**!eebee
mountain	**intaba**	ee**ntah**bah
river	**umlambo**	oo**mlah**mbaw
well/oasis	**iqula**	ee!**q**!oolah

Entertainment *Ukonwaba*

What's playing at the theatre?	**Kudlalani ethiyetha?**	kooDLah**lah**nee ehtee**yeh**tah
How much are the seats?	**Yimalini ukungena?**	yeemah**lee**nee ookoo**ngeh**nah
Is there a discotheque in town?	**Ikho idisko edolphini?**	**ee**ko ee**dee**skaw ehdawlo**pee**nee
Would you like to dance?	**Ungathanda ukudansa?**	oongah**tah**ndah ookoo**dah**nsah
Thank you. It's been a wonderful evening.	**Enkosi. Bekumnandi kakhulu.**	eh**nkaw**see. behkoo**mnah**ndee kah**koo**loo

TELLING THE TIME, see page 156/DATE, see page 157

Shops, stores and services *livenkile–Nezoncedo*

Where's the nearest …?	**Iphi i … eseduze?**	eepee ee … ehseh**doo**zeh
baker's	**bheyikhari**	behyee**kah**ree
barber	**kulungiswa iinwele**	kooloo**ngee**swah een**weh**leh
bookshop	**ivenkile yeencwadi**	eeveh**nkee**leh yen!c!**wah**dee
chemist's	**khemisti**	keh**mee**stee
department store	**venkile enkulu**	veh**nkee**leh eh**nkoo**loo
grocery	**venkile ethengisa ukutya**	veh**nkee**leh ehteh**ngee**sah oo**koo**dlah
post office	**posi**	**paw**see
supermarket	**suphamakethe**	soopahmah**keh**teh
toilets	**indlu yangasese**	**ee**nDLoo yahngah**seh**seh

General expressions *lizitsho ezivamile*

Where's the main shopping area?	**Ziphi iivenkile?**	**zee**pee eeveh**nkee**leh
Do you have any …?	**Unayo i …?**	oo**nah**yaw ee
Can I try it on?	**Ndingayilinganisa?**	ndeengah**yee**leengah**nee**sah
How much is this?	**Yimalini lento?**	yeemah**lee**nee **leh**ntaw
Please write it down.	**Khawuyibhale phansi.**	kahwooyee**bah**leh **pah**nsee
That's too much.	**Iduru kakhulu.**	ee**doo**roo kah**koo**loo
How about … rand?	**Ndingakunika amarandi angu … ?**	ndeengahkoo**nee**kah ahmahrahndee ahngoo
No, I don't like it.	**Cha. Andiyithandi.**	!c!**ah**. ahndeeyee**tah**ndee
I'll take it.	**Ndizayithatha.**	ndeezahyee**tah**tah
Do you accept credit cards?	**Niyawathatha amacredithi khadi?**	neeyahwah**tah**tah ahmah!c!reh**dee**tee **kah**dee

black	**mnyama**	**mny**ahmah	orange	**orenji**	o**reh**njee
blue	**luhlaza**	loo**hlah**zah	red	**bomvu**	**baw**mvoo
brown	**ntsundu**	**ntsoo**ndoo	white	**mhlophe**	**mlaw**peh
green	**luhlaza**	loo**hlah**zah	yellow	**mthubi**	**mtoo**bee

NUMBERS, see page 158

I want to buy …	**Ndifuna ukuthenga …**	ndee**foo**nah ookoo**teh**ngah
anti-malaria tablets	**amapilisi emalaria**	ahmahpee**lee**see ehmah**lah**eeyah
aspirin	**iyeza lokudambisa iintlungu**	ee**yeh**zah lawkoodah**mbee**sah **eentloo**ngoo
batteries	**amabhetri**	ahmah**beh**tree
newspaper	**Iphepha**	ee**peh**pah
American	**laseMelika**	lahsehmeh**lee**kah
English	**laseBritani**	lahsehbree**tah**nee
postcard	**posikhadi**	posee**kah**dee
sun-tan cream	**amafutha welanga**	ahmah**foo**tah weh**lah**ngah
soap	**isepha**	ee**seh**pah
toothpaste	**intlama yamazinyo**	een**tlah**mah yahmah**zee**nyaw
a half-kilo of apples	**uhafu wekhilo lama apile**	oo**hah**foo weh**kee**law lahmah ah**pee**leh
a litre of milk	**ilitha yobisi**	ee**lee**tah yaw**bee**see
I'd like … film for this camera.	**Ndifuna ifilmu e … lalekhamera.**	ndee**foo**nah ee**fee**lmoo eh … lahlehkah**meh**rah

Souvenirs *Ezenkumbulo*

imbiza	ee-mbeezah	clay pot for cooking
inqawe	een!**q**!**ah**weh	long-stemmed wooden smoking pipe
ingqayi	een!**gq**!**ah**yee	small decorated clay pot
iqhiya	ee!**qh**!**ee**yah	women's head scarf
isithebe	eesee**teh**beh	flat plate for drying meal
ukhukho	oo**koo**kaw	grass mat
ungobozi	oongaw**baw**zee	large grass plate
ungxowa	oong!**x**!**aw**wah	leather tobacco pouch

At the bank *Ebhankini*

Where's the nearest bank/currency exchange office?	**Iphi ibhanki yokutshintsha imali eseduze?**	**ee**pee eebahnkee yawkoo**tshee**ntshah ee**mah**lee ehseh**doo**zeh
I want to change some dollars into …	**Ndifuna ukutshintsha amadola ndiwenze ama …**	ndee**foo**nah ookootsheentshah ahmah**daw**lah ndee**weh**nze ahmah

What's the exchange rate?	**Yini ireyithi okutshintshwa ngayo?**	**yee**nee eereh**yee**tee awkoo**tsheen**tshwah **ngah**yaw

At the post office *Eposini*

I want to send this by …	**Ndifuna ukuthumela lento nge …**	ndee**foo**nah ookootoo**meh**lah **leh**ntaw ngeh
airmail	**moya**	**maw**yah
express	**ndlela esheshisayo**	**nDLeh**lah ehshehshee**sah**yaw
I want some …-rand stamps.	**Ndifuna iitampu zamarandi ayi …**	ndee**foo**nah ee**tah**mpoo zahmahrahndee ahy-ee
What's the postage for a letter to America?	**Yimalini ukuposa ileta eliya eMelika?**	yeemah**lee**nee ookoo**paw**sah ee**leh**tah eh**lee**yah ehme**lee**kah
Is there any mail for me?	**Likho iposi elize kum?**	**lee**kaw ee**paw**see eh**lee**zeh **koom**
My name is …	**Igama lami ngu …**	ee**gah**mah **lah**mee ngoo

Telephoning *Ukushaya ucingo*

Where's the nearest public phone?	**Iphi ifowuni yawonkewonke eseduzane?**	eepee eefo**woo**nee yahwawnkeh**waw**nkeh ehsehdoo**zah**neh
Hello. This is … speaking.	**Molo. U … lona othethayo.**	**maw**law. oo … **law**nah oteh**tah**yaw
I want to speak to …	**Ndifuna ukuthetha no …**	ndee**foo**nah ookoo**teh**tah naw
When will he/she be back?	**Uzabuya nini?**	oozah**boo**yah **nee**nee
Will you tell him/her that I called?	**Uzomxelela akuba bendifowunile?**	oozawm!x!**ehleh**lah ookoo**bah** behndeefowoo**nee**leh

Time and date *Ixesha*

English expressions for telling the time are commonly used by Xhosa speakers.

EMERGENCIES, see page 158/NUMBERS, see page 159

in the morning	**kusasa**	koo**sah**sah
during the day	**emini**	eh**mee**nee
in the evening	**entambama**	ehntah**mbah**mah
at night	**ebusuku**	ehboo**soo**koo

Sunday	**iCawe**	ee!**c**!**ah**weh
Monday	**uMvulo**	oo**mvoo**law
Tuesday	**uLwesibili**	oolwehsee**bee**lee
Wednesday	**uLwesithathu**	oolwehsee**tah**too
Thursday	**uLwesine**	oolweh**see**neh
Friday	**uLwesihlanu**	oolwehsee**HLah**noo
Saturday	**uMgqibelo**	oom!**q**!ee**beh**lo
January	**uMdumba**	oo**mdoo**mbah
February	**uMthupha**	oo**mtoo**pah
March	**ukwindla**	oo**kwee**ndlah
April	**uThazimpunzi**	ootahzee**mpoo**nzee
May	**uCanzibe**	oo!c!ah**nzee**beh
June	**uSilimela**	ooseelee**meh**lah
July	**uNtulikazi**	oontoolee**kah**zee
August	**eyeKhala**	ehyeh**kah**lah
September	**eyoMsintsi**	ehyaw**msee**ntsee
October	**eyeDwarha**	ehyeh**dwah**-hah
November	**eyeNkanga**	ehyeh**nkah**ngah
December	**eyoMnga**	eh**yaw**mngah

Note that English names of the months are commonly used.

yesterday	**izolo**	ee**zaw**law
today	**namhlanje**	nah**mHLah**njeh
tomorrow	**ngomso**	**ngaw**msaw
spring	**intlakohlaza**	eentlahkaw**HLah**zah
summer	**ihlobo**	ee**HLaw**baw
autumn (fall)	**ukwindla**	oo**kwee**nDLah
winter	**ubusika**	ooboo**see**kah

Numbers *Izinombolo*

0	**unothi**	oo**naw**tee
1	**-nye**	nyeh
2	**-mbini**	**mbee**nee
3	**-thathu**	**tah**too
4	**-ne**	neh
5	**hlanu**	**HLah**noo
6	**-thandathu**	tah**ndah**too
7	**-sixhenxe**	see!**xh**!**ehn**!x!eh
8	**-sibhozo**	see**baw**zaw
9	**-sithoba**	see**taw**bah
10	**-shumi**	**shoo**mee
11	**-shumi elinanye**	**shoo**mee ehlee**nah**nyeh
12	**-shumi elinambili**	**shoo**mee elheenah**mbee**lee
13	**-shumi elinantathu**	**shoo**mee ehleenah**ntah**too
14	**-shumi elinane**	**shoo**mee ehlee**nah**neh
15	**-shumi elinanhlanu**	**shoo**mee ehleenah**nHLah**noo
16	**-shumi elinantandathu**	**shoo**mee ehleenahntah**ndah**too
17	**-shumi elinesixhenxe**	**shoo**mee ehleenehsee!**xh**!**ehn**!x!eh
18	**-shumi elinesibhozo**	**shoo**mee ehleenehsee**baw**zaw
19	**-shumi elinesithoba**	**shoo**mee ehleeneheе**taw**bah
20	**amashumi amabili**	ahmah**shoo**mee ahmah**bee**lee
21	**amashumi amabili nanye**	ahmah**shoo**mee ahmah**bee**lee **nah**nyeh
30	**amashumi amathathu**	ahmah**shoo**mee ahmah**tah**too
40	**amashumi amane**	ahmah**shoo**mee ah**mah**neh
50	**amashumi amahlanu**	ahmah**shoo**mee ahmah**HLah**noo
60	**amashumi ayisithandathu**	ahmah**shoo**mee ahyeeseetah**ndah**too
70	**amashumi ayisixhenxe**	ahmah**shoo**mee ahyeesee!**xh**!**ehn**!x!eh
80	**amashumi ayisibhozo**	ahmah**shoo**mee ahyeesee**baw**zaw
90	**amashumi ayisithoba**	ahmah**shoo**mee ahyeesee**taw**bah
100	**ikhulu**	ee**koo**loo
101	**ikhulu nanye**	ee**koo**loo **nah**nyeh
200	**amakhulu amabini**	ahmah**koo**loo ahmah**bee**nee
500	**amakhulu amahlanu**	ahmah**koo**loo ahmah**HLah**noo
1,000	**iwaka**	ee**wah**kah

first	**kuqala**	koo!**q**!**ah**lah
second	**-sibini**	see**bee**nee
once/twice	**kanye/kabini**	**kah**nyeh/kah**bee**nee
a half	**uhafu**	oo**hah**foo

Emergency *Ezoncendo*

Call the police	**Biza amapolisa**	**bee**zah ahmahpaw**lee**sah
Get a doctor	**Biza ugqirha**	**bee**zah oo!**gq**!**ee**-hah
Go away	**Hamba**	**hah**mbah
HELP	**NCEDA**	**n**!**c**!**eh**dah
I'm ill	**Ndiyagula**	ndeeyah**goo**lah
I'm lost	**Ndilahlekile**	ndeelahhleh**kee**leh
Leave me alone	**Ndiyeke**	ndee**yeh**keh
STOP THIEF	**YIMA SELA**	**yi**mah **seh**lah
My … have been stolen.	**I … yami itshontshiwe.**	ee … **yah**mee eetshaw**ntshee**weh
I've lost my …	**Ngilahlekelwe yi …**	ngeelahHLeh**keh**lwe yee
handbag	**-sikhwama**	see**kwah**mah
passport	**pasipoti**	pahsee**paw**tee
luggage	**mpahla**	**mpah**HLah
wallet	**spaji**	**spah**jee
Where can I find a doctor who speaks English?	**Ndingamfumanaphi gqirha othetha isiNgesi?**	ndeengahmfoo**nah**pee oo!**gq**!**ee-h**ah aw**teh**tah eeseen**ge**see

Guide to Xhosa pronunciation

Vowels

Letter	Approximate pronunciation	Symbol		Example
a	like **a** in hard	ah	**paka**	**pah**kah
e	like **e** in red	eh	**ewe**	**eh**weh
i	like **ee** in see	ee	**sisi**	**see**see
o	like **a** in **a**ll	aw	**molo**	**maw**law
u	like **oo** in book	oo	**zu**	zoo

Consonants

d, f, h, j, l, m, n, r, s, sh, v, w, y, z		as in English		
dl	similar sound to **hl** below	DL	isidlo	ee**see**DLO
g	always like **g** in go	g	igama	ee**gah**mah

TELEPHONING, see page 156

hl	place your tongue to the side of your mouth and expel air; like the Welsh sound **ll** in **Ll**ewelyn	HL	**kakuhle**	ka**koo**HLeh
ts	hissing sound made by placing your tongue just above your teeth and ejecting air	ts	**itswele**	ee**tsweh**leh
tsh	similar to **dge** in ju**dge**	tsh	**tshin-tsha**	**tsheen-**tshah
ty	similar to **dge** in ju**dge**	ty	**ukutya**	oo**koo**tyah

Note: **bh**, **kh**, **ph**, **rh** and **th** are aspirated sounds; pronounce as **b**, **k**, **p**, **r** and **t** respectively, while forcefully expelling air.

Clicks

Clicks are a peculiarity of the Xhosa and Zulu languages, originating from Hottentot. The symbols ! ! should alert you to these clicks, but we can provide only approximate descriptions of how to pronounce them.

c	place your tongue at the back of the teeth and suck in, as when expressing annoyance	!c!	**cawe**	!c!ahweh
ch	as **c** above, but suck in more air	!ch!	**cha**	!ch!a
gc	as **c** above, but pronounce more voiced	!gc!	**ugcado**	oo!**gc**!**ah**do
q	place your tongue on the roof of your mouth and suck in	!q!	**qanda**	!**q**!**ahn**dah
qh	as **q** above, but suck in more air	!qh!	**iqhiya**	ee!**qh**!**ee**yah
gq	as **q** above, but pronounced more voiced	!gq!	**ngqo**	n!gq!aw
x	place your tongue on your upper right jaw then pull it down; as if urging on a horse	!x!	**uxolo**	oo!**x**!**aw**law
xh	as **x** above, but suck in more air	!xh!	**xhosa**	!**xh**!**aw**sah
gx	as **x** above, but pronounce unvoiced	!gx!	**nengxo-lo**	nen!**gx**!**aw**-law

Yoruba

Basic expressions *Gbólóhùn kéékèèké*

Yes/No.	**Bẹ́ẹ̀ ni/Bẹ́ẹ̀ kó.**	beh-eh nee/beh-eh ko
Please.	**Ẹ jọ̀ọ́.**	eh jaw-aw
Thank you.	**Ẹ ṣe é.**	eh shay-ay
I beg your pardon?	**Kí lẹ wí?**	kee leh wee

Introductions *Ìfira-ẹni hàn*

Good morning.	**Ẹ káàárọ̀.**	eh ka-a-a-raw
Good afternoon.	**Ẹ káàsán.**	eh ka-a-sa^n
Good night.	**Ó dàárọ̀.**	o da-a-raw
Good-bye.	**Ó dàbọ̀.**	o da-bo
My name is …	**Orúkọọ̀ mi ni/Èmi ni …**	oh-roo-kaw-aw mee nee/ay-mee-nee
Pleased to meet you.	**Inú-ùn mi-ín dùn láti ríi yín.**	ee-noo-oo^n mee-ee^n doo^n la-tee ree-ee yee^n
What's your name?	**Kí ni orúkọ yín?**	kee nee o-roo-kaw yee^n
How are you?	**Ṣé dáadáa ni?**	shay da-a-da-a nee
Fine thanks. And you?	**Dáadáa ni. Ìwọ náà ńkọ̀?**	da-a-da-a nee. ee-waw na-a n-kaw
Where do you come from?	**Níbo lẹ ti wá?**	nee-bo leh tee wah
I'm from …	**Láti … nì mo ti wá.**	la-tee … nee mo tee wa
Australia	**Ọsirélíà**	aws-re-lee-ah
Britain	**Ilẹ̀ẹ Gẹ̀ẹ́sì**	ee-leh-eh geh-eh-see
Canada	**Kánádà**	ka-na-da
South Africa	**Gúúsù kẹ̀ Aáfíríkà**	goo-oo-soo keh aa-fee-ree-kah
USA	**Ilẹ̀ Amẹ́ríkà**	ee-leh a-meh-ree-kah
I'm with my …	**Èmi àti …**	ay-mee a-tee
wife	**ìyàwóò mi**	ee-yah-woh-o mee
husband	**ọkọọ̀ mi**	aw-kaw-aw mee
children	**àwọn ọmọọ̀ mi**	a-wo^n aw-maw-aw mee
parents	**àwọn òbîì mi**	a-wo^n o-bee-ee mee
boyfriend/girlfriend	**ọ̀rẹ́ẹ̀ mi**	aw-reh-eh mee

GUIDE TO PRONUNCIATION, see page 176/EMERGENCIES, see page 175

Questions *Ìbéèrè*

When?	**Nígbà wo?**	nee-gba wo
Why?	**Kí ló dé?**	kee lo day
How?	**Báwo ni?**	baa-wo nee
Who is this/that?	**Ta lèyí/nìyí?**	ta lay-yee/nee-yee
What is this/that?	**Kí lèyí/nìyẹn?**	kee lay-yee/nee-yeh^{n}
Where is/are …?	**Níbo ni … wà?**	nee-bo nee … wah
Where can I get/find …?	**Níbo ni mo ti lè rí …?**	nee-bo nee mo tee lay ree
How far?	**Báwo ló ṣe jìnnà tó?**	ba-wo lo shay jee-naa toh
How long?	**Báwo ló ṣe pẹ́ to?**	ba-wo lo shay peh toh
How much?	**Èló ni?**	ay-lo nee
Can you help me?	**Ẹ jọ̀wọ́, ẹ ràn mí lọ́wọ́?**	eh jo-wo eh ra^{n} mee lo-wo
What does this mean?	**Kí ni ìtumọ̀ èyí?**	kee nee ee-too-mo ay-yee
I understand.	**Ó yé mi.**	o yay mee
I don't understand.	**Kò yé mi.**	ko yay mee
Please speak slowly.	**Ẹ jọ̀ọ́, ẹ rọra sọ̀rọ̀ jẹ́ẹ́jẹ́ẹ́.**	er jaw-aw eh raw-ra saw-ro jeh-jeh
Can you translate this for me?	**Ǹjẹ́ ẹ lẹ̀ túmọ̀ èyí fún mi?**	n-jeh eh leh tu-maw ay-yee foo^{n} mee
Can I have …?	**Ṣé ẹ lè fún mi ní …?**	shay eh lay foo^{n} meenee
Do you speak English?	**Ṣé ẹ gbọ́ Gẹ̀ẹ́sì?**	shay eh gbaw geh-eh-see
I don't speak Yoruba.	**Mi ò gbọ́ Yorùbá.**	mee o gbaw yo-roo-ba

It's … *Ó …*

big/small	**tóbi/kéré**	too-bee/kay-ray
cheap/expensive	**pọ̀/wọ́n**	paw/waw^{n}
early/late	**yá/pẹ́**	ya/kpeh
good/bad	**dáa/burú**	da-a/boo-roo
hot/cold	**gbóná/tutù**	gbo-na/too-too
near/far	**wà nítòsí/jìnnà**	wa nee-toh-see/jeen-na
old/young	**dàgbà/jẹ́ ọ̀dọ́**	dag-ba/jeh aw-daw
vacant/occupied	**ṣófo/kò ṣófo**	sho-fo/ko sho-fo

Hotel–Accommodation *Ibùgbé–Òtẹ̀ẹ̀lì*

We've reserved two rooms.	**A ti ní kí wọn ó fi yàrá méjì silẹ̀ fún wa.**	a tee nee kee waw^n o fee ya-ra may-jee see-leh foo^n wa
Here's the confirmation.	**Ẹrí rẹ nìyí.**	ay-ree reh nee-yee
Do you have any vacancies?	**Ǹjé ẹ ní ààyè?**	n-jey eh nee a-a-yay
I'd like a … room.	**Mo fé yàrá kan …**	mo fay ya-ra kahn
single	**kékeré**	kay-kay-ray
double	**títóbi**	tee-toh-bee
with twin beds	**pẹ̀lúu ibùsùn**	peh-luu ee-boo-soo^n
with a double bed	**pẹ̀lú ibùsùn oníha méjì**	peh-loo ee-boo-soo^n o-nee-ha may-jee
with a bath	**pẹ̀lú ilé ìwẹ**	peh-loo ee-lay-ee-weh
with a shower	**pẹ̀lù ṣáwà**	peh-loo sha-wa
We'll be staying …	**A ó dúró níbí …**	a o doo-ro nee-bee
overnight only	**lálẹ òní**	la-leh o-nee
a few days	**fún ọjọ́ díẹ̀**	foo^n aw-jaw dee-eh
a week	**ọ̀sẹ̀ kan**	aw-seh kah^n

Decision *Ìpinnu*

May I see the room?	**Ṣé mo lè wo yàrá ọ̀hún?**	sheh mo leh wo ya-ra aw-hoo^n
That's fine. I'll take it.	**Ó dáa. Mà á gbà á.**	o da-a. ma-a gba a
No. I don't like it.	**Kò wù mí.**	ko woo mee
It's too …	**Ó … jù.**	o … joo
dark/small	**ṣókùnkùn/kéré**	shó-koo^n-koo^n/kay-ray
noisy	**láriwo**	la-ree-wo
Do you have anything …?	**Ṣé ẹ ní omîn …?**	shay eh nee o-mee-ee^n
better/bigger	**tó dáa/tóbì**	toh da-a/to-bee
cheaper	**rọ̀jú**	raw-joo
quieter	**tí kò láriwo**	tee ko la-ree-wo
May I please have my bill?	**Ẹ jọ̀ọ́ mo fẹ́ẹ̀ mọ iye tí mà á san.**	eh jaw-aw mo feh-eh maw eeyeh tee ma-a sa^n
It's been a very enjoyable stay.	**Mo gbádun ibí gan-an.**	mo gba-doo^n ee-bee ga^n-a^n

DATE, see page 173/NUMBERS, see page 174

Eating out *Jìjẹnu níta*

I'd like to reserve a table for 4.	**Ẹ bá mi fi ààyè èniyàn mérin sílè.**	eh ba mee fee a-a-yay eh-nee-ya^{n} meh-ree^{n} see-leh
We'll come at 8.	**A ń bọ láàgo mẹ́jọ.**	a n-baw laa-go meh-jaw
I'm hungry.	**Ebi ń pa mí.**	ay-bee npa mee
I'm thirsty.	**Òùngbẹ ń gbẹ mí**	o-oo^{n}-gbeh n gbeh mee
I'd like …	**Mo fẹ́ oúnjẹ …**	mo feh o-oo^{n}-jeh
breakfast/lunch	**àarọ̀/ọ̀sán**	a-a-roh/aw-sa^{n}
dinner	**alẹ́**	a-leh
Do you have local dishes?	**Ṣé ẹ lóúnjẹ?**	shay eh lo-oo^{n}-jeh
What do you recommend?	**Èwo lẹ rò pó dáa?**	ay-wo leh ro po da-a
Do you have vegetarian dishes?	**Ṣe ẹ ní ouńjẹ ti kò ní ẹran?**	shay eh nee o-oo^{n}-jeh tee ko nee eh-ran

Breakfast *Oúnjẹ àárọ̀*

I'd like some …	**Mo fẹ́ …**	mo feh
bread/butter	**buredi/bọ́tà**	boo-ray-dee/baw-tah
eggs	**ẹyin**	eh-yee^{n}
jam	**jáàmù**	ja-a-moo
rolls	**búrédì kéékèèké**	booray-dee kay-kay-kay

Meat *Eran*

I'd like some …	**Mo fẹ́ …**	mo feh
beef	**ẹran màálúù**	eh-ra^{n} ma-a-loo-oo
chicken	**adìẹ**	a-dee-eh
goat	**ewúrẹ́/ògúfe**	ay-woo-reh/o-goo-fay
lamb	**ẹran àguntan**	eh-ra^{n} a-goon-ta^{n}
pork	**ẹran ẹlẹ́dẹ̀**	eh-ra^{n} eh-leh-deh
ẹ̀gusí ẹran màálúù àti ọbẹ̀	eh-goo-see eh-ra^{n} ma-a-loo-oo a-tee aw-beh	beef and melon seed stew
ọbẹ̀ ẹ̀gúsí ẹti ẹran adiẹ	aw-beh eh-goo-see ay-tee eh-ra^{n} a-dee-eh	melon seed soup and chicken stew
ọbẹ̀ ilá àti ìgbín	aw-beh ee-lah a-tee ee-gbeh^{n}	okra soup and snail stew

NUMBERS, see page 174/TIME, see page 173

baked	**bíbéèkì**	bee-bay-ay-kee
boiled	**sísè/bíbọ̀**	see-say/bee-baw
fried	**dídín**	dee-dee^n
grilled/roast	**yíyan/sísun**	yee-yaa^n/see-soo^n
stewed	**sísèpọ̀**	see-say-kpaw
underdone (rare)	**kó má jinná jù**	ko ma jee-nah joo
medium	**kó jinná díẹ̀**	ko jee-nah dee-eh
well-done	**kó jinná daadaa**	ko jee-nah daa-daa

Fish and seafood *Ẹja àti ẹran inú òkun*

ewéédú àti ọbẹ̀ ẹja	ay-way-ay-doo a-tee o-beh eh-jah	green leaf soup and fish stew
ọbẹ̀ ẹja aborí	aw-beh eh-jah a-bo-ree	cat fish stew
ọbẹ̀ ẹja òkú èkó	aw-beh eh-jah o-koo ay-ko	mackerel stew
ọbẹ̀ alákàn	aw-beh a-la-ka^n	crab stew
ọbẹ̀ edé	aw-beh ay-day	shrimp stew
ọbẹ̀ ẹja ọ̀bọ̀kún	aw-bay eh-ja aw-baw-koo^n	fresh fish stew
ọbẹẹ gbẹ̀gìrì àti panla	aw-beh-eh gbeh-gee-ree a-tee kpa-n-la	bean soup and stock fish stew

Vegetables *Èfọ́*

beans	**ẹ̀wà**	eh-wah
cabbage	**kábéèjì**	kah-bay-ee-jee
carrots	**kárọ́ọ̀tì**	ka-raw-aw-tee
onion	**àlùbọsà**	a-loo-baw-sah
peas	**ẹ̀wà**	eh-wah
potatoes	**ànàmọ́/pòtétò**	a-na-maw/kpo-tay-to
spinach	**ẹ̀fọ́**	eh-faw
pẹpẹ súùpù	kpeh-kpeh so-oo-kpoo	pepper soup

Fruit *Èso*

apple	**ápù**	a-kpoo
banana	**ọ̀gẹ̀dẹ̀**	aw-geh-deh
lemon	**ọsàn wẹ́wẹ́**	aw-sam way-weh
mango	**máńgòrò**	ma-n-go-ro
orange	**ọsàn/orombo**	aw-san/o-ro-mbo
pineapple	**ọ̀pẹ̀-òyìnbó**	aw-kpeh o-yeen-bo

tangerine	**tanjarîînì**	ta-n-ja-ree-ee-nee
ice-cream	**áís krìmù**	a-ees kree-ee-moo

Drinks *Ohun mímu*

beer	**bíà**	bee-a
(hot) chocolate	**ṣokoléètì**	sho-ko-lay-ay-tee
coffee	**kọfí**	kaw-fee
black	**láìní mílîìkì**	la-ee-nee mee-lee-ee-kee
with milk	**pẹ̀lú mílîìkì**	peh-loo meelee-ee-kee
fruit juice	**omi èso mímu**	o-mee ay-so mee-moo
apple juice	**omi ápù**	o-mee a-kpoo
orange juice	**omi ọsàn**	o-mee aw-sa^n
mineral water	**omi inú àpátá**	o-mee ee-noo a-kpa-ta
tea	**tîì**	tee-ee
wine	**wáìn-nì**	wa-ee^n-nee
red/white	**pupa/funfun**	kpoo-kpoo/foo^n-foo^n
emu	eh-moo	palm wine; sweet/sour taste, slightly alcoholic
ọ̀gọ̀rọ̀	oh-gaw-raw	raffia palm wine; sweet

Paying *Sísanwó*

This is too … bitter/sweet	**Èyí ti … jù. korò/dùn**	ay-yee tee … joo ko-ro/doo^n
That's not what I ordered.	**Kìí ṣe ìyẹn nì mo bèèrè fún.**	kee-ee shay ee-yeh^n nee mo bay-ay-ray foo^n
I'd like to pay.	**Mo fẹ́ẹ̀ sanwó.**	mo fay-ay sa^n-wo
I think you made a mistake in the bill.	**Mo rò pé ẹ ṣẹ àsìṣe nípa ìye owó yìí.**	mo ro kpay eh sheh a-shee-shay nee-kpa ee-yeh o-wo yee-ee
Can I pay with this credit card?	**Ṣé mo lè fi ike ìsanwó yìí sanwó.**	shay mo lay fee ee-kay ee-sa^n-wo yee-ee sa^n-wo
Is service included?	**Ṣé ẹ ti ro owó iṣẹ́ tiyín mọ́ ọn.**	shay eh tee ro o-wo ee-shay tee-yee^n maw-aw^n
I'm full.	**Mo (ti) yó.**	mo (tee) yo
We enjoyed it, thank you.	**A gbádùn-un rẹ̀, ẹ ṣe é.**	a gba-doo^n-oo^n ray eh shay ay

NUMBERS, see page 174

Travelling around *Rírin ìrìn-àjò káàkiri*

Plane *Ọkọ̀ òfuurufú/Ẹropleenì*

Is there a flight to Lagos?	**Ṣé ọkọ̀ ẹropleenì Èkó wà?**	shay aw-kaw eh-ro-play-ay-nee ay-ko wa
What time do I check in?	**Ìgbà wo ni kí n lọọ wọlé?**	ee-gba wo nee kee n law-aw waw-lay
I'd like to … my reservation on flight no. …	**Mà á fẹ́ẹ́ … ààyè mi nínú ọkọ̀ nọ́mbà …**	ma-a feh-eh … a-a-yay mee nee-noo aw-kaw naw-m-ba
cancel/change	**kánsù/pààrọ̀**	ka-n-soo/kpa-a-raw
confirm	**gba ìdánilójú**	gba ee-da-nee-lo-joo

Train *Ọkọ̀ ojú irin*

I want a ticket to Ìbàdàn.	**Mo fẹ́ tíkẹ́ẹ̀tì Ìbàdàn.**	mo feh tee-keh-eh-tee ee-ba-da^{n}
single (one-way)	**ti àlọ nìkan**	tee a-loh nee-ka^{n}
return (roundtrip)	**ti àlọ àti àbọ̀**	tee a-law a-tee a-baw
first class	**onípò kìn-ínní**	o-nee-kpoh kee^{n}-ee-nee
second class	**onípò kejì**	o-nee-kpo kay-jee
How long does the journey (trip) take?	**Wákàtí mélòó ni ìrìnàjò ọhún?**	wa-ka-tee may-lo-o nee ee-ree^{n}-a-jo aw-hoo^{n}
When is the … train to Ile-Ife?	**Àkókò wo ni ọkọ Ilé-Ifẹ̀ yóó gbéra …?**	a-ko-ko wo nee aw-kaw ee-lay ee-feh yo-o gbay-ra
first	**akọ́kọ́**	a-kaw-kaw
next	**èyí tó tẹ̀ lé e**	ay-yee toh teh lay ay
Is this the right train to Òsogbo?	**Ṣé ọkọ̀ òṣogbo nìyí?**	shay aw-kaw o-sho-gbo nee-yee

Bus–Coach *Bọ́ọ̀sí–Bọ́ọ̀sì ńlá-ńlá*

What bus do I take to the centre?	**Bọ́ọ̀sì wo ni kí n wọ̀ dé Ìgboro?**	baw-aw-see wo nee kee n waw day ee-gbo-ro
How much is the fare to …?	**Èló ni owó ọkọ̀ dé …?**	ay-lo mee o-wo aw-kaw day
Will you tell me when to get off?	**Ẹ jọ̀ọ́ ẹ sọ ibi tí mà á ti sọ̀kalẹ̀ fún mi?**	eh jaw-aw eh saw ee-bee tee ma a tee saw-ka-leh foon mee

TELLING THE TIME, see page 173

Taxi *Taksí*

How much is it to …?	**Èló ni dé …**	ay-lo nee day
Take me to this address.	**Ẹ jọ̀ọ́, ẹ gbé mi lọ sí àdírẹ́ṣì yìí.**	eh jaw-aw ay gbay mee law see a-dee-reh-see yee-ee
Please stop here.	**Ẹ jọ̀ọ́, ẹ dúró níbí.**	eh jaw-aw eh doo-ro nee-bee

Car hire–Automobile rental *Káà híháyà/ríréǹtì*

I'd like to hire a car.	**Mo fẹ́ẹ̀ hááyàa káà.**	mo feh-eh ha-a-ya-a kaa
I'd like it for a day/week.	**Mo fẹ́ ẹ fún ọjọ́/ọ̀sẹ̀ kan.**	mo feh eh foo^n aw-jaw/ aw-seh ka^n
Where's the nearest filling station?	**Níbo ni ilé epo tó súnmọ ibi yìí jù wà?**	nee-bo nee ee-lay ay-kpo toh soo^n-maw ee-bee yee-ee joo wa
Full tank, please.	**Ẹ jọ̀ọ́, ẹ jẹ́ kó kún.**	eh jaw-aw eh jeh ko koo^n
Give me … litres of petrol (gasoline).	**Ẹ fún mi ní líta petrol (gasoline) …**	eh foo^n mee nee lee-ta pay-trol (ga-so-leen)
How do I get to …?	**Báwo ni mo ṣe lè dé …**	ba-wo nee mo shay lay day
I've had a breakdown at …	**Ọkọ̀ọ̀ mi-ín ti bàjẹ́ …**	o-kaw-aw mee-ee^n tee ba-jeh
Can you send a mechanic?	**Ẹ jọ̀ọ́ ṣé ẹ lè fi mẹkáníìkì hàn mí?**	eh jaw-aw shay-eh lay fee meh-ka-nee-ee-kee ha^n mee
Can you mend it?	**Sé o lè tún un se?**	shay olay too^n oon shay

☞ Go straight ahead.	**Ẹ máa lọ tààràtà.** ☜
It's down there on the left/right.	**Òun nìyẹn nísàlẹ̀ yẹn lápá òsì/ọ̀tún.**
opposite/behind …	**lódìkejì/lẹ́yìn-in …**
next to/after …	**lẹ́gbẹ̀ẹ́/níkọjáa …**
north/south	**lárìíwá/ní gúúsù**
east/west	**ní ìlà-oòrùn/ ní ìwọ̀ oòrùn**

Sightseeing *Àrìnká láti rí gbogbo ìlú*

Where's the tourist office?	**Níbo ni ilé-iṣẹ́ àjọ arìnrìn-àjò?**	nee-bo nee ee-lay ee-shay a-jaw a-ree^{n}-ree^{n}-a-jo
Is there an English-speaking guide?	**Ǹyẹ́ atọ́nà tó gbọ́ gẹ̀ẹ́sì wà?**	n-jay a-taw-na toh gbaw geh-eh-see wa
Where is/are the …?	**Níbo ni … wà?**	nee-boh nee … wa
botanical gardens	**ọgbà igi àti ewéko**	aw-gba ee-gee a-tee ay-way-ko
castle	**ilé ńlá-nla**	ee-lay n-la-n-la
chief's house	**ilé ìjòyè**	ee-lay ee-joh-yay
church	**ṣọ́ọ̀ṣì**	shaw-aw-shee
city centre	**àárin ìgboro**	a-a-ree^{n} ee-gbo-ro
harbour	**ibùdó ọkọ̀ ojú omi**	ee-boo-do aw-kaw o-joo o-mee
market	**ọjà**	aw-ja
museum	**mùsíòmù**	moo-see-aw-moo
President's palace	**ilé ààrẹ**	ee-lay a-a-reh
shops	**ṣọ́ọ̀bù**	shaw-aw-bu
When does it open/close?	**Ìgbà wo ni wọ́n ń ṣí i/tì í?**	ee-gba wo nee waw^{n} n shee-ee/tee-ee
How much is the entrance fee?	**Èló lowó ìwọlé?**	ay-lo lo-wo ee-waw-lay

Countryside *Ìhí oke*

desert	**aṣálẹ̀**	a-sha-leh
farm	**oko**	o-ko
footpath	**ojú ọ̀nà ẹsẹ̀**	o-joo aw-na eh-seh
game reserve	**ọgba ẹranko**	aw-gba eh-ra^{n}-ko
lake	**adágún-odò**	a-da-goo^{n}-o-do
mountain	**òkè**	o-keh
river	**odò**	o-doh
savannah	**ilẹ̀ẹ pápá**	ee-leh-eh kpa-kpa
well/oasis	**kànga/ṣẹ̀lẹ̀rú**	ka^{n}-ga/sheh-leh-roo

Entertainment *Ìdárayá*

What's playing at the theatre?	**Eré wo ni wọ́n ń ṣe ní tíátà?**	eh-reh woh nee waw^{n} n shay nee tee-a-ta

DAYS OF THE WEEK, see page 174

How much are the seats?	**Èló lowó ìwọlé?**	eh-lo lo-wo ee-waw-leh
Would you like to go out with me tonight?	**Ṣé wà á bá mi jáde lálẹ́ yìí?**	shay wa a ba mee ja-day la-leh yee-ee
Is there a discotheque in town?	**Ṣé ilé-ijó (dískò) wà nígboro?**	shay ee-lay-ee-jo (dee-sko) wa nee-gbo-ro
Would you like to dance?	**Ṣé o fẹ́ẹ́ jó?**	shay o feh-eh jo
Thank you. It's been a wonderful evening.	**O ṣe é. Mo gbádùn alẹ́ yìí gan-an ni.**	o-shay ay. mo gba-doo^{n} a-lay yee-ee ga^{n}-a^{n} nee

Shops, stores and services *Ṣọ́ọ̀bù*

Where's the nearest …?	**Níbo ni … tó súnmọ́ tòsí jù?**	nee-bo… toh soo^{n}-maw toh-see joo
baker's	**ilée búrẹ́di**	ee-lay-ay boo-reh-dee
bookshop	**ilé ìtàwé**	ee-lay ee-ta-way
butcher's	**ìsọ̀ ẹlẹ́ran**	ee-saw eh-leh-ra^{n}
chemist's	**ilé ìta oogun**	ee-lay ee-ta o-o-goo^{n}
dentist	**ilée dókítà eléyín**	ee-lay-ay do-kee-ta ay-lay-yee^{n}
department store	**ṣọ́ọ̀bù ńlá-ńlá**	shaw-aw-boo n-la-n-la
grocery	**ìṣọ̀ alátẹ**	ee-saw a-la-teh
hairdresser/barber	**ilée onídìrí/bábà**	ee-lay-ay o-nee-dee-ree/ba-ba
newsagent	**ìṣọ̀ oníwèé ìròyìn**	ee-saw o-nee-way-ay ee-ro-yee^{n}
post office	**ilé-ìfìwé ránṣẹ**	ee-lay ee-fee-way ra^{n}-sheh
supermarket	**ọjà ṣọ́ọ̀bù ńlá-ńlá**	aw-ja shaw-aw-boo n-la-n-la
toilets	**ilé-ìgbọ̀nsẹ̀**	ee-lay ee-gbawn-seh

General expressions *Ìsọ̀rọ̀ nípa orísirísi nǹkan*

Where's the main shopping area?	**Níbo ni ọjà tó tóbií wà?**	nee-bo nee aw-ja toh toh-bee wa
Do you have any …?	**Ṣé ẹ ní …?**	shay eh-nee
Do you have anything …?	**Ṣe ẹ ní nǹkankan tó …?**	shay eh nee n-nka^{n}-ka^{n} toh
better	**dára ju èyí lọ**	da-rah joo-ay-yee-law

NUMBERS, see page 174

cheaper	**dínwó**	dee^{n}-wo
larger	**tóbi**	toh-bee
smaller	**kéré ju èyí lọ**	kay-ray joo ay-yee law
Can I try it on?	**Ṣé mo lè wọ̀ ọ́ wò?**	shay mo lay waw aw wo
How much is this?	**Èló ni èyí?**	ay-loh nee ay-yee
Please write it down.	**Ẹ jọ̀ọ́ ẹ kọ ọ́ sílẹ̀.**	eh jaw-aw eh kaw-aw see-leh
That's too much. How about … naira?	**Ìyẹ́n ti pọ̀ jù. Náírà … ńkọ́?**	ee-ye^{n} tee paw joo. na-ee-ra … n-kaw
No, I don't like it.	**Rárá, kò wù mí.**	ra-ra ko woo mee
I'll take it.	**Mà-á mú un.**	ma-a moo oo^{n}
Do you accept credit cards?	**Ṣé ẹ máa ń gba ike ìsanwó?**	shay eh ma-a n gba ee-kay ee-san-wo

black	**dúdú**	doo-doo	blue	**búlúù**	boo-loo
brown	**pípọ́n**	kpee-po^{n}	green	**aláwọ̀ ewé**	a-la-waw ay-way
orange	**aláwọ̀ ọsàn**	a-la-waw aw-sa^{n}	red	**pupa**	kpoo-kpa
yellow	**yẹ́lò**	yeh-lo	white	**funfun**	foo^{n}-foo^{n}

I want to buy …	**Mo fẹ́ẹ̀ ra …**	mo feh-eh ra
anti-malaria tablets	**oògùn ibà**	o-o-goo^{n} ee-ba
aspirin	**aspinrín-ìn**	a-speen-ree^{n}-ee^{n}
batteries	**bátìri**	ba-tee-ree
newspaper	**ìwé ìròyìn**	ee-way ee-ro-yee^{n}
English	**Gẹ̀ẹ́sì**	geh-eh-see
American	**Amẹ́ríkà**	ar-meh-ree-ka
shampoo	**ọṣẹ ìfọrun**	aw-sheh ee-faw-roo^{n}
soap	**ọṣẹ**	aw-sheh
toothpaste	**ọṣẹ ìfọyín**	aw-sheh ee-faw-yee^{n}
a half-kilo of apples	**ìdajì ìwọ̀n-ọn kílò ápù kan**	ee-da-jee ee-wo^{n}-o^{n} kee-lo a-poo ka^{n}
a litre of milk	**lítàa wàrà kan**	lee-ta-a wa-ra ka^{n}
I'd like … film for this camera.	**Mo fẹ́ fíìmù fún kámẹ́rà yìí.**	mo feh fee-ee-moo foo^{n} ka-meh-ra yee
black and white	**dúdú àti funfun**	doo-doo a-tee foo^{n}foo^{n}
colour	**aláwọ̀ [kọ́lọ̀]**	a-la-waw [kaw-law]

TELLING THE TIME, see page 173

Souvenirs *Mnl-an ìtàn*

àdìrẹ	a-dee-reh	locally-dyed fabric
àpò aláwọ	a-kpo a-la-waw	leather bag
bàtà aláwọ	ba-ta a-la-waw	leather shoes
dùndún	doo^{n}-doo^{n}	talking drum
ère	ay-ray	statue
ìkòkò/apẹ Ìlọrin	ee-koo-koo/a-kpeh ee-lo-ree^{n}	pots made in Ilorin
ọ̀pá ìtìlẹ̀	aw-kpa ee-tee-leh	decorated walking stick

At the bank *Ní ilé ìfowópamọ́sí*

Where's the nearest bank/currency exchange office?	**Níbo ni báǹkì/ilé ìpààrọ̀ owo to súnmọ́ tòsí jù ú wà?**	nee-boh nee ban-kee/ ee-lay ee-kpa-a-raw o-wo toh soo^{n}-maw toh-see joon-wa
I want to change some dollars/pounds into naira.	**Mo fẹ́ẹ́ pààrọ̀/ṣẹ dọ́là/ ponùn díẹ̀ sí Náírà.**	mo feh-eh kpa-a-ro/ sheh daw-la/pon-oo^{n} dee-eh see na-ee-ra
How many dollars/ pounds to the naira?	**Èló ni dọ́là/pọ́n-ùn sí Náírà?**	ay-loh nee daw-lar/ po^{n}-oo^{n} see na-ee-ra

At the post office *Ní ilé ìfiwéránṣẹ́*

I want to send this by …	**Mo fẹ́ẹ́ fi èyí ránṣẹ́ (póòsìì) èyí ní …**	mo feh-eh fee ay-yee ran-sheh (kpo-o-see-ee) ay-yee nee
airmail	**íámeèlì**	ee-a-may-ay-lee
express	**ẹksprẹ́ẹ̀sì**	eh-kspreh-eh-see
registered mail	**rẹ́gístà**	reh-gees-ta
I want …-naira stamps.	**Mo fẹ́ sitámpù oní náírà …**	mo feh see-tam-kpoo o-nee na-ee-ra
What's the postage for a letter/postcard to America?	**Èló ni fún lẹ́tà/káàdì dé Amẹ́ríkà?**	ay-lo nee foo^{n} leh-tar/ ka-a-dee day a-meh-ree-ka
Is there any mail for me? My name is …	**Ǹjẹ́/Ṣé mo ní lẹ́tà? Onikọ mi ni …**	n-jay/shay-mo nee leh-ta. o-nee-kaw mee nee
Can I send a telegram/fax?	**Ṣé mo lè ṣe télí-gráàmù/fáàksì níbí?**	shay mo lay shay teh-lee-graamoo/fa-a-ksee nee-bee

Telephoning *Títẹlifóònù*

Where's the nearest public phone?	**Níbo ni ènìyàn-án ti lè tẹlifóònù tó sún-mọ́ tòsí jù?**	nee-bo nee ay-nee-ya^n-an tee leh teh-lee-foo-noo toh soo^n-mo toh-see joo
May I use your phone?	**Ṣé mo lè lo fóònù yín?**	shay mo lay lo fo-o-^{n}oo yee^n
I want to make an international call to…	**Mo fẹ́ẹ̀ fóònù sí ókè òkun …**	mo feh-eh fo-o-noo see o-kay o-koo^n
Hello. This is … speaking.	**Hẹ̀lóò … ló ń sọ̀rọ̀.**	heh-lo-o … lo-n saw-raw
I want to speak to …	**Mo fẹ́ẹ̀ bá … sọ̀rọ̀.**	mo feh-eh ba … saw-raw
When will he/she be back?	**Nígbà wo ní yóò dé?**	nee-gba wo nee yo-o day
Will you tell him/her that I called?	**Ẹ sọ fún un pé mo pè é?**	eh saw foo^n oon kpay mo kpay ay

Time and date *Àkókò àti ọjọ́*

What's the time/hour?	**Aago mélòó ló lù?**	a-a-go may-lo-o lo loo
It's …	**Aago …**	a-a go
five past one	**kan-án kọjá ìṣẹ́jú márún-uń**	ka^n-an kaw-ja ee-sheh-joo ma-roo^n-oo^n
quarter past three	**mẹ́taá kọjá ìṣẹ́jú mẹ́ẹ̀ẹ́dógún**	meh-ta-a kaw-ja ee-sheh-joo meh-eh-eh-do-goo^n
twenty past five	**márùn-uń kọjá ogún ìṣẹ́jú**	ma-roo^n-oo^n kaw-ja o-goo^n ee-sheh-joo
half-past seven	**méje ààbọ̀**	may-jay a-a-bo
twenty-five to nine	**mẹ́sàn-án kù ìṣẹ́jù mẹ́ẹ̀ẹ́dọ́gbọ̀n**	meh-sa^n-a^n koo ee-sheh-joo meh-eh-eh-do-gbaw^n
ten to ten	**mẹ́wàá ku ìṣeju mẹ́wàá**	meh-waa koo ee-sheh-joo meh-waa
noon/midnight	**ọ̀sán/òru**	aw-sa^n/o-roo
in the morning	**ní àárọ̀**	nee a-a-raw
during the day	**ní ọ̀sán**	nee aw-sa^n
in the evening	**ní ìrọ̀lẹ́**	nee ee-raw-leh
at night	**ní alẹ́**	nee a-leh

yesterday/today	**àná/òní**	a-na/o-nee
tomorrow	**ọ̀la**	aw-la
rainy season (mid April-October)	**ìgbà òjò**	ee-gba o-jo
dry season (mid October-April)	**ìgbà ẹ̀ẹ̀rùn**	ee-gba eh-eh-roo^n

Sunday	**Sánńdè**	sa^n-n-day
Monday	**ọjọ́ọ Mọ́ndè**	aw-jaw-aw maw^n-day
Tuesday	**ọjọ́ọ Túùsdeè**	aw-jaw-aw too-oos-day-ay
Wednesday	**ọjọ́ọ Wẹ́ẹ̀sdeè**	aw-jaw-aw weh-ehs-day-ay
Thursday	**ọjọ́ọ Tọ́ọ̀sdeè**	aw-jaw-aw taw-aw-s-day-ay
Friday	**ọjọ́ọ Fúráìdeè**	aw-jaw-aw foo-ra-ee-day-ay
Saturday	**ọjọ́ọ Sátidé**	aw-jaw-aw sa-tee-day
January	**Jánúárì**	ja-noo-a-ree
February	**Fẹ́bọ́árì**	feh-bo-a-ree
March	**Máàṣì**	ma-a-shee
April	**Épirì**	ay-kpee-ree
May	**Méè**	meh-eh
June	**Júùnù**	joo-oo-noo
July	**Júláì**	joo-la-ee
August	**Ọ́gọ́ọ̀sì**	o-go-o-see
September	**Sẹ̀tẹ́mbà**	seh-teh-m-ba
October	**Ọ̀któbà**	awk-toh-ba
November	**Nòfẹ́mbà**	no-feh-m-ba
December	**Dìsẹ́mbà**	dee-seh-m-ba

Numbers *Òǹkà*

0	**òdo/òfo**	o-doh/o-fo
1	**ọ̀kan/kan**	aw-ka^n/ka^n
2	**méjì**	may-jee
3	**mẹ́ta**	meh-ta
4	**mẹ́rin**	meh-reen
5	**márùn-ún**	ma-roo^n-oo^n
6	**mẹ́fà**	meh-fa
7	**méje**	meh-jay
8	**mẹjọ**	meh-jo
9	**mẹ́sàn-án**	meh-sa^n-a^n
10	**mẹ́wàá**	meh-wa-a

11	**mọ́kànlá**	maw-ka^{n}-la
12	**méjìlá**	meh-jee-la
13	**mẹ́tàlá**	meh-ta-la
14	**mẹ́rìnlá**	meh-ree^{n}-la
15	**mẹ́ẹ̀ẹ́dógún**	meh-eh-eh do-goo^{n}
16	**mérìdín lọ́gún**	meh-ree-dee^{n} lo-goo^{n}
17	**métàdínlógún**	may-ta-dee^{n}-lo-goo^{n}
18	**méjìdínlógún**	may-jee-dee^{n}-lo-goo^{n}
19	**mọ́kàndínlógún**	maw-ka^{n}-dee^{n}-lo-goo^{n}
20	**ogún**	o-goo^{n}
21	**mọ́kànlélógún**	maw-kan-lay-lo-goo^{n}
30	**ọgbọ̀n**	aw-gbo^{n}n
40	**ogójì**	o-go-jee
50	**àádọ́ta**	a-a-daw-ta
60	**ọgóta**	aw-gaw-ta
70	**àádọ́rin**	a-a-daw-ree^{n}
80	**ọgọ́rin**	aw-gaw-ree^{n}
90	**àádọ́rùn-ún**	a-a-daw-roo^{n}-oo^{n}
100	**ọgọ́rùn-ún**	aw-gaw-roo^{n}-oo^{n}
101	**mọ́kàn-lélọ́gọ́rùn-ún**	maw-kan-lay-law-gaw-roo^{n}-oo^{n}
200	**igba**	ee-gba
500	**ẹ̀ẹ́dẹ́ gbẹ̀ta**	eh-eh-deh gbeh-ta
1,000	**ẹgbẹ̀rún**	eh-gber-roo^{n}
100,000	**ẹgbẹ̀rún lọ́nà ọgọ́rùn-uń**	eh-gbeh-roo^{n} law-na aw-gaw-roo^{n}-oo^{n}
first	**èkíní**	ay-keen-nee
second	**èkejì**	ay-kay-jee
once	**lẹ́ẹ̀kan**	leh-eh-ka^{n}
twice	**lẹ́ẹ̀mejì**	leh-eh-may-jee
a half	**ìdajì**	ee-da-jee
a quarter	**ìdá mẹ́rin**	ee-da meh-ree^{n}

Emergency *Pàjáwìrì*

Call the police	**Pe ọlọ́pàá**	kpay aw-law-pa-a
Get a doctor	**Pe dókítà**	kpay do-kee-ta
Go away	**Kúrò/Máa lọ**	koo-ro/ma-a law
HELP	**É GBÈ MÍ O**	eh-gba mee o
I'm ill	**Araà mi ò yá**	a-ra-a mee o-ya
I'm lost	**Mo sọnù**	mo saw-noo
Leave me alone	**Fi mí sílẹ̀**	fee mee see-leh
STOP THIEF	**DÚRÓ OLÈ**	doo-ro o-lay

TELEPHONING, see page 172

My … have been stolen.	**Wọn ti jí … mi.**	waw^n tee jee … mee
I've lost my …	**Mo ti sọ … mi nù.**	mo tee saw … mee noo
handbag	**àpò ìfàlọ̀wọ́**	a-kpo ee-fa-law-waw
passport	**páàspọ̀ọ̀tì**	kpa-as-kpaw-aw-tee
luggage	**àpótí**	a-kpo-tee
wallet	**àpamọ́wọ́**	a-kpa-maw-waw

Guide to Yoruba pronunciation

Letter	Approximate pronunciation	Symbol		Example
Consonants				
b, d, f, h, j, k, l, m, n, p, r, t, w, y		as in English		
g	like **g** in **g**o	g	**gé**	geh
gb	like **gb** in bi**gb**oy	gb	**gbà**	gba
p	like **kp** in bac**kp**ain	kp	**kpa**	kpa
s	like **s** in **s**ee	s	**sun**	soo^n
ṣ	like **sh** in **sh**irt	sh	**ṣe**	sheh
Vowels				
a	like **ar** in **Ar**abic	a/ah	**ara**	a-ra
e	like **a** in l**a**te	ay	**ewé**	ay-way
ẹ	like **e** in **e**gg	eh	**ẹsẹ̀**	eh-seh
i	like **ee** in b**ee**	ee	**igi**	ee-gee
o	like **o** in c**o**ld	o/oh	**orí**	o-ree
ọ	like **aw** in r**aw**	aw	**ọwọ́**	aw-waw
u	like **oo** in t**oo**	oo	**ìlù**	ee-loo

Like French, Yoruba has nasalized vowels: **an**, **ẹn**, **ọn**, **in**, **un**, which are pronounced partly through the nose. The **n** is not pronounced as a separate consonant and is indicated in our phonetic transcription by ^{n}.

Tones

Yoruba is a tonal language. Each syllable has one of 3 tones: high pitch (´), low pitch (`) or mid pitch (no mark). However, for simplicity, we have not included tonal indicators in our phonetic transcriptions.

Zulu

Basic expressions *Izisho ezelula*

Yes./No.	**Yebo./Cha.**	**yeh**baw/ǀ**c**ǀ**ah**
Please.	**Siza.**	**see**zah
Thank you.	**Ngiyabonga.**	ngeeyah**baw**ngah
I beg your pardon?	**Uxolo?**	ooǀ**x**ǀ**aw**law

Introductions *Ukwazisana*

Good morning/ Good afternoon.	**Sawubona.**	sahwoo**baw**nah
Good-bye.	**Uhambe kahle/ Usale kahle.**	oo**hah**mbeh **kah**HLeh/ oo**sah**leh **kah**HLeh
My name is …	**Igama lami ngu …**	ee**gah**mah lah**mee** ngoo
Pleased to meet you.	**Ngiyajabula ukukwazi.**	ngeeyahjah**boo**lah ookoo**kwah**zee
What's your name?	**Ngubani igama lakho?**	ngoo**bah**nee ee**gah**mah **lah**kaw
How are you?	**Unjani?**	oon**jah**nee
Fine thanks. And you?	**Ngiyaphila. Wena unjani?**	ngeeyah**pee**lah. **weh**nah oon**jah**nee
Where do you come from?	**Ubuyaphi?**	ooboo**yah**pee
I'm from …	**Ngibuya …**	ngee**boo**yah
Australia	**Australia**	awseetreh**lee**yah
Britain	**Brithani**	bree**tah**nee
Canada	**Canada**	kah**nah**dah
Ireland	**Ireland**	ahyah**leh**ndee
USA	**Amelika**	ahmeh**lee**kah
I'm with my …	**Ngino … wami.**	**ngee**naw … **wah**mee
wife	**nkosikazi**	nkawsee**kah**zee
husband	**myeni**	**myeh**nee
children	**bantwana**	bah**ntwah**nah
parents	**bazali**	bah**zah**lee
boyfriend/girlfriend	**isithandwa**	eesee**tah**ndwah
I'm on vacation.	**Ngikuholide.**	ngeekoohaw**lee**deh
I'm on business.	**Ngize ngebhizinisi.**	**ngee**zeh ngehbeezee**nee**see

GUIDE TO PRONUNCIATION/EMERGENCIES, see page 190

Questions *Imibuzo*

When?/How?	**Nini?/Kanjani?**	**nee**nee/kahn**jah**nee
Why?/Which?	**Ngoba?/Yiphi?**	**ngaw**bah/**yee**pee
What is this/that?	**Yini le/leya?**	**yee**nee leh/**leh**yah
Who is this/that?	**Ngubani lo/loya?**	ngoo**bah**nee law/**law**yah
Where is …?	**Iphi i …?**	**ee**pee ee
Where are …?	**Ziphi izi …?**	**zee**pee **ee**zee
Where can I find …?	**Ngingayitholaphi?**	ngeengah**yee**taw**lahpee**
How far?	**Kude kangakanani?**	**koo**deh kahngahkah**nah**nee
How long?	**Isikhathi esingakanani?**	eesee**kah**tee ehseengahkah**nah**nee
How much?	**Kangakanani?**	kahngahkah**nah**nee
Can you help me?	**Ungangisiza?**	oongahngee**see**zah
What does this mean?	**Isho ukuthini lento?**	**eeshaw** ookoo**tee**nee **leh**ntaw
I understand.	**Ngiyezwa.**	ngee**yeh**zwah
I don't understand.	**Angizwa.**	ah**ngee**zwah
Please speak slowly.	**Ngicela ukhulume ngokungasheshi.**	ngee!**c**!**e**lah ookoo**loo**meh ngawkoongah**sheh**shee
Can you translate this for me?	**Ungangihumu-shela lento?**	oongahngeehoomoo-**sheh**lah **leh**ntaw
Can I have …?	**Ngicela i …?**	ngee!**c**!**e**lah ee
Do you speak English?	**Uyasikhuluma isingisi na?**	ooyahseekoo**loo**mah eesee**ngee**see nah
I don't speak Zulu.	**Angisikhulumi isiZulu.**	ahngeeseekoo**loo**mee eesee**zoo**loo

It's … *I/Ku …*

beautiful/ugly	**-nhle/-mbi**	-nHLeh/-mbee
better/worse	**-ngcono/-mbi kakhulu**	-**n**!**gc**!**aw**naw/-mbee kah**koo**loo
big/small	**nkulu/ncane**	**nkoo**loo/**n**!**c**!**ah**neh
cheap/expensive	**-shibhile/-biza**	-shee**bee**leh/-**bee**zah
good/bad	**-nhle/mbi**	-nHLeh/mbee
hot/cold	**-shisa/-banda**	-**shee**sah/-**bah**ndah
near/far	**duzane/kude**	doo**zah**neh/**koo**deh

Hotel–Accommodation *Ihotela–Indawo yokuhlala*

We've reserved two rooms.	**Sikhulumele amakamelo amabili.**	seekooloo**meh**leh ahmahkah**meh**law ahmah**bee**lee
Do you have any vacancies?	**Ninawo amakamelo akhululekile?**	nee**nah**waw ahmahkah**meh**law ahkoolooleh**kee**leh
I'd like a … room.	**Ngingathanda ukuthola ikamelo …**	ngeengah**tah**ndah ookoo-**taw**lah eekah**meh**law
single	**lomuntu munye**	law**moo**ntoo **moo**nyeh
double	**labantu ababili**	lah**bah**ntoo ahbah**bee**lee
with twin beds	**elinomubhede emibili**	ehleenawmoo**beh**deh ehmee**bee**lee
with a bath	**elinebhavu**	ehleeneh**bah**voo
with a shower	**elineshawa**	ehleeneh**shah**wah
We'll be staying …	**Sizohlala …**	seezaw**HLah**lah
overnight only	**lobusuku kuphela**	lawboo**soo**koo koo**peh**lah
a few days	**amalanga ambalwa**	ahmah**lah**ngah ah**mbah**lwah
a week (at least)	**(ngaphezu) kweviki**	ngah**peh**zoo kweh**vee**kee

Decision *Ukukhetha*

May I see the room?	**Ngicela ukubona lekamelo?**	nee!**c**!**eh**lah ookoo-**baw**nah lehkah**meh**law
That's fine. I'll take it.	**Lilungile. Ngizolithatha**	leeloo**ngee**leh ngeezawlee**tah**tah
No. I don't like it.	**Cha. Angilithandi.**	!**ch**!**ah**. ahneelee**tah**ndee
It's too …	**Li … kakhulu.**	lee … kah**koo**loo
dark/small	**mnyama/ncane**	**mnyah**mah/n!**c**!**ah**neh
noisy	**nomusindo**	nawmoo**seen**daw
Do you have anything …?	**Ninalo eli … kunaleli?**	nee**nah**law ehlee … koonah**leh**lee
better/bigger	**ngcono/khulu**	n!**gc**!**aw**naw/**koo**loo
cheaper/quieter	**shibhile/thulile**	shee**bee**leh/too**lee**leh
May I please have my bill?	**Ngicela iakhawunti yami?**	ngee!**c**!**eh**lah ee-ahkah-**woo**ntee **yah**mee
It's been a very enjoyable stay.	**Bekumnandi ukuhlala lapha.**	behkoo**mnah**ndee ookoo**HLah**lah **lah**pah

Eating out *Ukudla ngaphandle*

I'd like to reserve a table for 4.	**Ngicela ukubekelwa itafula labantu abane.**	ngee!**c**!**eh**lah ookoobeh**keh**lwah eetah**foo**lah lah**bah**ntoo ah**bah**neh
We'll come at 8.	**Sizofika ngo eyithi.**	seezaw**fee**kah ngaw **eh**yeetee
I'm hungry.	**Ngilambile.**	ngeelah**mbee**leh
I'm thirsty.	**Ngomile.**	ngaw**mee**leh
I'd like …	**Ngicela …**	ngee!**c**!**eh**lah
breakfast	**ibhilakufesi**	eebeelahkoo**feh**see
lunch	**indlamini**	eenDLah**mee**nee
dinner	**idina**	ee**dee**nah
Do you have a set menu?	**Ninayo imenyu?**	nee**nah**yaw ee**meh**nyoo
Do you have local dishes?	**Ninako ukudla kwalendawo?**	nee**nah**kaw oo**koo**DLah kwahleh**ndah**waw
What do you recommend?	**Yini emnandi?**	**yee**nee eh**mnah**ndee
Do you have vegetarian dishes?	**Ninako ukudla okungenanyama?**	nee**nah**kaw oo**koo**DLah awkoongehnah**nyah**mah

Breakfast *Isidlo sasekuseni*

May I have some …?	**Ngicela i …?**	ngeh!**c**!**eh**lah ee
bread/butter	**sinkwa/bhatha**	**see**nkwah/**bah**tah
cereal	**siriyeli**	seeree**yeh**lee
eggs	**qanda**	!**q**!**ah**ndah
jam	**jamu**	**jah**moo
rolls	**amaroli**	ahmah**raw**lee

Starters *Izidlo zokuqala*

amahewu	ahmah-**heh**woo	thin, fermented drinking porridge with sugar
izidumba	eezee**doo**mbah	type of potato, boiled
imfe	**ee**mfeh	type of sweet sugar cane
izinkobe	eezee**nkaw**beh	boiled kernels of maize or sorghum with salt
izindlubu	eezee**nDLoo**boo	variety of nut, boiled
umqwayiba	oom!q!wah**yee**bah	biltong: cured meat strips, dried in the sun

Meat *Inyama*

I'd like some …	**Ngifuna …**	ngee**foo**nah
beef	**inyama yenkomo**	een**yah**mah yeh**nkaw**maw
chicken	**inkukhu**	een**koo**koo
goat	**imbuzi**	eem**boo**zee
lamb	**inyama yezinyane lemvu**	een**yah**mah yehzee-**nyah**neh **leh**mvoo
pork	**inyama yengulube**	een**yah**mah yehngoo**loo**beh

Meat and fish are usually referred to by the way they are cooked, e.g. **inyama eyosiwe** (roasted meat); **inhlanzi ethosiwe** (fried fish).

baked	**-bhakiwe**	-bah**kee**weh
boiled	**-bilisiwe**	-beelee**see**weh
fried	**thosiwe**	taw**see**weh
grilled/roast	**-yosiwe**	-yaw**see**weh
underdone (rare)	**-sebomvu**	-seh**baw**mvoo
medium	**engavuthwe kakhulu**	ehngah**voo**tweh kah**koo**loo
well-done	**evuthisisiwe**	ehvooteesee**see**weh

Vegetables *Izithelo*

beans	**ubhontshisi**	oobawn**tshee**see
cabbage	**iklabishi**	eeklah**bee**shee
carrots	**ikhelodi**	eekeh**law**dee
potatoes	**amazambane**	ahmahzah**mbah**neh
rice	**irayisi**	eerah**yee**see
spinach	**imifino**	eemee**fee**naw
amasi	ah**mah**see	stiff corn or sorghum porridge with sour milk
imbuba	eem**boo**bah	beans with corn meal
isidudu	eesee**doo**doo	pumpkin mixed with sorghum or corn meal
isijabane	eeseejah**bah**neh	spinach mixed with stiff corn porridge
isinkwa sombila	eesee**n**kwah saw**mbee**lah	corn bread; normally served with sour milk
ujeleza	oojeh**leh**zah	melon-like vegetable mixed with corn meal

Fruit & dessert *Izithelo ne dizethi*

apple	**iapula**	ee-ah**poo**lah
banana	**ubhanana**	oobah**nah**nah
lemon	**ilemoni**	eeleh**maw**nee
orange	**iolintshi**	ee-aw**lee**ntshee
plum	**ipulamu**	eepoo**lahmoo**
strawberries	**amastrobheri**	ahmahstraw**beh**ree
cake	**ikhekhe**	ee**keh**keh
ice-cream	**iayisikhrimu**	ee-ahyeesee**kree**moo

Drinks *Iziphuzo*

beer	**ubhiye**	oo**bee**yeh
(hot) chocolate	**ukhokho**	oo**kaw**kaw
coffee	**ikofi**	ee**kaw**fee
black	**elimnyama**	ehlee**mnyah**mah
with milk	**elinobisi**	ehleenaw**bee**see
fruit juice	**ijuzi**	ee**joo**zee
apple	**yeapula**	yeh-ah**poo**lah
orange	**yealintshi**	yeh-aw**lee**ntshee
mineral water	**amanzi omthombo**	ah**mah**nzee aw**mtaw**mbaw
tea	**itiye**	ee**tee**yeh
wine	**iwayini**	eewah**yee**nee
red/white	**ebomvu/emhlophe**	eh**baw**mvoo/ eh**mHLaw**peh
amahewu	ahma**heh**woo	non-alcoholic drink made from sour corn meal
umqombhothi	oom!q!aw**mbaw**tee	alcoholic drink from fermented sorghum

Paying *Kubhadala*

I'd like to pay.	**Ngicela ukukhokha.**	ngee!**c**!elah ookoo**kaw**kah
I think you made a mistake in the bill.	**Ngibona sengathi nenze iphutha kule akhawunti.**	ngee**baw**nah seh**ngah**tee **neh**nzeh ee**poo**tah **koo**leh ahkah**woo**ntee
Can I pay with this credit card?	**Ngingakhokha ngale credithi khadi?**	ngeengah**kaw**kah **ngah**leh !**c**!**reh**deetee **kah**dee
We enjoyed it, thank you.	**Bekumnandi. Siyabonga.**	behkoo**mnah**ndee. seeyah**baw**ngah

NUMBERS, see page 189

Travelling around *Ukuhamba*

Plane *Indiza*

Is there a flight to Nairobi?	**Ikhona indiza eya eNayirobi?**	ee**kaw**nah een**dee**zah **eh**yah ehnahyee**raw**bee
What time do I check in?	**Kufuneka ngifike nini e ephothi?**	koofoo**neh**kah ngee**fee**-keh **nee**nee eh eh**paw**tee
I'd like to … my reservation.	**Ngicela uku … isihlalo engibekelwe.**	ngee|**c**|**eh**lah ookoo … eesee**HLah**law ehngeebeh**keh**lweh
cancel	**khansela**	kahn**seh**lah
change	**tshintsha**	**tshee**ntshah
confirm	**qinisela**	|q|eenee**seh**lah

Train *Isitimela*

I want a ticket to Durban.	**Ngicela ithikithi eliya eDurban.**	ngee|**c**|**eh**lah eetee**kee**tee eh**lee**yah ehdoorbahn
single (one-way)	**eliyayo kuphela**	ehlee**yah**yaw koo**peh**lah
return (roundtrip)	**elibuyayo**	ehleeboo**yah**yaw
first class	**ikilasi loku qala**	eekee**lah**see lawkoo |**q**|**a**lah
second class	**ikilasi lesibili**	eekee**lah**see lehsee**bee**lee
How long does the journey (trip) take?	**Luthatha isikhathi esingakanani loluhambo?**	loo**tah**tah eesee**kah**tee ehseengahkah**nah**nee lawloo-**hah**mbaw
When is the … train to Dodoma?	**Sihamba nini isitimela … esiya eDodoma?**	see-**hah**mbah **nee**nah eeseetee**meh**lah … ehseeyah ehdaw**daw**mah
first	**esokuqala**	ehsawkoo|**q**|**ah**lah
next	**esizayo**	ehsee**zah**yaw
last	**esokugcina**	ehsawkoo|**gc**|**ee**nah

Bus–Coach *Ibhasi*

Is there a bus today?	**Ikhona ibhasi namhlanje?**	ee**kaw**nah ee**bah**see nah**mHLah**njeh
What bus do I take to the centre?	**Ngithatha yiphi ibhasi ukuya phakathi ngqo?**	ngee**tah**tah **yee**pee ee**bah**see oo**koo**yah pah**kah**tee **n**|**gq**|**aw**
How much is the fare to …?	**Yimalini ukuya e …?**	yeemah**lee**nee oo**koo**yah eh

TELLING THE TIME, see page 189

Will you tell me when to get off?	**Uzongitshela uma kufanele ngehle?**	oozawngee**tsheh**lah **oo**mah koofah**neHL**eh **ngeh**hleh

Taxi *Ithekisi*

How much is it to …?	**Yimalini ukuya e …?**	yeemah**lee**nee oo**koo**yah eh
Take me to this address.	**Ngiyise kulekheli.**	ngee**yee**seh koolehk**eh**lee
Please stop here.	**Ngicela ume lapha.**	ngee!**c**!elah oomeh **lah**pah

Car hire (rental) *Ukuqasha imoto*

I'd like to hire (rent) a car.	**Ngingathanda ukuqasha imoto.**	ngeengah**tah**ndah ookoo-!**q**!**ah**shah ee**maw**taw
I'd like it for a day/week.	**Ngizoyisebenzisa ilanga linye/iviki.**	ngeezawyeesehbeh**nzee**sah ee**lah**ngah **lee**nyeh/ ee**vee**kee
Where's the nearest filling station?	**Ikuphi ifilingi steshini eseduze?**	ee**koo**pee eefee**lee**ngee steh**shee**nee ehseh**doo**zeh
Give me … litres of petrol (gasoline).	**Nginike amalitha angu … ephethiloli.**	ngeh**nee**keh ahmah**lee**tah ahngoo … ehpehtee**law**lee
How do I get to …?	**Ngifika kanjani e …?**	ngee**fee**kah ka**njah**nee eh
I've had a breakdown at …	**Ngiphukelwe yimoto e …**	ngeepoo**keh**lweh yee**maw**taw eh
Can you send a mechanic?	**Ungathumela umakheniki?**	oongahtoo**meh**lah oomahkeh**nee**kee
Can you mend it?	**Ungayilungisa?**	oongahyeeloo**ngee**sah

Go straight ahead.	**Qhubeka ngqo.**
It's down there on the left/right.	**Ilapha ezansi ngasonxele/ngasokudla.**
opposite/behind …	**bhekene ne/ngasomuva kwe …**
next to/after …	**eceleni kwe/ukwendlula i …**
north/south	**enyakatho/eningizimu**
east/west	**empumalanga/entshonalanga**

NUMBERS, see page 189

Sightseeing *Ukubona indawo*

Where's the tourist office?	**Likuphi ihovisi lezivakashi?**	lee**koo**pee ee-haw**vee**see lehzeevah**kah**shee
Is there an English-speaking guide?	**Ukhona umkhaphi okhuluma isingisi?**	oo**kaw**nah oo**mkah**pee awkoo**loo**mah eesee**ngee**see
Where is/are the …?	**Iphi i/Ziphi izi …?**	**ee**pee ee/**zee**pee **ee**zee
botanical gardens	**ngadi**	**ngah**dee
church	**sonto**	**saw**ntaw
city centre	**umphakathi dolobha**	oompah**kah**tee daw**law**bah
game reserve	**isiqiwu**	eesee!**q**!**ee**woo
market	**makethe**	mah**keh**teh
museum	**imyuziyemu**	eemyoozee**yeh**moo
shops	**tolo**	**taw**law
When does it open?	**Ivulwa nini?**	ee**voo**lwah **nee**nee
When does it close?	**Ivalwa nini?**	ee**vah**lwah **nee**nee
How much is the entrance fee?	**Kungenwa ngamalini?**	koo**ngeh**nwah ngahmah**lee**nee

Entertainment *Ukuzijabulisa*

What's playing at the theatre?	**Kudlalani kuthiyetha?**	kooDLah**lah**nee kootee**yeh**tah
How much are the seats?	**Yimalini ukungena?**	yeemah**lee**nee ookoo**ngeh**nah
Would you like to go out with me tonight?	**Ungathanda ukuphuma nami namhlanje ebusuku?**	oongah**tah**ndah ookoo**poo**mah nahmee nah**mHLah**njeh ehboo**soo**koo
Is there a discotheque in town?	**Ikhona idisko lana?**	ee**kaw**nah ee**dee**skaw **lah**nah
Would you like to dance?	**Uyafuna ukudansa?**	ooyah**foo**nah ookoo**dah**nsah
Thank you. It's been a wonderful evening.	**Ngiyabonga. Bekumnandi kakhulu.**	ngeeyah**baw**ngah. behkoo**mnah**ndee kah**koo**loo

isibhaca (eesee**bah**!c!ah) dance by teams of men to the accompaniment of drums; a popular tourist entertainment

TELLING THE TIME, see page 189

Shops, stores and services *Izitolo, nezoncedo*

Where's the nearest…?	**Iphi i … eseduze?**	eepee ee … ehseh**doo**zeh
baker's	**bhikawozi**	beekah**waw**zee
bookshop	**sitolo sezincwadi**	see**taw**law sehzee**n**ǀ**c**ǀ**wah**dee
butcher's	**silaha**	see**lah**ah
chemist's	**khemisi**	keh**mee**see
department store	**sitolo esikhulu**	see**taw**law ehsee**koo**loo
grocery	**sitolo sokudla**	see**taw**law saw**kooDL**ah
newsagent	**umthengisi wamaphepha**	oomteh**ngee**see wahmah**peh**pah
post office	**posi**	**paw**see
supermarket	**suphamakethe**	soopahmah**keh**teh
toilets	**indlu yangasese**	**ee**nDLoo yahngah**seh**seh

General expressions *Izisho ezivamile*

Where's the main shopping area?	**Ziphi izitolo?**	**zee**pee eezee**taw**law
Do you have any …?	**Unayo i …?**	oo**nah**yaw ee
Do you have anything …?	**Unayo into e …?**	oo**nah**yaw **ee**ntaw eh
cheaper	**shibhile kuna**	shee**bee**leh **koo**nah
better	**ingcono kuna**	een**ǀgcǀaw**naw **koo**nah
larger	**nkulu kuna**	**n**koo**loo** **koo**nah
smaller	**ncane kuna**	**n**ǀ**c**ǀ**ah**neh **koo**nah
Can I try it on?	**Ngingayilinganisa?**	ngeengahyee**lee**leengah-**nee**sah
How much is this?	**Yimalini lento?**	yeemah**lee**nee **leh**ntaw
Please write it down.	**Ngicela uyibhale phansi.**	ngeeǀ**c**ǀ**e**lah ooyee**bah**leh **pah**nsee
That's too much.	**Ubiza kakhulu.**	oo**bee**zah kah**koo**loo
How about … shillings?	**Ngingakunika amashilingi angu …?**	ngeengahkoo**nee**kah ahmahshee**lee**nee ahngoo
No, I don't like it.	**Cha. Angiyithandi.**	ǀ**ch**ǀ**a**. ahngeeyee**tah**ndee
I'll take it.	**Ngizoyithatha.**	ngeezawyee**tah**tah
Do you accept credit cards?	**Niyawathatha amacredithi khadi?**	neeyahwah**tah**tah amahǀcǀreh**dee**tee **kah**dee

black	**mnyama**	**mnyah**mah
blue	**luhlaza**	loo**hlah**zah
brown	**nsundu**	**nsoon**doo
green	**luhlaza**	loo**hlah**zah
orange	**umbala we olintshi**	oo**mbah**lah weh aw**lee**ntshee
red	**bomvu**	**baw**mvoo
yellow	**liphuzi**	lee**poo**zee
white	**mhlophe**	**mhlaw**peh

I want to buy …	**Ngifuna ukuthenga …**	ngee**foo**nah ookoo**teh**ngah
anti-malaria tablets	**amapilisi womkhuhlane wokuqhuqha**	ahmahpee**lee**see wawmkoo**HLah**neh wawkoo!**qh**!**oo**!qh!ah
aspirin	**aspirini**	ahspee**ree**nee
batteries	**amabhetri**	ahmah**beh**tree
bottle opener	**isivulo samabhodlela**	eesee**voo**law sahmahbawDL**eh**lah
newspaper	**iphepha**	ee**peh**pah
American	**laseMelika**	lahsehmeh**lee**kah
English	**laseNgilandi**	lahsehngee**lah**ndee
shampoo	**ishampu**	ee**shah**mpoo
sun-tan cream	**ukhilimu welanga**	ookee**lee**moo weh**lah**ngah
soap	**insipho**	een**see**paw
toothpaste	**umuthi wokuxubha**	oo**moo**tee wawkoo!**x**!**oo**bah
a half-kilo of apples	**uhafu wekhilo lama apule**	oo**hah**foo weh**kee**law lahmah ah**poo**leh
a litre of milk	**ilitha yobisi**	ee**lee**tah yaw**bee**see
I'd like … film for this camera.	**Ngifuna ifilimu e … lalekhamera.**	ngee**foo**nah eefee**lee**moo eh … lahlehkah**meh**rah

Souvenirs *Izikhumbuzo*

amagcebesha	ahmah!gc!eh**beh**shah	elaborate bead necklace
idlelo	eeDL**eh**law	small tobacco calabash
ihluzo	ee**HLoo**zaw	grass beer strainer
imbenge	ee**mbeh**ngeh	flat grass dish
imbiza	ee**mbee**zah	clay pot for cooking
isikhetho	eesee**keh**taw	big grass spoon
umkhamba	oo**mkah**mbah	clay beer pot

At the bank *Ebhange*

Where's the nearest bank/currency exchange office?	**Iphi ibhange yokutshintsha imali eseduze?**	ee**pee** ee**bah**ngeh yawkoo**tshee**ntshah ee**mah**lee ehseh**doo**zeh
I want to change some dollars.	**Ngifuna ukutshintsha amadola ngiwenze.**	ngee**foo**nah ookoo**tshee**-ntshah ahmah**daw**lah ngee**weh**nzeh
What's the exchange rate?	**Yini ireyithi okutshintshwa ngayo?**	**yee**nee eereh**yee**tee awkoo**tshee**ntshwah **ngah**yaw

At the post office *Eposini*

I want to send this by …	**Ngifuna ukuthumela lento nge …**	ngee**foo**nah ookootoo-**meh**lah **leh**ntaw ngeh
airmail	**moya**	**maw**yah
registered mail	**posi lokurejistwa**	**paw**see lawkooreh**jee**stwah
I want…-shilling stamps.	**Ngifuna izitembu zamashilingi ayi …**	ngee**foo**nah eezee**teh**mboo zahmah-shee**lee**ngee ahyee
What's the postage for a letter/postcard to America?	**Yimalini ukuposa incwadi/iposikhadi eliya eMelika?**	yeemah**lee**nee ookoo**paw**sah **ee**n¦c¦wahdee/ eepawsee**kah**dee eh**lee**yah ehmeh**lee**kah
Is there any mail for me? My name is …	**Likhona iposi elize kimi? Igama lami ngu …**	lee**kaw**nah ee**paw**see eh**lee**zeh **kee**mee. ee**gah**mah **lah**mee ngoo

Telephoning *Ukushaya ucingo*

Where's the nearest public phone?	**Likuphi ucingo lawonkewonke eliseduze?**	lee**koo**pee oo¦**c**¦**ee**ngaw lahwawnkeh**waw**nkeh ehleeseh**doo**zeh
Hello. This is … speaking.	**Sawubona. U … lona okhulumayo.**	sahwoo**baw**nah. oo … **law**nah awkooloo**mah**yaw
I want to speak to …	**Ngifuna ukukhuluma no …**	ngee**foo**nah ookookoo**loo**mah naw

NUMBERS, see page 189